LUXURY

PRAISE FOR *LUXURY: A RICH HISTORY*

'In this truly "rich history" Peter McNeil and Giorgio Riello show us why luxury matters, why—in other words—it is not just a concern of the super-rich of past and present. Their acute and timely book explains the economics and politics of luxury and explores what it has meant in terms of privilege, display, and experience from ancient times to today. No previous work has tackled this complex and ever-changing phenomenon with such range and erudition or illustrated it with such a dazzling array of stories and examples. The book will be indispensable reading for anyone wishing to understand why the wealthy have always wanted to live differently and what this has signified for the rest of us.'

Stephen Gundle, author of *Glamour: A History*

'Peering into the past through this informed, engaging kaleidoscope has been a great time travel. Exploring the definitions of luxury both conceptual and material as they manifest the *zeitgeist* of their time. The inherent contradictions of opulence versus understatement, its elusiveness, its pleasure seeking nature, objects of desire to be coveted; and how power, privacy and comfort always find their place in the dialogue on luxury.'

Charlotte Moss, author and interior designer

'Luxury is a hot topic, not least because there is a lot of money to be made from the new global luxury consumer. Selling luxury brands rests in part on how we define the concept of luxury—is it a function of rarity, cost, authenticity, distinction, excess, pleasure? McNeil and Riello take a completely new, *materialistic* approach to luxury, beginning with the objects themselves—and what extraordinary objects they are! This is an absolutely fascinating book, rich in insights and pleasures.'

Valerie Steele, Director of the Museum at the Fashion
Institute of Technology, New York

LUXURY
a rich history

PETER McNEIL & GIORGIO RIELLO

OXFORD
UNIVERSITY PRESS

OXFORD

UNIVERSITY PRESS

Great Clarendon Street, Oxford, OX2 6DP
United Kingdom

Oxford University Press is a department of the University of Oxford.
It furthers the University's objective of excellence in research, scholarship,
and education by publishing worldwide. Oxford is a registered trade mark of
Oxford University Press in the UK and in certain other countries

Published in the United States of America by Oxford University Press
198 Madison Avenue, New York, NY 10016, United States of America

British Library Cataloguing in Publication Data
Data available

Library of Congress Control Number: 2015954095

ISBN 978-0-19-966324-8

Printed in Great Britain by
Clays Ltd, St Ives plc

Links to third party websites are provided by Oxford in good faith and
for information only. Oxford disclaims any responsibility for the materials
contained in any third party website referenced in this work.

To our friends, our great luxury in life

PREFACE AND ACKNOWLEDGEMENTS

The genesis of the idea for this work came several years ago as we were sitting around talking during two cold winter Augusts in Sydney. While fashion has a long history and has now amassed a large body of studies, luxury—we observed—had received little attention. What seemed to be missing was an analysis of the meaning and importance of luxury across time.

A decade ago, this issue would have been easily dismissed by arguing that luxury was either a niche topic—the whimsical choices of the elites—or of little interest to either serious scholars or the majority of readers. Yet, in the last few years, luxury has become a 'hot topic'. In an age of rampant individualism, of rising economic inequality, and of puritanical attitudes to social mores, luxury has become commonplace in our daily newspapers, lamenting the vulgarity of the super-rich, in billboards advertising the same commodities that are supposed to be so vulgar, and in the general desire to aim for something better, something different, and something exclusive.

Yet our students have been surprised to learn that debates about luxury had a long history reaching far back in time and place. The topic of luxury seemed so connected to the fashion studies and material culture that we often studied and taught, sometimes using alternate words, that we began to ask where the 'luxury debate' had gone in recent years. We worked on establishing a research network, which was generously funded by the Leverhulme Trust. Over the two years of its activity, the International Network 'Luxury and the Manipulation of Desire', coordinated by Giorgio Riello and Rosa Salzberg at the University of Warwick, allowed collaboration with Glenn Adamson, Marta Ajmar, Christopher Breward, Jonathan Faiers,

Catherine Kovesi, Peter McNeil, Luca Molà, Maria Giuseppina Muzzarelli, Ulinka Rublack, Bill Sherman, John Styles, and Qing Wang. We are grateful to all of them and the dozens of scholars who joined us at events organized in London (V&A and The Shard), Coventry (University of Warwick), Bologna (the University of Bologna), and Florence (Villa I Tatti and the European University Institute). A grant from the Australian Academy of the Humanities International Science Linkages Humanities and Creative Arts Programme (ISL-HCA) allowed Giorgio to spend time in Australia to develop this book. This project was further developed in conversation with colleagues at the EUI in Fiesole and at the University of Padua.

Many people must be thanked. First, we thank our colleagues and friends who endured us writing another book simultaneously with other projects and even a new job for Peter at Aalto University, Helsinki, and a new position at Warwick for Giorgio. We wish to mention in particular Simon Lee and Richard Butler. Our colleagues Maxine Berg, Anne Gerritsen, and Giovanni Luigi Fontana did much to support, inspire, and critique this project. The next round of thanks must go to our indefatigable and always cheerful friends and occasional assistants Masafumi Monden in Sydney and Clare Tang in London, and to the very erudite and worldly Virginia Wright, who took a strong web-based pencil to our text. To all of you, we are very grateful. We thank the anonymous readers who commented on our proposal and Matthew Cotton, our editor at Oxford University Press, for his patience, surely a great luxury.

Special thanks must go to Kevin L. Jones, FIDM Museum Curator, and Christina Johnson, FIDM Museum Associate Curator. They kindly showed us part of the wonderful FIDM Museum collection and arranged for its special photography. Our thanks also to Justin Hobson, Country Life Picture Library; Kristen McDonald, Lewis Walpole Library, Yale University; Matthew Martin and Jenny Moloney, National Gallery of Victoria; Sanda Miller; Elizabeth Fischer, Director of Jewelry Design, Haute École de Design, Geneva; Adelheid Rasche and Hildegard Ringena, Lipperheidesche

Kostümbibliothek Berlin; Martin Kamer, Zug; Maurizio Marinelli; Caro-lyn Cartier; Ilaria Vanni; Mingming Cheng; Desley Luscombe, and Amy Evans for their help. Concetta Laciaux of LuxAdvisory, and Lifen Zhang, Editor-in-Chief, FTChinese.com, provided much needed help with the understanding of contemporary luxury. Titi Halle, Michelle Majer, and Billy de Gregorio continue to support our projects through their advice at Titi Halle/Cora Ginsburg New York. Lillian Williams (Paris and Aix-en-Provence) was very hospitable in showing Peter a part of her private collection of eighteenth-century artefacts. Finally, we also thank the staff of the Abegg-Stiftung, the Victoria & Albert Museum, the Los Angeles County Museum of Art, the Virginia Museum of Fine Arts, and our other museum friends around the world. We thank photographer and fashion theorist Alexander Su for sharing his photograph of a pawnshop in Sydney, and our picture researcher, Fo Orbell. Shalen Singh helped greatly in the final stages of the typescript, and Simon Lee read the sections on the great brands.

Peter McNeil and Giorgio Riello
Christmas 2015

CONTENTS

LIST OF ILLUSTRATIONS

Introduction

Luxury: A Rich History and a History of Riches

The opposite of luxury is not poverty because in the houses of the poor you can smell a good 'pot au feu'. The opposite is not simplicity for there is beauty in the corn-stall and barn, often great simplicity in luxury, but there is nothing in vulgarity, its complete opposite.

Gabrielle 'Coco' Chanel as told to the photographer Cecil Beaton in 1966.

WHAT IS YOUR LUXURY?

To ask 'What is your luxury?' might appear a banal question. Yet, the very subject of this book remains elusive. If we ask a group of people what is their luxury, replies include a wide variety of material artefacts ranging from branded products to jewellery, fast cars to fancy clothing. Others will mention gourmet meals, exotic vacations, and spa pampering—immaterial luxuries that cannot be put in a vault—or a wardrobe. The younger set definitely includes the latest technologies and ownership of an apartment in those cities of spiralling prices. Those who actually can afford or already own all of these are much more philosophical and recount that their 'true' luxury is time ('quality time' to be precise), to be spent with friends and family or in the relaxation of switching off one's bleeping cellphone—all 'free luxuries', but ones difficult to achieve in today's managerial society.

Coco Chanel, the great *couturière* of the twentieth century, was cannier in her reply. For her, luxury was not necessarily something material or something that could be experienced. To her it was a concept, an idea. Yet, she resisted telling us what this idea might be, and identified instead its opposite. That—according to Coco—was neither poverty nor simplicity, but vulgarity. Both our imagined focused group and Chanel would find the story that we are going to tell rather surprising, even upsetting. One wonders, for instance, what Coco made of the fact that—myth or reality—Cleopatra dissolved a pearl worth 10 million sesterces (roughly $15 million in 2015 money) in vinegar, one of the greatest acts of whimsical luxury consumption in human history?[1] This book includes luxuries as varied as coconut shells, cut flowers, household plumbing, porcelain cups, buildings that fell down under the weights of their domes, relics, crowns that could not be worn, fake jewellery, and real pieces of jewellery in the shape of flower pots. These are clearly not among the 'top-ten' luxury items anyone would mention. Yet they all embodied the best of luxury in their specific time and place. They gave pleasure—and sometimes also a great deal of pain—to their owners, makers, and financiers. They were treasured and handed down, melted or collected, discarded or sent into a museum's vault.

We start with a very materialistic approach to luxury and its history as a counterbalance to the many academic studies that have treated luxury as an analytical category.[2] We are certainly not the first to write about luxury in history, but our approach is somewhat different, as we wish to place people and objects at the forefront of our story. There are many excellent books and articles detailing the importance of the concept of luxury, of the debates that it raised historically, and of how luxury intersected with morality, religion, the economy, and society in different periods, from antiquity to the present day.[3] We start instead with the objects themselves, as we think that they reveal a great deal about the ideas, cultural practices, and aspirations of people of different means and social conditions across time. Rather than impose a general framework of analysis, we wish to consider the forms that luxury assumed in different periods, encountering on the way a number of memorable characters: vain princes, rich American brides, British aristocrats, US presidents who lacked dinner services, skilful decorators, *bon viveurs*, gigolos, acerbic gossip writers, and rich 'ladies who lunched'. Many of these figures are now considered so eccentric as to require explanation.

All books—as good or as bad as readers might judge them—have a plan and a plot. Ours is to make the long history of luxury accessible, and to convince the reader that what we today think of as luxury is not an immutable category. Our point of departure—and indeed of arrival—in the historical narrative that we present is the very present. Luxury is all around us. One of the authors was once surprised to find a bar of soap in a university's student dormitory whose package proclaimed it to be 'luxury soap', when clearly it was not. We are told in the daily press of the growth of a new 'luxury industry' and the excesses of the richest in the world, be they Saudi prices, Russian oligarchs, or Chinese billionaires. Since the early 2000s, luxury as a theme and a topic has returned with a vengeance, to be used in monographs and journalistic articles, in discussions regarding decadence and bad taste, or the financial inequality of present-day societies. Luxury has become a commonplace point of conversation, both conceptually and materially. The luxury brands have helped to satisfy a demand for luxury that came not just from a few high net worth consumers, but first and foremost from society at large. Some talk about a 'democraticization of luxury', an expression that alludes to the fact that luxury has clearly expanded its meaning and the forms through which it manifests itself.[4] We note also that the topic still divides us, and appears morally revolting to some, even though they might themselves find pleasure in art, crafts, libraries, wines, property, and international travel.

WHAT IS LUXURY?

So far we have skirted around the definition of luxury by asking what is *your* luxury or what luxury might have been for a person in the fifteenth rather than the nineteenth century. Luxury is contingent: it depends on what a society assumes to be 'beyond' the expected. Very often this is the fruit not of mere cultural relativism but of an interplay between society's expectations and the availability and capacity of producing material things and services. Later in the book, we explain how flowers out of their season were until the 1960s a great luxury and an item of enormous expense. This was due to the fact that, before the creation of international systems of cultivation and the ability to move goods by air freight, flowers complied to the pattern of the seasons. Roses on St Valentine's Day were something as unexpected as expensive. Today they can be purchased at corner super-markets every day.

Is it possible, however, to generalize and find unchanging characteristics for luxury? The philosopher and sociologist Yves Michaud, in a recent study of contemporary luxury, tells us that luxuries 'effectively signify rarity, cost, change, transformation, expenditure, distinction, excess...and, we should not forget, pleasure'.[5] The French intellectual Georges Bataille included luxury among a number of 'unproductive' items of expenditure together with bereavement, wars, religious services, the building of monuments, games, the arts and performing arts, non-reproductive sexual activities—a rather varied list that includes several forms of luxury, some of which often come free.[6] Clearly the emphasis is put on the fact that luxury—and by extension a history of luxury—is about the *extra*-ordinary, that which goes beyond the everyday, the affordable, and the mundane. On the one hand, luxury is uplifting both spiritually and materially; on the other, it is seen as 'unproductive' and therefore useless in any society that privileges economic and social rationality. As most commodities work on the principle of price (the higher the price, the lower the demand), luxury makes a virtue of the opposite. Price must be high in order to convey value, sometimes a value that can hardly be reified in terms of money. True luxury is either inestimable or completely free.

There is, therefore, a dimension of luxury that cannot be captured through the lucid rationality of an accountant, or perhaps—dare we say— by an earnest sociologist or marketing expert. Luxury—today as in the past—plays with a mixture of feelings and emotions. We are wearied by historians' ability to capture and understand the emotions of those people who preceded us. Yet we must at least try to give some psychological depth to our forebears. Our narrative, based on wide changes over time, is punctuated by stories that provide 'flesh and blood' to a history that is not just about economic means, social conventions, and cultural practices, but also about cautious investment, whimsical acts, sexual ambiguity, and the mere pleasure to dazzle and charm. As we will see, luxury has been linked throughout history to a series of concepts, including: authenticity and truthfulness (to own a Van Gogh and not a copy); depth (though luxury is often accused of being shallow); acculturation (the fact that luxury thrives on knowledge, sometimes of arcane facts); self-realization (here we study a long list of rich people with a need to display how rich they are and were); and eroticism (the sheer pleasure of texture and material allure).

Luxury's slipperiness is therefore not just the fruit of the emotional logic that governs it. It is also a concept and a material practice that is relative, and has been so throughout history. A banal example might explain the concept thus: the Queen of England lives in great luxury; yet even the most daring tabloid journalists would not feel entitled to accuse the Queen of exercising uncontrolled desires or being a 'slave to luxury' by the fact that she travels in a Bentley, wears custom-made dresses on most occasions, and give parties for a thousand people at a time. This is because the Queen is the state and the state uses luxury as one of the tools of its façade. It would be considered unforgivable if the Queen were forced to travel in a Mini metro or go to Top Shop for her suits. By contrast, a pop star who is chauffeured in a Bentley, wears custom-made dresses, and gives parties for a thousand people (and indeed many names might come to your minds) is considered extravagant by many and also immoral, dissolute, and decadent by the same press that hold the Queen up as an example for the nation.

The example of the pop star suggests a further characteristic of luxury that one can observe across time: the fact that luxury has always been divisive. As is the case for fashion, it is based on the principle of exclusion, the sharp division between those who have and those who have not. Today luxury is seen as the embodiment of growing income inequality within states and communities, and also between different nations in the world. This is not new, although in the past luxury and inequality were seen as part of how a hierarchical society was structured: something that was acknowledged, rather than seen as a problem. This book, however, is adamant that luxury is *not* the cause of inequality, though it might be one of its effects. When societies aim towards income and social equality (as postwar societies did), luxury—or at least the public discussion of luxury—seems to disappear. By contrast, societies in the second decade of the twenty-first century, in which 1 per cent of the population owns 49 per cent of the world's wealth, lead luxury to the fore.

Luxury comes with a mixed reputation. The slippage between *luxuria* (lust and dissipation), *luxus* (softness and opulence), and luxury is indicative of the fact that, in ancient times (and when the concept of luxury re-emerged strongly in the west European sixteenth century), it was clearly not perceived as being among the virtues. It was connected instead with some of the deadliest of sins. It was considered as another form of unregulated desire that went hand in hand with *vanitas* (vanity), pomp, sumptuous spending, and expensive ornamentation. Its personification was female, something that connected luxury to the bodily appetites. It is not surprising that luxury has long been seen as an object of desire that acts as a temptation or testing of one's moral strength.[7] This has therefore required, as we will see in this book, the taming of luxury through a variety of acts, some of which were legislative (called the 'sumptuary laws'), to temper luxury's most negative effects by limiting it and sometimes punishing its devotees. Today, this might appear an unusual position, though many still agree that it is morally and economically sensible to tax luxuries and discourage their consumption.

Finally, a great many ideas about what luxury might be and what it might mean come not from history but from various theories. The nineteenth and twentieth centuries saw the birth of the modern social sciences—sociology first in the 1890s and later anthropology and economics. Luxury has played an important role in all of them, with the key scholars such as Thorstein Veblen, Georg Simmel, and Werner Sombart dedicating a great deal of attention to what might appear at first sight the relatively niche field of luxury.[8] Veblen's 'conspicuous consumption' theory is to luxury what the theory of gravity is to physics, in the words of the art historian Glenn Adamson.[9] Many theorists, who were generally observing their own time and place, have speculated about luxury. They include philosophers, sociologists, historians, and writers such as Olivier Assouly, Maxine Berg, Christopher Berry, Jean Castarède, Richard Goldthwaite, Philippe Perrot, Jan de Vries, Dana Thomas, and Evelyn Welch.[10] Their ideas are the key in structuring the intellectual framework of this book, which moves beyond the queues at Louis Vuitton and the stories of the brands.

A HISTORY OF LUXURY

This book shows that history has a great deal to reveal about the complexity and richness of luxury. The book's subtitle, 'A Rich History', does not imply that this is a history of the rich and their toys, but rather that our work is an attempt to recover the richness of the term through its own history. We do so by starting with antiquity, when both the Greeks and the Romans found that luxury was a slippery concept and a matter of great concern. Accumulation of wealth, the creation of splendid artefacts, and the building of sumptuous villas allowed some to 'live the life'. Luxury emerged as a divisive issue, an indicator of inequality, and, some argued, a waste of personal and collective resources. Yet many of the luxuries of the ancient world retained enduring appeal among collectors and men of letters in the following centuries. The antique—the rare object from the past—has been since the Middle Ages a prop of cultural luxury among the intellectual and political elites of Europe and beyond. Collectors in the Renaissance and grand tourists to Italy and Greece in the eighteenth century found their luxury in ruins and the excavated items from sites such as Herculaneum and Pompeii. Across Europe, the splendour of court life in many rising nation states was embodied in a variety of luxury items. Splendid textiles and dresses, priceless jewellery, and great houses were meant to express magnificence and splendour, especially that of rulers and their courtiers. They competed to secure the best that art, woodwork, goldsmithing, and textile-weaving could produce in a game of grandeur such as can still be seen in Louis XIV's enormous and unrivalled palace at Versailles.

The eighteenth century was, however, a period of profound change for luxury. Next to traditional luxury goods for the very rich and the noble, a new series of more affordable luxuries became available to consumers with more modest means. Goods coming from Asia fuelled desire across European society for commodities such as tea and coffee, teacups and Indian cottons. They were soon imitated, which sparked a fashion for things oriental, thus expanding the taste for *chinoiserie*, *japonaiserie*, and *turqueries*, a passion that continued well into the nineteenth and early twentieth centuries. One area of particular importance for luxury consumption was domestic space. We consider in Chapter 4 the birth of modern living, in the noble residences of cities such as Paris and London, and their owners' choices of furniture, furnishing, and comforts. Today we think of luxury as items that are a part of personal consumption, especially for the adornment of the body, but a history of luxury cannot fail to notice that perhaps the area of greatest luxury spending has been interior decoration: inlaid furniture, chaises longues, marble mantelpieces, and extremely expensive plumbing systems produced enormous bills and were considered by many—rich and poor alike—as the great luxuries in life.

In the final three chapters, we move into the twentieth century and onto more familiar terrain. Chapter 5 shows how the opulence that characterized the end of the nineteenth century through a superfluity of forms gave way in the post-First World War period to a more restrained luxury. Coco Chanel was among those at this time who argued that luxury was not necessarily physically embodied in artefacts: diamonds could therefore be replaced by imitation paste, silk or velvet by a wool jersey. One did not need to flaunt money in materials and craft, but luxury could be expressed in nearly imperceptible ways. Yet, this was no 'democratic' move in any sense of the word. Luxury was the superior taste for those 'in the know' and those 'who counted' in society, and it continued to cost a great deal. Chanel was partisan in a titanic struggle between the protectors of elite forms of luxury (today referred to as 'metaluxury' or 'über luxury') and the fact that the affluent society of the twentieth century made available to many for the first time the things that had before been considered to be the great luxuries, from chocolate to central heating. Via cosmetics and domestic appliances, passing through nylon stockings and Bakelite handbags and radio sets, we eventually reach today's luxury world of branded products and new technologies.

The final two chapters focus on the role of consumers and producers of luxury since the 1980s. Today's consumers think that luxury is something that everyone should aspire to. Advertising, the Internet, and the conspicuous presence of shops that claim to sell us the latest luxury objects make luxury as much a topic of debate as a much-loved pursuit such as golf or travel. We lift the lid on the luxury brands, investigating their financial structures, their claims to authenticity, their power (in the media, but it turns out in particular in the courts of law), and their shifting appeal (which waxes and wanes). We see branded products and their production, distribution, purchase, and consumption as part of a new form of twenty-first-century capitalism ('luxury capitalism'), very different from the industrial capitalism of the nineteenth and the service-based capitalism of the twentieth century. Our aim here is not one of accusation (terrific works such as Naomi Klein's books serve that function well), but to raise the issue of how much today's luxury is contingent on specific sociocultural and economic contexts, very different not just from that of the Renaissance courts but also from that of the socially minded post-Second World War Western economies, now being unravelled, for better or worse.

1

Luxury, Antiquity, and the Allure of the Antique

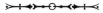

O ne might be mistaken for thinking that luxury is a recent thing, a phenomenon that developed slowly over the course of history, becoming particularly pronounced in our modern wealthy societies. In reality, luxury dates back to prehistoric times. The world-famous Upper Palaeolithic cave paintings at Lascaux in France, dated to *c.*15,300 BCE, are not just among the earliest examples of human art, they are also one of the earliest forms of luxury: something that was not strictly necessary, and even more so in a society with very limited resources. The Lascaux paintings point also to a further aspect of luxury: it might be decorative, but it is neither superficial nor plain useless. Luxury has a function in society, be it to embellish oneself, to dream of another life, or simply to show that one can afford not just that which is strictly necessary, but also something extra.

LUXURY AND TIME

More intriguing, perhaps, is the idea that one's luxury might not just be produced in the immediate present. Something can be rare and unusual precisely because it comes from *another* time. Today we are used to the concept that the best and most costly furniture is 'antique', that paintings by the Renaissance masters are expensive, not to mention objects of great value such as Roman coins and Ming vases. The list could continue and extends to 'collectables' of more recent manufacture, including a great deal of twentieth-century art, design, and jewellery. It is evident that the appeal of these objects is at least partially that their supply is limited. They are rare because they can no longer be produced: there is no Michelangelo to paint another Sistine chapel for a Russian oligarch, even if many of them could certainly afford one. But the 'antique' is also rare because a great deal of it has simply disappeared. Millions of canvases were painted in the Dutch golden age; however seventeenth-century Dutch paintings are now valuable because the great majority has not survived.

Rarity might explain why we value objects from the past, things that are not just 'old' but 'antique'. Indeed, there is sufficient demand to deserve an entire sector, that of the auction houses and antique dealers, although the latter are currently in decline as tastes in luxuries change. Yet the appeal of the 'old-antique' is not just the result of its rarity. There are many things in the present day that are equally rare and expensive. However, unlike objects churned out by today's factories or artisanal workshops, the antique has also the added value of *time*. In the same way in which wine gets better with age, so a piece of furniture 'matures' over time. It bears the signs of time that no new object can possess. This is called 'patina', and it refers to the tarnish that forms on the surface of metals and stone, or the sheen on wooden furniture produced by age and wear and tear. Patina makes things look timeworn and thus differentiates them from modern equivalents. Patina serves to add rather than to subtract value. While most things lose value by ageing (indeed this could be extended also to the appeal of humans), some things become more valuable: grandfather's Rolls locked in the garage is not simply old but an 'antique car'. Patina becomes a cultural attribute by which we value things that have a history. Better still if this is one that can be documented over time.

This attitude towards the old, and the cultural propensity to value it, are linked to the greatest luxury of them all: to be able to play with time. If we are rich, we might afford to travel around the world, but no one can travel in time. We might extend our earthly life by buying the best medical care available; however, no billionaire can live 150 years or travel back to a previous century. Yet some of us might be able to surround ourselves and acquire the best that the past had to offer: splendid textiles, luxurious furnishings, works of art, and expensive leather-bound books. By collecting 'beautiful things' from the past we are able, if not to relive the past, at least to appreciate what is no longer.

This playfulness between present and past is a luxury per se: call it a dream of immortality, or the extension of one's life beyond the confines of one's time. The reality is that such a phenomenon is not recent at all. The ancient Mesopotamians, for example, valued Old Babylonian monuments, and in c.1900–1800 BCE they spent a great deal of time compiling a catalogue of monuments that were at least 500 years old.[1] The best examples of ancient luxuries have been preserved precisely because of a dream of immortality. Royal and wealthy Ancient Egyptians were keen to build vast tombs that acted as 'palaces of eternity' where they surrounded themselves with everything they would need. Luxury objects promised a future life after the terrestrial one had ended. Pyramids were both monuments to eternity and the most direct statement of exhibitionism. And we owe to such conspicuous funerary waste some of the most important works of art ever produced by humankind.

We might think that later civilizations were less obsessed with both luxury and death, but if we consider this first-century AD rock crystal *amphoriskos*, an 8.5-centimetre-high two-handled vessel with two braided gold chains (Figure 1.1), we realize that luxury, time, and death remained strongly entwined throughout antiquity. The vessel was probably used to contain essences and oils. It was an object of extreme luxury that possibly has reached us because it was buried with its owner. It usurped the inexpensive *pyxides* (vessels) made of wood, or blown glass, that held cosmetics and perfumes that in themselves were often not expensive.[2] The

Fig. 1.1. Rock Crystal *amphoriskos*. Mediterranean–Roman, first century CE. Rock crystal and gold. 8.4 x 4.9 cm. A golden chain holds the stopper from falling. In the post-war period, the Swiss textile industrialist Werner Abegg and his American-born wife Margaret created the world's most significant private foundation for historic textiles, the Abegg Stiftung (established 1961), with a museum and innovative conservation facilities. In order to contextualize the textile collections, many of which were extremely luxurious and rare, they purchased objects such as this perfume vase to show the *gesamtkunstwerk* (total environment) of luxury that pervaded the upper levels of societies such as Ancient Rome.

material of which it was made, rock crystal, was said by Pliny the Elder (23–79 CE) to have come from mountains and to have naturally cooling powers like ice.

Objects like these—the luxuries of antiquity—have been at the centre of the collecting practices of rich people over the past five or six centuries, with enormous amounts of time and a great deal of money spent amassing splendid collections of artefacts. These luxuries have, in turn, come to form important components of many major museum collections. They are often thought of as 'artworks', but many—if not all—were functional, at least in some way. Most art was described in ancient languages through words akin to 'craft'. Most objects had more than one function, and many 'exhibit a surplus of order and aesthetic organisation which goes beyond the narrowly functional'.[3] Many of the individual luxuries described in this book, whether we consider them today as 'craft', 'decorative', 'applied arts', or 'art', fall into this useful categorization. Whether they were designed as artworks or not (and 'art' is largely a Western concept), many of them are little masterpieces.

THE ROMANS OF THE DECADENCE

The Romans of the Decadence (Musée d'Orsay, 1847) is a monumental 7-metre-wide canvas by the French painter Thomas Couture that fascinated the viewers of the nineteenth century (Figure 1.2). Its subject matter refers to a text by the Roman poet Juvenal (*c.*66–140CE): 'Crueller than war, vice fell upon Rome and avenged the conquered world.' The orgiastic painting also alluded to the glittering decadence of the mid-nineteenth-century Paris in which it was painted. We should not be led to believe that the past offers just a series of material things that are today appreciated as luxuries. Egyptian, Greek, and in particular Roman antiquity—up to the fall of the Roman Empire in 476 CE—set all the major features of luxury. The late Republican and the Imperial Roman periods clearly show the

Fig. 1.2. Thomas Couture (1815–79), *The Romans of the Decadence*, 1847. Oil on canvas. 472 x 772 cm. This sensational canvas was designed to pique the interest of contemporary Parisian and other viewers who could only but compare it with the splendours of mid-nineteenth-century Paris, the centre of good living, sensuality, and luxuries. Two visitors to the right—properly clad—look on unimpressed.

emergence of many of the ideas that we associate with the topic. Antiquity also presents us with some surprises that challenge our established assumptions about what luxury is and what it might mean.

Just as today luxury is a divisive issue, so it was in antiquity. Because of its alluring qualities, luxury was seen as the ultimate temptation. To resist luxury meant to show firmness of character; to embrace it was a sign of feebleness and at times degeneracy and effeminacy. To the democratic Greeks, luxury was simultaneously troubling but also a type of evidence that their society was 'doing well' and expanding its borders. Plato saw luxury as connected to the idea of utopia, the land of the 'lotus-eaters'. The Comic playwright Hermippus, contemporary of Aristophanes (*c.*446–386 BCE), wrote:

Now tell me, Muses, dwellers on Olympus:
Which goods Dionysus brought over here for men on his black ship . . .

From Egypt, rigged sails and books. And from Syria, further, frankincense.
And fine Crete provides cypress for the gods,
And Libya ivory in plenty for sale.
Rhodes, raisins and sweet-dream figs.
Moreover, from Euboea—pears and fat apples.
Slaves from Phrygia, and from Arcadia mercenaries...
Paphlagonians provide the acorns of Zeus and shining
Almonds. For they are the ornaments of a feast.
Phoenicia, further, palm-fruit and fine wheat-flour.
Carthage, carpets and cushions of many colours.[4]

As the historian of the ancient world David Braund explains, these utopian lists are connected to comedy and are not at all positive. That a democracy such as Athens was in fact making new luxuries available to many—rearing cock fowls and calling them 'Persian birds', raising pheasants and calling them 'Phasian birds', and even breeding peacocks for consumption by the late fifth century BCE—was a cause of anxiety to the old oligarchy, as such luxuries normally sat at the tables of foreign despots.[5]

Since Roman times the very definition of luxury has been based on a semantic slippage between the words *luxus* (meaning splendour, pomp, but also sensuality) and its derivative *Luxuria* (riot, excess, and extravagance). Neither word had a positive connotation, and luxury was therefore held to be problematic and negative on many levels. Roman commentators claimed that luxury was also the source of other vices. Cicero, for instance, concluded that from luxury 'avarice inevitably springs, while from avarice audacity breaks forth, the source of all crimes and misdeeds'.[6]

Already in Roman times, many believed that luxury produced selfishness and undermined civic spirit and a sense of community of interests, a trope that is still with us today.[7] The Roman writer and intellectual Pliny the Elder was particularly critical of the spread of luxury across Roman society, something that he saw as a sign of greed and wastefulness. Luxury was a vice that threatened to destabilize the nation and that symbolized decadence in the history of Rome. Even those who were less inclined to dismiss luxury wholesale or see it as the source of all evil did not fail to brand it as negative. Another first-century Roman, the rhetorician Quintilian, believed material riches to be the most common but unsuccessful way to hide moral weakness: 'A tasteful and magnificent dress...lends added dignity to its wearer; but effeminate and luxurious apparel fails to adorn the body and merely reveals the foulness of the mind.'⁸ Luxury was good when it bestowed honour on its owner but not when it simply covered faults. It was even worse when luxury became the pretext to better oneself in a society in which birth rather than money or material possession was what counted. The observant Horace (65–8 BCE) laughed at the affectation that accompanied luxury: 'I am sorry', he joked, 'for those who like to know how the Phasian bird differs from the crane of wintry Rhodope, what sort of goose has the largest liver, why a Tuscan boar is tastier than an Umbrian, and what seaweed makes the most comfortable bed for slippery shellfish'.⁹ Apparently, luxury was also the source of pretentiousness.

Horace hints at another perplexing aspect of luxury in Roman life: the fact that it entailed sophistication. It broke from the idea of Roman society as embracing a simple way of living. The simple way is a Greek ideal: the Athenian philosopher Plato in the fourth century BCE had already suspected the 'many will not be satisfied with the simpler way of life'. He clearly worried about material accumulation and complained about the habits of his fellow Athenians:

> They will be for adding sofas, and tables, and other furniture; also dainties, and perfumes, and incense, and courtesans, and cakes, all these not of one sort only, but in every variety; we must go beyond the necessaries of which I was first speaking, such as houses, and clothes, and shoes: the arts of the painter and the embroiderer will have to be set in motion, and gold and ivory and all sorts of materials must be produced.¹⁰

The simplicity of past times versus the sophistication (and corruption) of the present was a theme dear to those who lamented the decline and loss of the *mos maiorum* (the customs of the ancestors). The critique of luxury played no small part in this.

By claiming that luxury was an illness of the present—rather than an innate 'character fault' in any human society—Roman commentators created the need to explain whence luxury had developed. They saw it as quintessentially 'foreign' and therefore alien to the true and olden spirit of the Roman polis. This is why luxury was often represented as coming from 'the Orient', something that came as part and parcel of the success of the Empire's conquest of North Africa and Asia. It was said that luxurious habits had been adopted when Sulla, during his campaign in Asia (87–82 BCE), had allowed his men to indulge in both the carnal and venal pleasures of the East. Livy (64 or 59 BCE–17 CE), on the other hand, thought that corrupt Eastern luxury arrived in Rome a century earlier with the triumph of Manlius Vulso in 186 BCE when 'foreign luxuries were brought to the city by the army from the east'.[11] He said that this licentious army had brought back 'bronze couches, costly cloth spreads, tapestries, and . . . magnificent furniture, table with single pedestals and side-tables'.[12] Pliny the Elder singled out instead spices and perfumes (first used by the Persians according to him) from the East.[13] Others complained about the abundance of Oriental gold, gems, and silken fabrics, of slaves, and exotic animals ranging from elephants to rare birds. Roman villas were, according to Juvenal, stuffed with Greek art-works, ivories, silver and silken fabrics including cloth of purple.[14] But they all agreed that the Orient was to be blamed for having introduced new and appealing goods, another recurrent theme in the history of luxury. The range of artefacts criticized—rich furnishings, spices and foods, textiles, vessels and cloths—remain fairly constant until our own times as the most desirable luxuries.

Wickedness requires a villain: the anti-hero. For the Romans—and we might stretch to include also the way in which they are written about in today's tabloid newspapers and magazines—this was the figure of the *nouveau riche*. Here is Cicero describing a Greek former slave, Chrysogomus, in less-than-flattering prose. He not only freed himself but became rich and lived a luxury lifestyle that clearly greatly troubled Cicero. It is worthwhile citing at length:

> He has a nice property outside the city, just for the pleasure of it, and several other pieces of land, all of them attractive, and not far away. His house is full of Corinthian and Delian ware, including, of course, his famous cooker ... But never mind that: how much sculpted silver, how many tapestries, how many paintings, how many statues, how much marble do you think he has at home? What about his staff, the number of them and their varied occupations? I pass by the ordinary professions, cooks, bakers, valets. He has so many people engaged in amusing his mind and his ears, that the whole neighbourhood resounds continually with music of voice, string, woodwind and all night partying. What do you think the daily expense must be of a life like that? How much wine do you think they get through? What must those parties be like? Good ones, I should think, in that kind of house, if house is the word for this factory of impropriety, this warehouse of all the vices.[15]

For the Romans, to whom the *domus* was the inner *sanctorum* of family life, to see it labelled as the 'warehouse of all the vices', the brothel of *luxus* and *luxuria*, must have made it titillating reading. Here might be found 'Indian gold, Tyrian purple, Arabian cinnamon, and mother-of-pearl'.[16] Bacchanals (from Bacchus, god of wine) were a pastime of the Roman rich but also the source of great anxiety: the *luxux mensae* (the luxury of the table), as Tacitus called it, was becoming one of the most common luxuries of Roman society. The expenditure on food reached such levels that laws were introduced setting limits in relation to one's position and wealth. Sumptuary laws—laws governing the expenditure on luxuries—come about from a mismatch between economic wealth and political power.[17] Newly enriched people attempted to challenge the power of traditional elites through conspicuous consumption and the magnificence of their parties. Men vied with each other in the splendour of their entertainments, and the new 'equestrian' class who could engage in overseas rather than local agricultural trade tried to make a mark where there were limited

political places: 'men displayed their riches in order to impress the elector-
ate and secure the offices that were their due.'[18]

Sumptuary laws—as we will see in the following chapters—remained
important features of the history of conspicuous consumption until the
eighteenth century. Yet, unlike the medieval and *ancien régime* sumptuary
laws that regulated mostly expenditure on clothing and adornment, the
Roman ones focused on expenditure on feasts. They regulated what types
of foods could be consumed, how much one could spend for a single meal,
and even the number of guests one could have for dinner in any single day.
The Romans enjoyed a version of *haute cuisine* in which one food was
made to resemble another; one of their favourite delicacies was sows'
udders, which appear in both texts and funerary sculpture on the head-
stones of butchers.[19] They enjoyed delicacies such as fattened fowls, peacock, oysters, ham, wild boar, and fig-peckers, a bird that was eaten whole,
sometimes all combined together in a *paté en croûte*, even though this was
forbidden by law (only one bird might be eaten at a dinner and fattening
was outlawed).

Laws limiting food and other luxury consumption must have been quite
often disregarded, as by the time of Caesar more drastic measures were
needed and guards were sent from market to market to seize all manner of
forbidden foodstuffs even before they could reach the tables of wealthy
Romans.[20] They include dried figs and imported Atlantic oysters.[21] Rice,
chickpeas, black pepper, olives, melons, pistachios, almonds, pine kernels,
dates, pomegranates, and to some extent peaches were also imported into
Central Europe, where they are found mainly in Roman officers' quar-
ters.[22] At a Roman villa in Switzerland, in the town of Avenches (Aventi-
cum), hundreds of bones from pigs' trotters as well as the feet of hare and
chicken have been excavated.[23] Dates and olives packaged in long, thin
amphorae were also found at this site; imported dates have also been found
as far afield as Cologne and Tours.[24] Small songbirds were consumed in
very large amounts by the Roman rich.

Partying required not just expensive wine and exotic food but also lavish accoutrements in the form of silverware; the most expensive and sought after was antique silver. It was not uncommon to mix silverware of different manufactures and different periods. This appears to be the case in the famous finding in a Roman villa at Posanella a Boscoreale in Campania in 1895, where an impressive 109 pieces of silverware (mainly tableware) were found. These were bought for half a million French Francs (around $15 million in 2015 money) by Baron Edmond de Rothschild for his collection, but he eventually decided to donate the bulk of it to the Louvre Museum, where they are to be found today.[25] The House of Menander yielded 118 such dining vessels. The surviving silver tableware shows the refinement of the Roman elite: it includes spoons and ladles for the wine, several trays used for serving food, salt cellars, and containers for spices and sauces. The silver cups are decorative masterpieces showing mythological scenes and political subjects such as episodes from the lives of Augustus and Tiberius. These and other decorative cups were functional objects as well as being objects of conversation for those eating and drinking at the long banquet, and later reclining on the semicircular dining couches with matching marble tables favoured by the Romans.[26]

Of particular concern to moralists and satirists such as Juvenal was the practice of disguising practical furniture such as dining tables with inappropriate materials: silver was bad but ivory was even worse. Juvenal also comments satirically that clearly it was better to have a bevy of pretty pageboys (*exoleti*) arranged according to their nationality, size, and hair colour serving the drinks rather than coarse householders.[27] The older servant boys had painted faces and their long hair was plaited and woven. Only the young men with developing beards did heavy work.[28] It is believed that the iconography of the beautiful and gracious serving page passed into the Christian iconography of the Adoration of the Magi.[29] Once again, there is a long continuity in this type of conspicuous consumption; in the nineteenth century there was a premium on tall footmen matching in size, and the wages diminished for good-looking men in the great houses of England and France as they aged, unless they advanced to become a butler.

The Romans were less interested than modern societies in clothing. Fashion did exist, but expenditure on clothing was not great compared to modern societies. An exception was, however, the use of jewellery, magnificent examples of which are still visible today in the most important museums in Europe and North America. Precious metals held and continue to exert an important cultural value in society. Gold and silver, but also gemstones, are both items of decoration and objects of intrinsic worth: they are beautiful and expensive. While they are often invested with deep meaning (think about engagement rings), they can also serve as a visible expression of wealth. A good example would be the small earring shown in Figure 1.3, measuring just over 3 centimetres and weighing no more than one gram. This apparently simple piece of jewellery was in fact a highly sought-after artefact that included both a stone and a pearl all the way from Asia. It was crafted in the most exquisite and refined taste.

Women would wear bracelets (*armillae*), rings, earrings, necklaces (*monilia*), golden chains to their waists, veils made of silver or gold thread (*retuculae*), all made of gold imported from Egypt, Spain, Britannia, and Dalmatia and further embellished with stones from the Middle East, or pearls from the Red Sea and the Indian Ocean. The much desired *Chryso-lithi*—peridot or topaz—came from India or Ethiopia and *smaragdi* or emeralds from Scythia. Gems were also copied in glass and worn by prostitutes and actresses.[30]

It therefore appears not coincidental that the first sumptuary laws forbidding the immoderate display of wealth (the lex Oppia of 215 BCE) focused on jewellery. In particular it forbade 'women from owning more than half an ounce of gold', as well as 'wearing multi-coloured clothing, and go[ing] around town in a chariot with the exception of religious festivities'.[31] At the time there was resentment at displays by women, who

Fig. 1.3. Earring with pearl and emerald pendant, Roman, 2–3 century CE. The earring consists of a simple gold ring; from this is suspended a gold element incorporating a pearl and a white emerald. Such jewellery, with its air of abstraction rather than naturalism, had a major impact on the 'archaeological' revivals of the mid- to late nineteenth century as well as on Arts and Crafts and Studio jewellery well into the twentieth century.

were possibly using real gold implements for religious ceremonies. It is believed that some of the hostility was directed at a way of life imported from the East by way of Aemilia, wife of Scipio (236–183 BCE), the famous conqueror of the Carthaginians under Hannibal.[32] In 184 BCE Cato the Elder, at that time Censor of Rome, taxed luxuries including women's clothes, jewellery, and vehicles very heavily.[33] Many Roman elegiac poems featured luxury goods to make a point. Propertius argued that Cynthia might wear 'elaborate hairstyles, seductive Coan silks [an almost transparent silk from the Island of Cos], or perfume from the Orient' so as to provide inspiration; Tibullus ranked silk with expensive products, including Tyrian purple and pearls (2.4.28–9), and noted that that the famous transparent Coan silk was sometimes also striped with gold (2.3.53–4), making it even more expensive.[34]

Men too wore gold jewellery. The wearing of the gold ring was initially limited only to senators and a small group of notables. However, the practice became so widespread among the populace that a decree of 23 CE limited the wearing of the gold ring only to those whose fathers and grandfathers were free. Freed slaves could wear a silver ring and slaves only iron rings.[35] Moralists also complained about ever wider classes of men wearing the fine silks and colours to which the elites were entitled.[36]

The luxury debate in Roman times extended even to the adoption of children. In an argument that has some parallels with the contemporary debate as to whether it is unethical to purchase a baby through adoption or surrogacy, the Roman commentators criticized rich men who adopted others' children, expressly in terms of luxury. Luxury, it was claimed, was tearing apart the very fabric of Roman parenthood. Just as there was a critique of the desire to imitate nature, with inauthentic painted landscape scenes on the walls, so there was critique of adoption by the rich: 'For truly they do not know how to enjoy anything real, but in their sickness they need unnatural fakes of sea or land out of their proper places to delight them. Do you still wonder that, in their disdain for the natural, they now don't even like children—except those of others?'[37] Luxury leads also, in this view, to the desire to pursue a whole array of anti-social patterns such as sleeping with other men's wives and to usurp what was once a free state.[38]

LUXURY AND THE REDISCOVERY OF CLASSICAL ANTIQUITY

The importance of antiquity rests not just on the fact that most of the key characteristics of luxury as we know it today were established during

Greek and Roman times but also on the great beauty of antique objects to be found in private collections and museums around the world since the Renaissance. They display high levels of design and artisanal sophistication. Both the world of ideas and the artefacts of ancient societies are significant as they informed the mentality and material culture of the so-called rebirths of culture in the West. This started emphatically in the early fifteenth century when such relics became the passion of the rich and cultured elite of the period that has since been called the Renaissance (*Rinascimento* in Italian, literally 'rebirth').

Something not well known outside the world of art history and archaeology is the term *spolia*. Spolia refers to the reuse of pieces of the past, generally in architectural settings or ecclesiastical artefacts. Spolia often are superb examples of 'archaeological luxury' that connect a ruler or powerful person to the past for various political or dynastic reasons. They are generally Greek or Roman artefacts. A fine example is the *Ambo of Henry II* (*c.*1002–14 CE), a pulpit in Aachen Cathedral. Set into the framework of the structure are the most astonishing luxuries: a bronze plaque, Roman agate vessels, a Roman glass bowl, a Fatimid rock crystal cup and saucer, even Muslim chess pieces of chalcedon and agate, along with sixth-century ivories that are contemporary with Henry II.[39] Thick gold wire connected this composition. The aim was to connect Henry with imperial Christian rulership and Byzantine power. Another famous example is the Lothair Cross (Aachen, Treasury, *c.*835–69 CE) in which Emperor Otto III (980–1002 CE) inserted a Roman cameo and many more early gemstones on an already made-up jewelled crucifix. Rare stones such as sardonyx were frequently remounted by the medieval church and state.

Spolia are part of Western society's long and complex project of rediscovery of its ancient past, in particular the literary and artistic legacies of Greece and Rome. It was the humanistic culture of the fourteenth and fifteenth centuries that rediscovered long-lost texts from Greek and Roman literature (including the many passages quoted earlier about luxury in

Roman society). The rich elites of Europe prided themselves on re-establishing an intellectual lineage and a genealogy of ideas and taste with the ancient past. In doing so they created new forms of luxuries in the shape of precious manuscripts and printed editions of ancient texts, and also through the gathering of impressive collections of magnificent artefacts.

The place where a passion for collecting antiques first emerged was Italy. By the fourteenth century a large market for antiques was present in the city of Venice. In the following century, the rich rulers of cities such as Florence, Mantua, and Milan began amassing enormous—and enormously expensive—collections of ancient artefacts.[40] Cosimo de' Medici (1389–1464), founder of the princely dynasty that ruled over Renaissance Florence, collected gems that, together with vases in semi-precious stones, crystal, ancient medals, coins, and jewellery, were kept in his *studiolo* (literally 'little study-room'), a small display room in his palace in Florence. The collection became a family passion, and, after Cosimo's death, it was expanded by his son Piero and later by his grandson, the famous Lorenzo Il Magnifico (1449–92).

It is important to note that such collections were more about the sum of the parts than the individual object. Lorenzo enlarged the family collection by acquiring part of the collection that had belonged to Pope Paul II, which included one of the most celebrated objects of antiquity: the Farnese cup. Produced possibly in Hellenistic Egypt in the second century BCE, the cameo agate cup (really a plate) represents the Egyptian divine triad, Serapis–Isis–Harpocrates. It was one of the most sought-after objects of antiquity, not just because of its incredible beauty but also because of its provenance and royal associations. It was acquired in Egypt in 31 BCE for the Treasury of Rome, following the defeat of Antony and Cleopatra. After the fall of the Roman Empire, it was moved to Byzantium, and, with the sack of the city in 1204 during the fourth crusade, it made its way into the collection of Emperor Frederick II (1194–1250). In the following century it moved to the Persian court of Herat, but found its way back to Europe.

It was then acquired by King Alfonso V of Aragon, who resided in Naples in the 1450s and who sold it in turn to Pope Paul II. It was finally purchased in Rome by Lorenzo in 1471.

What came to be known as the Farnese cup (as it was later in the possession of the noble Italian Farnese family) encapsulates the passion for unique antique objects in a multi-generational fashion. Collecting both antiquities and rare things from other continents became a pastime of the wealthy elites of Europe. Sometimes vast collections indicated status and connections. The Farnese cup, for instance, materially and symbolically linked Lorenzo de Medici with popes, kings, and emperors. Yet, collecting was not just about belonging to a restricted elite. Such objects also conferred cultural value to newly acquired wealth. 'New money'—as in the case of the Medici family—acquired a lineage in time through the possession of antiquities. They became 'necessary luxuries' to endorse one's social position. And for those whose nobility and place on the social ladder was not questioned, they were a tool of competition. Many of these collections were a good way to make other powerful and rich people green with envy.

Giovanni Grimani, a wealthy Venetian patrician of the late sixteenth century, spent enormous amounts in collecting antiquities and later worried that he might have offended God, 'having spent on such vanities as great amount of money which could have been applied to works of charity'. Luxury raises moral dilemma, and Grimani finally resolved that, to save himself from sin (and hell), he had to give up his collection of medals and cameos. Yet he decided to pass it down to his nephew on the ground that the collection was essential to the 'honour of our house of the Grimani'.[41]

It was not just the classical past that enthused wealthy collectors. Good Christians like Grimani also had a passion for purported religious relics. Eleanor, Princess of Portugal, was an avid collector of saintly memorabilia that included hairs of the Virgin Mary, pieces of Christ's dress, a drinking bowl used by St Anthony of Padua, and a variety of other relics from thirty biblical figures and saints, from the Old Testament to Christ's passion. Her most treasured relic was a thorn from the crown of Christ that was kept in an expensive reliquary made in the German fashion.[42]

Over time the practice of collecting also spread to major noble families. Status was conveyed by acquiring well-known and beautiful objects that were often displayed in appositely constructed spaces. Between 1605 and 1607, Carlo Emanuele of Savoy had an entire gallery constructed in his palace in Turin to house his collection.[43] The less wealthy British aristocrats started relatively late in collecting antiques. A well-known example is Thomas, 21st Earl of Arundel (1585–1646), head of the noble house of Howard. Married to the daughter of the Earl of Shrewbury, in 1613 Arundel went on a spending spree to Italy accompanied by the emerging architect Inigo Jones. During his two-year tour of Venice, Florence, Siena, and other cities in Italy, he came back 'infected with an incurable collecting fever which was to recur in virulent bouts throughout the rest of his life', as the historian Jonathan Scott puts it.[44] The death of his rich father-in-law just a year after his return to Britain gave Arundel the funds to refurbish his London palace on the Strand. He created a gallery for the many statues that he had acquired in Italy. Later in life he acquired further collections, including unique pieces, such as the beautiful bronze head of a poet (possibly Sophocles, now at the British Museum), a prodigious collection of intaglios and cameos, marbles, busts, and contemporary paintings.[45]

LUXURY AND THE EIGHTEENTH-CENTURY GRAND TOUR

Over the following century, this passion for the antique expanded, partly owing to the fact that an increasing number of people visited Italy and saw first hand its ancient ruins during travels that could last for years and were termed 'the grand tour'. Rich, young, and male, the grand tourists of the eighteenth century encountered Italian antiquity by visiting not just Roman ruins but also the Palladian villas of the Veneto in the north-east of Italy built a couple of centuries earlier in classical style as summer retreats for rich Italian aristocratic families. Here they learned the classical language of architecture that they would later repeat in the facades, columns, and tympana of their villas, such as Houghton Hall (rebuilt in the 1730s), constructed in the cold and damp English countryside. Once reaching Rome, they were exposed to the Baroque architecture of the previous century—that also was 'antique' but not regarded as possessing the beauty or cachet of the gardens at Tivoli and the ruins of Ancient Rome. But if the grand tour was about discovery, nothing was more inspiring than the view of Herculaneum and Pompeii, the archaeological sites not far from Naples, both of which were excavated and properly rediscovered from the 1730s onwards (Figure 1.4). Trained to appreciate everything ancient, young English gentlemen found a new way to conceive of antiquity. Years of studying dead languages and of tedious Greek and Roman literature now came alive in the newly discovered streets, houses, and public spaces of these two cities that had been destroyed by the eruption of Vesuvius in 79 CE.

The rich sons of English aristocrats quickly became 'Latin lovers'. They appreciated not just the voluptuous pleasures on offer in the streets of Naples but also the more refined aesthetic sense of an ancient culture, famous for its pomp and luxury. The young Horace Walpole (1717–97), son of the British prime minister Sir Robert Walpole, was one of the privileged youths sent to admire the ruins at Herculaneum. He was hugely impressed by what he saw: 'a subterranean town...perhaps one of the noblest curiosities that ever has been discovered...There is nothing of the kind in the world.'[46] Like many others he was interested in ruins of temples, baths, and palaces, urns, statues, and shattered columns. One of the most famous British architects of the time, Robert Adam (1728–92), was to be seen digging at Herculaneum in what looked to him 'a coal-mine worked by galley slaves'.[47] All this was in the name of ancient culture.

The amazing thing about the eighteenth-century rediscovery of antiquity is that at the time it was really something very new. It started in 1738

Fig. 1.4. 'The Gate of Herculaneum' ('L'Entrée de Pompeii'), watercolour over etched out-line by Francesco Piranesi after Louis Jean Desprez, second half of the eighteenth century. Scenes such as this provided inspiration not just to antiquarians and architects, but also to the set-designers who provided the *mise-en-scène* for entertainments, fireworks, balls, and parties at palaces and villas in the eighteenth century, such as the designs by the famed Philip James de Loutherbourg for Versailles, where a separate department managed such affairs, known as the *menus plaisirs*.

when Queen Maria Amalia came to be interested in the statues that were lying about in the palace gardens. They had been found a few years earlier under the lava deposit of Mount Vesuvius. Maria Amalia wanted more and convinced her husband King Charles of the Two Sicilies to have the area dug. Over the following decade, Maria Amalia's dig came to be one of the marvels of Europe, a must in any journey to Italy. The appeal of Hercula-neum and Pompeii gave body to a long-standing interest in classical art and architecture. It revealed a world of people and not just buildings, fro-zen in the salacious and colourful frescos and the many everyday and domestic objects recovered from the excavation.

Fig. 1.5. 'A Cognocenti contemplating ye Beauties of ye Antique'. Hand-coloured etching by James Gillray, published in London, 11 February 1801. This caricature indicates the huge British public interest in taste and modern design, with a heavy hand of cynicism mixed in.

All this also provided a new way to 'buy' some culture. It was not just the occasional rich tourist who was interested in purchasing expensive things. Sir William Hamilton, British envoy to Naples between 1764 and 1800, was an avid collector and advertised the new discoveries across Europe through his publications. Hamilton was one of the best-known Italophiles of the eighteenth century, famous in old age not just for his wealth and his collection of antiquity but also for his beautiful second wife, Emma, whom he married when he was 60 and she was just 26. A caricature by the irreverent cartoonist Gillray shows an old and bent Sir William surrounded by grotesque ancient artefacts while looking through his spectacles at the bust of 'Lais', aka Lady Hamilton, with a fashionable hairdo but with no nose, mouth, or chin (Figure 1.5). She reappears among the set of portraits on the wall this time as 'Cleopatra', indecently décolleté and holding a bottle of gin. Next to her is 'Mark Antony', Cleopatra's lover. In reality, it is a portrait of Admiral Nelson, Emma's not-so-secret lover. Vesuvius' eruption concludes the orgasmic scene. 'Claudius', a profile of Hamilton himself, turns his back on the other pictures (as he knew and even encouraged his wife's liaison with Nelson), confined as he is to be an old 'mummy', properly labelled Midas, the ancient mythological figure who turned everything he touched into gold.

MAKING GOOD USE OF ANTIQUITY

The appeal of the ancient was not just reserved for the lucky few who could visit Herculaneum and Pompeii or to equally wealthy collectors. In Britain and eventually in continental Europe and North America, it sparked a fashion for the 'antique' that came to influence everything from architecture to interior decoration and dress. The architect Robert Adam drew on his studies of antiquity and from the deep pockets of his clients to refresh the language of luxury with a coat of 'ancient' paint: in the early 1760s no one could claim to be fashionable without indulging in some classical redecoration at home. Syon House (1761–2) and Lansdowne House (1765) were among the most admired Adam mansions in classical style. In France, too, Marie Antoinette had her apartments at Fontainebleau redone in classical style with furnishings made to look bleached white in the antique manner but actually made of luxurious and glittering mother-of-pearl inlays. Archibald Alison in his *Essay on the Nature and Principle of Taste* (1790) concluded that 'the taste which now reigns is that of the Antique'.[48]

The pottery produced by the English entrepreneur Josiah Wedgwood, as well as the furniture by Thomas Sheraton and George Hepplewhite, were much influenced by the Italian archaeological discoveries. New and old mixed together, with teasets and decorative items of classical inspiration being manufactured in state-of-the-art manufactories such as Wedgwood's own Staffordshire factory (appropriately named 'Etruria'), where the new Jasperware and Queen's-ware techniques invented by Wedgwood were deployed. What is distinctive about Wedgwood is that he used a Classical vocabulary to produce new luxuries made of completely new materials. He married novelty and the kudos of the antique. He combined fashion, elegance, and luxury to a level that no one before him had done. And, finally, he produced goods not just for a selected clientele of rich patrons but for the rising middle classes. Perhaps more than any book or scholarly work, Wedgwood was the single most important person in introducing the luxury of antiquity to the homes of eighteenth-century England.

A great deal of the history of luxury shows that one of the entitlements of money is to own not just the present but also the past. In fact, the aesthetic of the 'modern' in the eighteenth century borrowed fulsomely from that of the ancient. And it did so not for the purpose of venerating the ancient past of Egypt, Greece, or Rome, but to make the late-eighteenth-century present just as grandiose, with the added value of conferring status and social cachet on the owners. Such social capital was often acquired not by owning a genuine piece of antiquity, but by owning a fashionable item *inspired* by the ancient past. And entire industries, from interior decoration to porcelain and dress, flourished by borrowing from antique design. The items that they produced were not super-expensive but neither were they for everyone: what one can define as popular luxuries or *populuxuries*.

The idea that the antique could spark improvements across the British economy was also very much on the mind of another man of culture, the aristocrat Lord Elgin. He observed that the antique was quintessentially useful to design production:

> The very great variety in our manufactures, in objects either of elegance or luxury, offers a thousand applications for such details. A chair, a footstool, designs or shapes for porcelain, ornaments for cornices, nothing is indifferent, and whether it be in painting or a model, exact representations of such things would be much to be desired.[49]

At this time, Greek ('Grecian') models were becoming the fashion of the day in preference to Roman models. A friend of Hamilton, Elgin came to be interested in Greek antiquity when he was the British ambassador in Istanbul. Today Elgin is well known for having given his name to the world-famous 'Elgin marbles', now at the British Museum in London. Dismantled from the Parthenon in Athens, they were shipped to Britain in 1802 and became the centrepiece of his extensive collection of Greek antiquities in his large house in London. They were eventually sold to the British government at a fraction of the estimated £70,000 (around £5 million in 2015 money) that he had spent for their excavation and removal. Elgin's extensive collection of other Greek antiquities was also sold to the British government, a fate not uncommon for many such valuable objects. Disappointingly, he never managed to get the reward he really wanted: a United Kingdom peerage, as his own Scottish title did not allow him to have a seat in the House of Lords. Posed as a condition for the sale of the Parthenon's marbles, Elgin's request was gracefully turned down.

AT WHATEVER COST: REVIVALS

The rediscovery of antiquity created several problems for those who could afford and appreciate ancient art, as the majority of what was discovered found its way into vast public collections. By the early nineteenth century these came to form the outstanding archaeological museum of Naples. Rarity meant scarcity, pushing those with money and the right connections to acquire expensive artefacts through legal as well as illegal means. Unable to acquire the beautiful Roman frescos, many thought it worthwhile acquiring good copies. Yet not even copies were abundant, as the Italian museums guarded themselves against any copies being made. The few copies that were produced were sold in great secrecy and were sought after by collectors possibly on the ground more of their illegal status than of any artistic quality or closeness to the original. Yet this is also a story in which original and copy do not just live side by side, but often become one and the same thing. The Venetian Giuseppe Guerra was one of the many Italian artists who struggled to make ends meet in the early decades of the nineteenth century. Though not untalented, he made a fortune more as a fraudster than as an artist. Based in Rome, he not only copied ancient frescos from Pompeii and Herculaneum but also faked them by using pieces of ancient plaster and then sold them off claiming to have acquired them from some Neapolitan petty trader. The directors of the Neapolitan museums raised the alarm and managed to trace the fakes to Guerra in Rome. Passing themselves as customers, they commissioned more fakes from Guerra that they deemed of very good quality. In a reversal of what today is the market for fake leather bags and wallets, the Neapolitan government decided that the best deterrent was not to prosecute the skilled artist, but to display four imitations next to the original frescos accompanied by an inscription warning wealthy tourists against this type of fraud.[50]

The problem was that rich grand tourists neither knew nor minded that they were being defrauded and that copies were frequently passed off as the originals. In fact they generally preferred the 'improved' versions of classical antiques (Elgin himself had been keen to have his Greek marbles restored, though he was later convinced that prosthetic arms might have diminished the value of his precious statues). As in the ancient world, the modern collecting of antiques revealed that the borderline between taste, exclusivity, and luxury, on the one hand, and tasteless commodification for the masses, on the other, was a fine one. If Roman and Greek antiquity prompted a renewal of the grammar of ornament and a reshaping of refined taste, there was nevertheless the danger of 'overdoing' it, something that occurred all too often in that strange period of historicizing design between 1810 and 1840.

The potential for exploitation of the antique for the production of new luxury did not limit itself to the Classical period of Greece and Rome. The influence of Napoleon's campaign in Egypt between 1798 and 1801 swept through Europe in the shape of a new Egyptomania. Many people today focus on the 1920s mania for Egypt with the exciting opening of Tutankhamun's tomb in 1922. They forget about the rage for things Egyptian more than 100 years earlier, when ladies carried crocodile-shaped handbags and even funerary chapels and Christian churches had Egyptian tomblike door cases. The link with the original was here even more tenuous, and the new luxuries in Egyptian style produced in Europe often had little to do with ancient Egypt. The poet Robert Southey in his *Letters from England* (1807) remarked upon the fact that 'everything now must be Egyptian: the ladies wear crocodile ornaments, and you sit upon a sphinx in a room hung round with mummies, and with long black lean-armed long-nosed hieroglyphical men who are enough to make the children afraid to go to bed'.[51] Southey might well have been describing the set of the film Cleopatra at *Cinecittà* a century and a half later.

This Egyptian style included everything from headdresses to furniture and especially architecture. Egypt, with its rich Nile delta, featured as a synonym for luxury in the European consciousness. The eighteenth-century philosopher and economist Adam Smith had admired Egyptian innovations in agriculture. Egypt represented something that was opulent and grand, albeit for many too *nouveau riche*. Size mattered: the contemporary orientalist Quatremère de Quincy in an 1803 work complained about 'le luxe de l'Architecture égyptienne' that boasted 'enormous pillars, enormous walls, and enormous ceilings'.[52] The mammoth scale of Egyptian style was clearly not to everyone's taste, and many considered it quite vulgar. This was the case with the gigantic Egyptian-style plate service commissioned by Napoleon from the famous luxury porcelain factory at Sèvres (Figure 1.6). It was produced in two sets with sixty-six plates with Egyptian scenes, twelve board dishes, twelve dessert dishes, two sugar bowls, and two ice boxes in Egyptian style and as a final touch a centrepiece 22 feet long composed of seventeen separate pieces featuring the kiosk at Philae and another two temples together with an entire small colonnade, two colossal seated figurines, and a sweep of sphinxes from Karnak. This was top luxury on a scale suitable for Napoleon, who wove around him all the atmosphere of an oriental despot. One set was sent to the Russian Tsar Alexander I (when Napoleon was still a friend). The second set was a divorce gift for Napoleon's first wife, the Empress Josephine. Just as today's billionaires might give their wives luxury cars and villas as tokens of an amicable marital separation, so Napoleon thought to impress his soon to be ex-wife. Yet Josephine found it rather tasteless and had it sent back. Eventually, after the fall of Napoleon, the service—valued at an enormous £1,500—was gifted by the new Bourbon King Louis XVIII (brother of the unfortunate Louis XVI) to the Duke of Wellington—by now it was not very fashionable and therefore a perfect diplomatic present—and installed at Apsley House in London.[53]

The story of the Egyptian Sèvres set indicates that it is not just the intrinsic value of an object that makes it an item of luxury. Many collectors today emphasize that an object's provenance adds financial and cultural value. Large diamonds, for instance, draw their value from rarity but also from their previous owners. The 31.06-carat Wittelsbach–Graff Diamond, for

Fig. 1.6. Plate from the 'Egyptian Service', hard-paste porcelain, painted in enamels and gilt, showing the statues of Amenhotep III at Luxor, designed by Vivant Denon (1747–1825) and made at the Sèvres porcelain factory, France, 1810–12. One of sixty-six such plates, this scene, 'Statues dites de Mennon', is taken from the illustrations by Denon (1802) in the description of his journey to Egypt during Napoleon Bonaparte's 1798 campaign.

instance, sold in 2008 for £16.4 million, was not just one of the most expensive diamonds in the world, but also an object that had once belonged to King Philip IV of Spain (1605–65) and a variety of other monarchs over the centuries. This has been surpassed by the record $32.6 million recently paid for a vivid blue diamond formerly in the collection of the heiress Rachel 'Bunny' Mellon, which was sold at Sotheby's New York to a Hong

Kong collector and renamed 'Zoe'. However, most objects—including antiques—do not have such well-known provenance. In many cases, provenance is more or less arbitrarily invented. In 1748 Horace Walpole saw what he thought were Tudor-period chairs at Esher Place in Surrey, and believed them to have been the property of Cardinal Wolsey, who had lived there after 1519. A similar suite comprising ebony chairs at Berkeley Castle was believed to have furnished Francis Drake's cabin, while an ebony bed acquired by William Beckford for Fonthill Abbey was reputed to have furnished the chamber of King Henry VIII of England. We now know that this type of Tudor furniture was in reality made on the Coromandel Coast of India and imported into Europe by the English and Dutch East India Companies, possibly a century after their famous purported owners had died.

MEN, LUXURY, AND EXTRAVAGANCE

Readers might have noticed that most of the great patrons discussed so far were men, whereas in the contemporary marketplace it is women who are very much identified as the luxury consumers par excellence. The eighteenth-century figures Horace Walpole and William Beckford embody a moment of transition in the gendered notion of luxury. Unlike their noble predecessors who had collected luxuries and built splendid villas and palaces in the classic idiom, theirs was a more haphazard recovery of the past characterized by eccentricity and personal passion. They built and furnished some of England's most extraordinary mansions in a new style that borrowed not from antiquity but from the Middle Ages: the Gothic style. Strawberry Hill, built in Twickenham near London between 1748 and 1776 by Horace Walpole, and Fonthill, built by the wealthy William Beckford near Bath from 1796 onwards, are highly stylized projects directed by wealthy, eccentric, and privileged men. The dwellings were not follies, a type of space that is visited but not lived in, but houses and, in the case of Beckford and Walpole, their main residences.

Horace (Horatio) William Walpole, 4th Earl of Orford (1717–97), was a British writer and antiquarian. The third son of the prime minister Robert Walpole, Horace was a Member of Parliament (1741–68), but his main interests were copious correspondence, antiquarian researches, and amateur design. A voluminous and pedantic correspondent, he wrote with an eye to posterity, cataloguing the motives, appearances, and manners of the personalities of his day in 4,000 surviving letters.[54] He also published *The Castle of Otranto* (1764), which was the first 'gothic' novel. Walpole's most significant contribution to the visual arts was his development and promotion of 'Strawberry Hill Gothick', a style that led to a new strand of English architecture that moved away from Palladian symmetry and encouraged the recovery of a real or invented medieval gothic style.

From 1748 to 1776 Walpole had his residence, Strawberry Hill, repeatedly rebuilt in an asymmetrical pseudo-gothic mode. Additions to the original building included a gallery, cloister, oratory, and a tower (the Beauclerk Tower). Walpole pursued what art historian Charles Saumarez Smith calls an 'exercise in archaeology, recreating different periods of architecture from room to room'.[55] In old age, Walpole described his 'small capricious house' as 'a sketch by a beginner'.[56] It was conceived not just as a matter of self-conscious antiquarianism, but rather as a practical residence with a relationship to contemporary taste and sociability: 'In truth, I did not mean to make my house so Gothic as to exclude convenience, and modern refinements in luxury. The designs of the inside and outside are strictly ancient, but the decorations are modern,' wrote Walpole.[57]

Like Walpole, the son of a powerful and wealthy grandee, Beckford published an eccentric novel, *Vathek*, an orientalist tale of incest and murder.[58] In 1796 Beckford began to transform the family estate, 'Splendens', into his own gothic extravagance, Fonthill Abbey. Like Walpole's Strawberry Hill, it was outside urban space and scrutiny, Fonthill being on the edge of a wild landscape, and Beckford having built a 12-foot-high wall to keep out any onlookers. Even more so than Strawberry Hill, the house was

SOUTH WEST VIEW OF FONTHILL ABBEY, WILTSHIRE; THE SEAT OF WILLIAM BECKFORD ESQ.

Fig. 1.7. Drawing by John Buckler of the south-west view of Fonthill Abbey, Wiltshire, the seat of William Beckford, 1821. Brush drawing in grey wash, 35.1 x 45.7 cm. At this secluded villa the notorious William Beckford is said to have had gilded pageboys open the front door. It was one of the tallest residences in England until it collapsed.

about surface, not substance. Designed by architect James Wyatt, Fonthill included an enormous entrance hall with a corresponding 276-foot tower made of wood and Wyatt's mixture of 'compo-cement', which collapsed in 1800 and several times subsequently (Figures 1.7 and 1.8). As Beckford ecstatically wrote in a letter, when you looked up into the tower, it 'was lost in vapour . . . all was essence—the slightest approach to sameness was here untolerated—monotony of every kind was banished'.[59]

Beckford was infamous at the time, the subject of a public and scandalous affair with a well-born young man and forced to live abroad for a time with his wife.[60] Returning to England following the death of his wife,

Fig. 1.8. Print after John Buckler of the south-west view of Fonthill Abbey, Wiltshire, the seat of William Beckford after the collapse of the central tower, c.1825. Lithograph, printed on chine collé. A true 'folly', this was meant to be lived in, not simply visited for fun. Fonthill was on the edge of a wild landscape, and Beckford had built a 12-foot-high wall to keep out any onlookers. Even more so than Strawberry Hill, the house was about surfaces, not substance. Designed by architect James Wyatt, Fonthill included an enormous entrance hall with a corresponding 276-foot tower made of wood and Wyatt's mixture of 'compocement', which collapsed in 1800 and several times subsequently.

Beckford put his heart and soul into the construction of Fonthill. The essayist William Hazlitt described Fonthill as 'a glittering waste of laborious idleness, a cathedral turned into a toy-shop, an immense Museum of all that is most curious and costly, and, at the same time, most worthless, in the production of art and nature'.[61] The term 'toy-shop' strongly suggests that luxury was here at the service not of magnificence and status, but of fashion and surfaces. The use of the word 'toy' at that time indicated not innocent children's games, but jewellery and trifles such as gold snuffboxes or steel buttons. Hazlitt played the arbiter of 'good' luxury, in opposition to pure embellishment and frills. He found Beckford's taste as banal as that of a *marchand-mercier* (a French luxury dealer): 'Mr Beckford has undoubtedly shown himself an industrious bijoutier, a prodigious virtuoso, an accomplished patron of unproductive labour, an enthusiastic collector of expensive trifles', a sentence that would not be out of place as a critique of one of the many plutocrats of today.[62] Beckford created the much-remarked-upon three-day 'long weekend' entertainment of 1781 for himself at Fonthill, for which Marie-Antoinette's set and landscape designer, Jacques Philippe de Loutherbourg, who also worked at Drury Lane Theatre, designed magic lantern and other light effects inside Fonthill's Egyptian- style hall.[63]

Beckford and Walpole aspired not simply to become arbiters of taste, as many of their peers had done through culture and money. Their pursuit of culture was also intertwined with passion, anti-conformism, and a good dose of what Hazlitt and many of his contemporaries thought was the bad taste of the rich and effeminate. Rather than aspiring to immortal reputation and the longevity of their creations, they saw luxury as ephemeral and mainly for the duration of their indulged lives (they had no direct heirs). In the case of Beckford, his tower had to be rebuilt and repaired several times until the building was left to decay. Walpole wrote as early as 1761 that 'My buildings are paper, like my writings, and both will be blown away in ten years after I am dead'.[64] Yet, Walpole's legacy remained key to the shaping of nineteenth-century taste. Strawberry Hill became the destination of a great many Victorian middle-class tourists, eager to see Walpole's villa. In terms of the history of furnishings, the collections at Strawberry Hill also fuelled an interest in fantastical and incongruous juxtaposition, further popularized through Walpole's published *Description* of his house (1784) and the famous auction dispersal of 1842.

Luxury is not something of recent invention. The allure and repulsion of luxury were already a topic of discussion in ancient times. Roman authors complained about the decline of ancient mores, yet the splendour of private and civic buildings in Pompeii and Herculaneum did not fail to astonish contemporaries as well as their discoverers in the mid-eighteenth century. This fostered a new interest in Roman antiquity already present in the Middle Ages when precious cameos, busts, and pottery were seen as essential in the collections of princes and rich intellectuals. The antique became a sign of cultural lineage and a major item of expenditure. The grand tour, a long sojourn in the Italian peninsula sometimes lasting up to several years, was the occasion to acquire a variety of costly (and often not very authentic) items. This use of the antique as an accessory to intellectual aspiration continued over the nineteenth and twentieth century with periodic rediscoveries of Roman, Greek, Gothic, and opulent Egyptian style.

2

Luxury, the Church, and the Court in the Late Middle Ages and Renaissance

The Middle Ages are often portrayed as the 'dark ages'. Yet, in many ways they could have not been more splendid. Rich, glossy silks imported from China and the Middle East were made into liturgical vestments and draped the statues of Madonnas in splendid churches and cathedrals decorated with enormously expensive glass windows. The power and splendour of Church and state were interlinked. The local ruler of one of the many Italian states would have been no less sumptuous in his choice of clothing (called 'livery') and entertainment for himself than he was for his family and vast coterie of courtiers. By the fifteenth century, luxury was also visible in the choice of food and in the degree of formalized manners used at table and in social interactions. This was evident among the wealthy urban elites and mercantile classes but assumed unprecedented forms at court. Princes and kings created perfect settings in which to entertain friends and impress political enemies. Splendid chandeliers, ornate gilded interiors, mirrors, and precious damasks furnished enormous rooms used for feasts, balls, and *divertissements*. By the seventeenth century, all these elements had found their apogee at the court of Louis XIV, King of France, otherwise known as the *Roi-Soleil* (Sun King) because of the remarkable splendour of his court, unprecedented in Europe.

LUXURY AND SPIRITUALITY

The most important figure in the rehabilitation of splendour (and by default luxurious goods) in the Christian Church is Abbot Suger. Suger (1081–1151) was in charge of the great abbey of Saint-Denis, which is now in a rather desultory part of the edge of Paris. In the twelfth century this was a space of the most splendid experimentation in what is now known as the French gothic style. Suger rebuilt an older basilica with large areas of stained glass and thin stone traceries originally painted in polychrome colours that were 'intended to inspire reverence in the believer from the moment he crossed the threshold'.[1] Suger worked closely with the court of the future Louis VI and acquired various rare and precious relics, including the famous Egyptian or late Imperial Roman porphyry vase that he had remounted with eagle mounts for the monarch, now in the Louvre, known as 'Suger's Eagle'. The inscription on the vessel makes the point that marble might be rare, but the deep purple-coloured porphyry is rarer still. It is one of the hardstones associated with the long afterlife of the Egyptian Empire.

To Suger, beautiful and precious objects were not just material artefacts, but conveyed the spiritual power of God. Beauty could therefore be framed as divine, and splendour for the Church was no longer considered to be an aberration. This permitted the incorporation into church decoration and fittings of the most magnificent textiles, gold and silver, gems and semi-precious stones, enamels (molten glass), marbles, bronze and other metals, curious carvings, ivories, and also paintings with precious pigments, which suggested the transcendental power of religion. The Virgin in art could wear a habit of the costliest silk, and altar screens radiated a depth of colour and sensuality. Most important to Suger's vision was the abstract play of light from the famous stained-glass windows that came to define the French gothic era. Anyone who has experienced the beams of these lights understands the link between matter and spirit that he expounded.

By the fourteenth century it became common to expose the host (the bread that is the body of Christ). Precious sacred vessels of rock crystal and metal, known as 'monstrances', were fashioned for this purpose. The use of such crystal to house the relics of the saints also became common among wealthy congregations from the twelfth century. This trend accelerated with the arrival of many such relics from Constantinople after it had been plundered by the Fourth Crusade in 1204. Specialist workshops in Paris, the Meuse, Moselle, and also Venice fashioned rock crystals that had to be hollowed out very carefully. Crystals sometimes acted like magnifying glasses for the relics tucked in behind. Rock crystal had magic and allegorical power: 'according to Saint Augustine, crystal stood for the transformations of evil into good; for St Gregory the Great, it represented Christ.'[2] The ideas are drawn from the discussions of the nature and appearance of the heavenly Jerusalem in the Old and New Testaments. Goldsmiths fashioned the most charming angels to hold up altarpieces and reliquaries. Relatively realistic statuary began to take the place of Byzantine vessels that contained the holy artefacts. Rubies, pearls, and enamel cameos embellished the famous 'Well of Moses', created by the fourteenth-century Dutch/Burgundian artist Claus Sluter for the Carthusian monastery of Champmol, near Dijon, about which it has been commented that 'its radiant physical beauty and the dramatic intensity of the scene depicted attract attention more beautifully than the presence of relics'.[3]

The relationship between the clergy and luxury has a long and complex history in the early Christian Church. Men of the cloth required garments to wear at the altar as well as in the street, and considerable debate took place over the centuries as to how they should appear. Pope Innocent II (1130–43) banned the clergy from displaying 'gilded bridles, saddles, breastplates and spurs' outside the church.[4] The Fourth Lateran Council of 1215 demanded linen tunics, which clearly implied that the more luxurious silk was not considered reasonable. From the thirteenth century, 'what seems to have been sought is a stark visual contrast: dark, plain, and humble outside of the sanctuary, but bright, glistening, and ornamented within church'.[5]

Much of the textile culture of this period was paid for and sometimes also made by noble women. For presiding over the Mass, garments of great splendour and cost were created and paid for by donors. The cone-shaped overgarments worn by the priest during the celebration of the Mass were known as 'chasubles'. One of the most splendid surviving chasubles allegedly belonged to St Vitalis. Preserved today in the Abegg-Stiftung in Switzerland, it was made for the abbey of St Peter in Salzburg, Austria (Figure 2.1). It was probably produced by ladies of the aristocracy, who from the mid-ninth century began to create luxurious liturgical attire incorporating rare imported silks, silk and gold thread, woven

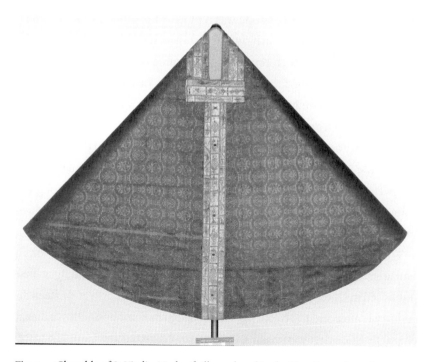

Fig. 2.1. Chasuble of St Vitalis. Made of silk produced in the Near East, eleventh century. Silk and gold, with river pearls and semi-precious stones.

silk bands, pearls, gems, and linen. Some sources suggest that the clergy themselves directed the work, which was conducted as a form of piety. St Vitalis died before 730 CE, and he cannot have worn this garment, which is constructed from eleventh- or twelfth-century silks richly embroidered with pearls and precious gems.[6]

LUXURY AND FASHION IN THE LATER MIDDLE AGES

Our image of a courtly society is today very much configured through tele-visual and movie dramas about the European Middle Ages. Famous come-dians such as Rowan Atkinson present a rather 'barbarian' society in which the rich and powerful lived in icy-cold castles feasting on large quantities of game and wildfowl. Historians, however, disagree with such a caricature and claim that medieval Europe was a more refined place than we imag-ine.[7] The development of fashion, for instance, has been attributed to the thirteenth and fourteenth centuries. A dynamic fashion system emerged within a conjunction of the competing polities of France, England, and Burgundy in the late Middle Ages, and around 1350 men began to dress very differently from women.[8] There was a new consciousness of the value of materiality and skills. The historian Georges Duby noted that people of the Middle Ages wished to celebrate their 'remarkable technical progress, the perfecting of tools', their ability to distinguish the 'shades among the colours', and the ability to unite within art both form and function, 'endow-ing it with grace'.[9]

The idea that the Middle Ages were far from dark comes from Johan Huizinga's famous work of history, *The Waning of the Middle Ages*, first published in Dutch in 1919. In this study of life in fourteenth- and fifteenth-century France and the Netherlands, Huizinga focused upon the medieval characteristics that pervaded the fifteenth-century Low Countries, the main European artistic and trading centre outside Italy. He presented the argument that the Middle Ages were not simply the prelude to the

Renaissance. Instead of seeing a moment of 'birth', he described instead 'the decay of overripe forms of civilization', concluding: 'No epoch ever witnessed such extravagance of fashion as that extending from 1350 to 1480.'[10] Subsequent scholarship has reinforced the notion that something very particular in the history of Western civilization took place in medieval Burgundy.

All this is summarized in one of the most popular paintings in the world, Jan van Eyck's *The Arnolfini Betrothal* (1434). Once thought to represent a wedding, it is now believed to represent a sacramental betrothal between a wealthy Italian textile merchant of the time, Giovanni Arnolfini, from the city of Lucca, and his bride-to-be, Giovanna, in a setting in the Flemish city of Bruges. The nature of his transcontinental trade is indicated not only in the fine woollen broadcloth, fur, and white linen that adorns both man and woman, and the small Turkey carpet, but also in the orange fruit, an exotic luxury that must have come from abroad, sitting on the window-sill. Even the little dog might represent a type of luxury; the Duke of Berry had 1,500 dogs, and 'René of Anjou felt compelled to construct a special fence to keep dogs off his bed'.[11] Lapdogs and hunting dogs were a sign of prestige.

Textiles were central to this new 'culture of appearances' (a term origi-nally coined for the eighteenth century but that applies to earlier periods too), with fine woollens and tapestries presented to visiting princes who voyaged to the rich Franco-Flemish towns.[12] One such luxury commodity that was even more uncommon (and not regularly presented in the north in this manner to visiting princes) was silk. Silk was more likely to be gifted to the Church—hence its survival in large quantities in ecclesiastical con-texts. The lust for silks is well known from the travels of Marco Polo, who marvelled at the types and qualities of silks made and worn across China and at the court of Kublai Kahn. His journey with his father and uncle from Venice to Asia in the late thirteenth century and subsequent published narratives revealed the trade in luxury goods in countries as diverse as Japan (which he read about but did not visit), Syria, Lesser Armenia, and as far south as the Hindu kingdoms of Ceylon and Sumatra.[13]

All this splendour began to filter back to Europe quite quickly, leading to attempts at producing similar products locally. Silk began to be produced in Europe in the early fourteenth century in places such as Lucca and Venice in Italy, where the secret of sericulture had been mastered from the Levant.[14] In a wool-producing country such as England, only silk braids and trimmings were made in the early Middle Ages. Silk was imported, however, from the Near East and China and eventually from Italy and Spain through a network of merchants. Many of these traders came via Paris and Bruges, the latter being a prosperous centre of luxury trade. Cloths of gold and figured silks without pile were the most expensive, followed by plain silks. After the 1330s new products like velvets began to be prominent.[15] The weave and lustre of 'infidel' textiles indicate a highly developed awareness of aesthetics. This pleasure was found not only in the components of dress, but also in trappings such as tents and equine decorations. Interestingly, this textile culture and interest in fashion are more clearly marked, according to many historians of the period, as a male interest.

The rise of fashion and the new impetus towards the consumption of foreign luxuries such as precious silks were not universally welcomed. Starting in the thirteenth century, local and later national governments attempted to control and curb conspicuous consumption. They passed hundreds of laws, called 'sumptuary laws', which established what each rank of society was entitled to consume. The rationale of such legislative intervention can be understood by looking at the preamble (the opening lines) of the sumptuary law of the French city of Montpellier in 1277, which stated that, the town 'wishing to avoid superfluous expense that was spent earlier on women's clothing and ornaments, and the danger for the soul that is [there] inherent, in honor of the highest Creator and for the utility of the town...', such a law had become necessary.[16]

The first sumptuary law in England, enacted in 1336, established that all men and women of whatever rank were forbidden from wearing clothing imported from outside England, Ireland, Wales, or Scotland. The same could be said of the wearing of fur, with the exception of the royal family, high prelates, earls, barons, and knights, as well as members of the clergy with an income of more than £100 a year.[17] Studies of the *Roman de la rose* (begun 1225–30, continued 1269–70), one of the most famous verse works of medieval France, indicate that much of the attention concerning luxury consumption was directed at men rather than women. Historian Sarah-Grace Heller notes how sumptuary laws promoted the ambitions of those who wished to expand their personal visibility.[18] Parts of the *Roman de la rose* concern 'deceit' by clothing, and many luxury fashions are described in the book, especially hats (furred and ribboned hats, floral garlands, unisex hats, to be worn by both women and men).[19]

French sumptuary laws, it has been argued, were different from other European laws in that they were concerned with food, clothing, and horses, but not funerals or social displays (apart from banqueting), which were a common object of sumptuary laws elsewhere in Europe.[20] French laws are not concerned with the silhouettes of garments in the thirteenth century; rather they focus on the nature and cost of the fabric. Philippe III's laws of 1279 set the number of robes that a man or a woman might possess to five for a duke and one for a bourgeois.[21] Imagine being told today how many sets of clothes one might own! Quite strict were the prohibitions for the bourgeoisie: 'No bourgeois man or women will wear *vair* [grey fur, generally squirrel], *gris*, or ermine fur, and they shall surrender all they have a year from next Easter. They shall not wear, nor be allowed to wear, gold or precious stones, nor crowns of gold or silver.'[22]

As with the French, Italian sumptuary laws attempted—and often failed—to limit not just the use of luxury cloth and clothing but also jewellery, cushions and coverlets, food and feasting, and expensive forms of transport such as chariots and palanquins.[23] For those who contravened the law, punishment followed. Fines were not uncommon for those who were found wearing forbidden items, and these fines were administered by specially employed officials who went from street to street and sometimes even entered people's private residences. Punishment could also extend to include the makers of forbidden items. In the cities of Forlì and Reggio Emilia in northern Italy in the mid-sixteenth century, for example, artisans producing forbidden garments, embroideries, or jewellery were fined 25 scudi and received three lashes.[24]

Within highly regulated Renaissance societies, most sumptuary laws were directed at women (even if men loved their horses, parties, and furs). The historian Catherine Kovesi points out that fashion is not an arcane sign system, but a visible and public indication of important matters. In a society such as medieval and Renaissance Italy, she argues, women relied much more than men on dress codes. Men could justify fine clothing by reference to their public roles; women lacked any such roles and were limited to the private sphere. Within this system, their clothes functioned as a type of 'voice'.[25] Young males, on the other hand, were accused of immodesty, effeminacy, and sometimes linked to charges of homosexuality via luxury consumption. The preacher Bernadino of Siena (1380–1444) published a sermon in which he claimed that, if parents sent their boys out of the house wearing fashionable clothes with low doublets, which showed parts of the legs and see-through shirts, then they were acting as pimps for their children.[26]

Sumptuary laws continued in the following centuries, being first repealed in England in 1603 and in other European countries over the course of the seventeenth and early eighteenth centuries. Yet historians agree that mere legislation might not have been sufficient to stop the rise of luxury and fashion. The very fact that these laws were periodically reissued and updated probably means that they were overall ineffective. Luxury and fashion became, instead, key phenomena both in the medieval courts and within the prosperous European cities of the Renaissance. Here one could find not just customers but also a variety of artisans busy providing luxury dress and trading in its components. The most skilful makers moved from place to place, sometimes avoiding corporate constraints and spreading new styles of, for instance, tailored clothes, textiles, embroideries, illuminated books, statuettes, and jewels. In this way, fashion and luxury became central to technological innovation and to the culture of hierarchical display that characterized late medieval and Renaissance Europe, especially in a courtly setting.

THE PURSUIT OF MAGNIFICENCE AT THE COURT OF HENRY VIII

The understanding of luxury within the courtly environment of the later Middle Ages and early modern period necessitates an appreciation of the concept of 'magnificence'. Magnificence, from the Latin *magnum facere*, literally means 'to do something great' and is closely related to the word *magnificentia*, which means both greatness and nobleness, but also generosity and pride. These were all virtues that a ruler had to embody in his actions, manners, and especially his choices of dress and luxurious spending. Renaissance rulers thus employed the newly confident artists, architects, and designers to assert the primacy of their court's power and culture. Magnificence was to be contrasted to mere 'pomp', the vain and ostentatious display of wealth through luxurious goods, something that medieval and early modern governments looked down upon and actively discouraged through laws and admonitions. The idea of magnificence, and the associated concept of splendour, had a long pedigree going back to antiquity, but in the Renaissance the two concepts became guiding concepts for any ruler. The humanist and poet Giovanni Pontano tells us in his 1498 philosophical and ethical treatise *De splendore*:

> It is appropriate to join splendour [*splendor*] to magnificence [*magnificentiae*], because they both consist of great expense and have a common matter that is money. But magnificence [*magnificentia*] derives its name from

the concept of grandeur and concerns building, spectacle and gifts while splendour [*splendor*] is primarily concerned with the ornament of the household [*ornamentis domesticis*], the care of the person, and with furnishings [*supelectile*] and in the display of different things.[27]

Magnificence and splendour were popular concepts not just in the Italian Renaissance courts but also at the French and English courts. Since 1485 England had enjoyed a period of relative prosperity and peace under Henry VII. When Henry VIII (1491–1547) succeeded his father in 1509, he inherited a full exchequer. He was a boy of 17 who read Latin and spoke French very well. One of the great events of his tumultuous life was the Field of the Cloth of Gold (*Camp du Drap d'Or*). Held near Calais in June 1520, this was a meeting arranged to increase the bond of friendship between England and France, when Henry came together with the handsome François I, King of France. The meeting lasted four weeks, with banquets, jousts, and general showing-off.[28] Although Henry VIII changed clothes constantly and had particularly fine tents and horse trappings, he realized that his English artists and designers were not as sophisticated as those working abroad, so he asked the great German artist Hans Holbein the Younger (1497–1543) to move to London along with other skilled artists and designers. Holbein, whom we associate with portrait painting, in fact designed everything from jewels to chimneypieces to clocks for Henry, to samples of embroidery for the ladies, using the then fashionable style of the grotesque.

Henry was a terror for the Church, and, after confiscating monastic lands, he lived at Whitehall, then one of the biggest palaces in the world with buildings covering 24 acres. He also built St James's Palace and Nonsuch in Surrey. Thomas Cromwell made him rich beyond imagination by dissolving the churches and monasteries. In old age Henry became very fat, as he could not play the sports he loved because of a leg injury. His waist increased from an attractive 34 to 54 inches (Figure 2.2). He adopted padded Germanic styles of dressing and laid on the gems, with some outfits

Fig. 2.2. *Henry VIII*, *c.*1560–80. Oil on panel after Hans Holbein the Younger.

covered in rubies set in gold and collars of pearls and jewels. It is said that those who laughed at his appearance suffered later.

Dress historian Maria Hayward, writing on the splendid clothes of Henry VIII, points out that, despite the rhetoric, 'visually and financially there would have been very little difference between magnificent and luxurious dress. Both would be sumptuous and expensive. The differ-ence ... is a moral one.'[29] The hats of Henry VIII were of black velvet, which was not very expensive in itself, but they were so covered in 'enamelled and engraved gold buttons, aglettes and jewelled brooches' that they were listed in his inventories next to the entry on plate (silver).[30] She points out that most foreign accounts of encountering the King had little to report on what he said, but much to say about what he wore.

Men liked their jewels very much and wore more than they have ever done, before or since: a painting of Robert Dudley, Earl of Leicester (attrib-uted to Steven van der Meulen, active 1543–68), indicates the many hun-dreds of pearls used as trimming on the sleeves of the doublet and as ties (Figure 2.3). Pearls also appear as trimmings on detachable sleeves on Venetian figures of the Virgin. Royal clothes were not locked in tradition, but had to change, as the English court was influenced by foreign fashions such as those from the realm of Burgundy.[31] The great fashion innovation of this period was the division of hose (stocking-like nether garments) into upper and lower. The codpiece or 'cod' was separate. A great luxury (and also, of course, a means of asserting a masculine presence), it was laced to the hose and doublet—and was, of course, also slang for scrotum.

LUXURY AND SPLENDOUR UNDER ELIZABETH I

Elizabeth I (1533–1603), daughter of Henry VIII, took magnificence to an ever greater extreme. In her famous Armada portrait, painted when she was nearly 60, she wears a front-fastening bodice with wings, decorated with bands of pearls and gem-studded bows and set with separate gems (Figure 2.4). The Ditchley portrait shows a dress of what is probably white silk with a secondary weft of silver. She has 45 jewelled buttons, 370 pearls, 300 pearls in necklace ropes, and earrings in the form of armillary spheres, tied with red ribbons. Her wired veil in two parts is edged with more jewels. The inventory of her wardrobe listed 1,900 items, including her clothes,

Fig. 2.3. *Robert Dudley, Earl of Leicester*, *c*.1560–5. Oil on oak panel attributed to Steven van der Meulen (fl. 1543–68).

Fig. 2.4. *Elizabeth I, Armada Portrait, c.*1588. Oil on panel attributed to George Gower (1540–96).

her fans, buttons, jewels, and lengths of silk. Dressing the Queen meant that each lady in waiting had a task, and a book was kept to record any jewels lost from the Queen. The circulation of jewels was a very important part of court culture. The miniatures given by Elizabeth I were a prized sign of great favour, and could be both melancholy and amusing at the same time: an eye shedding a tear and a heart pierced by an arrow spelled melancholy.

Luxury needed to be managed and required an army of trusty servants to receive, record, care, store, and mend garments, jewellery, weapons, and other royal paraphernalia. This position came to be known in France as the office of the King's Wardrobe. Under the French king Henri III (r. 1574–89), an executive office of the royal household was charged with providing not only the clothing of the King, but the livery ('issues') of cloth and furs of defined type and value for the nobility to gift to the poor, and a whole range of luxuries from ginger to candles. The King's tailors, who are known by name, were often a type of bureaucratic chief, responsible for everything from complete hangings for a royal bed, to the tens of thousands of furs bought to line livery. They made purchases from the regional fairs of England as well as from foreign merchants such as the Lucca silk-dealers and Baltic fur-traders.[32]

The role of the goldsmith was also central to the burgeoning trade in European high luxuries: he was an international figure also involved with the financial affairs of clients and trade generally. He had to move gold and silver from the Americas via Spain and Portugal and then might work in Nuremburg or London using diamonds from India, rubies from Burma, sapphires from Ceylon, emeralds from Colombia, and pearls grown on the Persian Gulf and off the coast of Ceylon. One of the most celebrated goldsmiths of the sixteenth century was the German Wenzel Jamnitzer, who served as court goldsmith to a succession of Holy Roman Emperors, including Charles V, Ferdinand I, Maximilian II, and Rudolf II (Figure 2.5). Extremely skilful in the production of jewellery boxes incorporating corals, shells, and hardstones encased in precious metal, he was also an inventor and a scholar of some reputation. He was probably the inventor of a machine for embossing metals and the author of *Perspectiva corporum regularium* ('Perspective of Regular Solids'), published in 1568.

Furs were also a very important part of global trade: *armions* (ermine) were the winter coat of the stoat, a member of the weasel family; those from the north were white in winter, except for the tip of the tail, which is black. You could substitute miniver, the white bellies of squirrels, which by the mid-sixteenth century was cheaper than ermine. Fashion was also on the move. Elizabeth knew about French cutting techniques and tried to get a French tailor to come to her court from Paris. Life-sized fashion dolls were sent between the French and Italian courts to communicate new trends.[33]

Fig. 2.5. *Portrait of the Goldsmith Wenzel Jamnitzer* (1507/8–85), *c*.1562–3 by Nicolas Neufchatel (previously attributed to Georg Pencz). 92.5 x 80 cm. Donated to the City of Geneva in 1805 according to consular decree of 1801 (Decree Chaptal) also called 'Sending Napoleon'. The goldsmith is depicted with the tools of his trade and the fruits of his labour. The ferns and leaves in the gilded vessel on the shelf are clearly fashioned from silver.

Medieval and Renaissance mindsets loved colours; to the well educated, colours had metaphysical as well as sensual qualities.[34] Elizabeth I owned rich gowns of mainly black and white, but also tawny, ash, dove, carnation, orange, peach, russet, crimson, 'hair colour', purple, bee colour, clay, drake's colour, horseflesh, lady's blush, partridge, and straw. New dyes were found all the time to extend the colour range.[35] The most vivid red was called lustie gallant, the palest maiden's blush. There was goose-turd green, pease-porridge tawny, and popinjay blue. None of Elizabeth I's complete garments survives, and barely any components; some are believed to be in the Danish Royal Collection.

Elizabeth developed the idea of the 'progress', in which she and her court moved across her realm. This was very clever, as she did not have to pay for her court when she was away. She greatly delighted in elaborate masques, a form of conspicuous consumption that was completely ephemeral and yet took up an enormous amount of time and money. Masques centred on the monarch, and she was generally invited to play a role in them. She borrowed the concept from Medici Florence. The idea was that noble lords and ladies would perform in masques and other theatrical devices on themes such as 'Triumph of the King and the Court'—masquers vanquished base enemies, who might be dressed as witches and hags, bacchic figures, grotesques, and carnival fools. They were cast away by members of the royal family dressed as Oberon, the Fairy King, the Divine Beauty, and the like. Nobles did not speak and had their faces hidden with a mask. Exquisite clothes were worn by the performers: some dancing before the Queen in 1600 wore 'a skirt of cloth of silver, a rich waistcoat wrought with silks and gold and silver, a mantel of carnacion taffeta cast under the arme, and their hair loose about their shoulders'.[36]

All of this was not about vanity so much as statecraft, organization, and economy. Elizabeth I's wardrobe did not exceed that of the other monarchs of Europe, about which she was well informed. She regarded these cloths and clothes as state treasure. But the pursuit of magnificence was not confined to dress. Architecture became in the early modern period a necessary expenditure for any ruler or nobleman. One historian of the period has written that Elizabethan architecture 'is not...of the mind but of the senses'.[37] Timber, stone, and brick offered colour, pattern, and quality. Architecture in the English-speaking world became part of the curriculum of magnificence and learning for the first time: 'Classical architecture was the built form of classical learning,' writes the architectural historian Christy Anderson.[38] The rise of the printed book played an important role in this: 'through the printed page architecture could now be studied independently of buildings themselves. Ancient architecture and inscriptions...and ideal cities were all topics available to the professional and amateur.'[39]

The completion of the great 'prodigy houses' of England was enriched with plunder in this period, especially after the defeat of the Spanish Armada in 1588: Longleat House, near Warminster (1567–80), with its facade showing the three classical orders and banqueting houses on the roof; Burghley House in Lincolnshire (1574–89), with its classical details deployed on the roofline; Aston Hall, Birmingham (1618–35), with its Long Gallery of Ionic pillars; Bolsover Castle in Derbyshire (1610s), with its Venus fountain and cold bath; and Wollaton Hall in Nottinghamshire (1580s), with its semi-correct Doric frieze (Figure 2.6). Many of these grand houses were fitted out in the hopes of the Queen visiting—a scenario that lasted until the reign of Queen Victoria.

Considerable investment went into the building of large palaces and houses. However, the real investment was in furnishing their splendid interiors. The walls might be brick or stone, sometimes rendered and painted, but the interiors were filled with tapestry, gold and silver plate, porcelain, and objects designed after Flemish and German woodcuts and Mannerist forms from France. One of the most famous and sensual objects surviving from this reign is the Sea-Dog Table, c.1597 (Figure 2.7).[40] Designed after the engravings of the French architect and designer Jacques

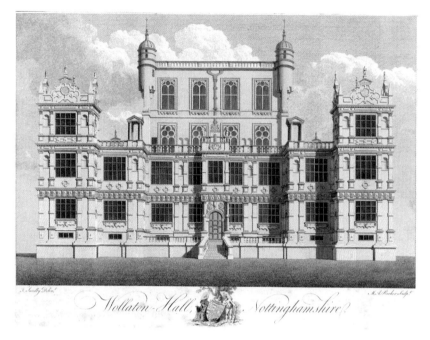

Fig. 2.6. Wollaton Hall, Nottinghamshire. Front view of the house, with pavilions with Dutch gables and acroterions, a tower with two cupolas, and arched windows behind the central building.

Androuet du Cerceau I, it sits on a base of carved tortoises, with four carved wooden seadogs with tails, pointed bosoms, and ostrich feather ears (which it is believed people caressed and rubbed as they studied the exotic inlaid walnut and marble sliding tabletop). It stood in the withdrawing chamber at Hardwick Hall in Derbyshire, home of Bess of Hardwick, one of the richest women in late sixteenth-century England. The top floor was built for a planned visit from the Queen. Sadly, by 1597 she was too old to visit. It is speculated that Bess used the tabletop to admire her jewels and *objets de vertu* when she was in residence. It was originally fitted with a carpet of needlework and a blue and gold fringe. That it was so erotic and owned by a woman cannot be coincidental. Seadog refers to the 'talbot' or dog that was a part of the arms of her fourth husband, George Talbot. Seadogs are

Fig. 2.7. Sea-Dog Table, c.1600. Inlaid walnut 875 mm (H); 1,480 mm (L).

chimera who can fly, walk, and swim. The tortoise base is a visual joke—as occurs also with so many Elizabeth jewels—'make haste slowly'. It took its place within a wholly cosmopolitan space where the carpets were from Constantinople and the porcelain was Chinese.[41]

Carpets were probably as important as silks in exciting the superrich of this time. Until the eighteenth century a carpet meant something covering furniture and only later applied to floors. As late as 1727 the *Chambers Cyclopoaedia* called it 'a sort of covering to be spread on a table, trunk, an astrade [dais] or even a passage or floor'.[42] It was generally the most decorative element in any room from the fifteenth to the seventeenth centuries, on tables and cupboards. Designs were sent from England to be worked into carpets in Turkey; they were later sent to India and China, as was also the case with porcelain. The fabrics used varied widely down the social scale. The rich had Eastern carpets from Turkey and Persia. The cheaper English equivalent was called Turkey-work. In 1523 Dame Agnes

Hungerford had fifty-four cushions, some of velvet and gold; 'six fine carpets for cupboards, three great carpets for tables (tapestry), as well as seven "bastard carpets" of poorer quality' or cut-down from old pieces.[43]

Prodigality and thrift were two sides of a continuum, and neither was acceptable for a ruler. Magnificence and modesty could also go together. Elizabeth was famous for spending a great deal on dress but saved money by visiting noble houses for part of the year, with the results that she bankrupted some of the major English noble families. In this sense, expenditure was rarely discussed in terms of exchange or in the context of a market, but as a form of representation or performance. When Elizabeth I died in 1603, her Stuart cousin James VI of Scotland inherited the throne of England and became James I. Even if Elizabeth I had embodied splendour, at her death in 1603 she left only £40,000 debt. However, just five years later, James I had accumulated debts worth £600,000. At the end of his reign in 1625, he owed a staggering £1 million (equivalent to $200 million in 2015 money).[44] Most of this money had been used not in waging war, but in a public and flamboyant display of conspicuous consumption. The cost of the garments of a king could be incredible: Charles I, son of James I, paid £266 for a scarlet silk suit with gold and silver embroidery in 1629, whereas a portrait by a great artist of the time such as Daniel Mytens cost only £66.[45] The royal family accumulated so much debt at this time that the funeral of Anne of Denmark (d. 1619) had to be delayed, as no one would supply the necessary black cloth.

DECORUM, MANNERS, AND COURT LIFE

The pursuit of luxury among early modern rulers and their retinue was predicated around the acquisition of enormously expensive artefacts, but experience of the mind and body was also valued: 'The things which can make life enjoyable remain the same,' commented Johan Huizinga. 'They are, now as before, reading, music, fine arts, travel, the enjoyment of nature, sports, fashion, social vanity...and the intoxication of the senses...The Renaissance wanted an unencumbered enjoyment of all of life.'[46] Yet the search for luxury was also underpinned by a series of ideas and concepts that are specific to the Renaissance. Generalization is difficult, as courts were widely different in their size and composition. The sixteenth-century Italian courts were different from the more decadent and wasteful courts of the seventeenth century, for instance. Cosimo I de Medici (1519–74), ruler of Florence, was even described as modest in his taste and expenditure. Medieval feasts, often portrayed today in films as excessive and extravagant, might not have been so wasteful after all. We should not assume, in fact, that the luxury of the table of the Middle Ages was about impressing people. The ceremony of the feast was closely related to Christ's Last Supper, and a seat next to the Lord was one of the greatest prizes. Giving a great feast was not just about impressing people. It was an act of 'generosity', a 'charitable act', a 'pious obligation', an attempt to 'secure the peace' and sustain 'the social order of the world'.[47] 'Loyalty is venison' ran the motto of the Danish Renaissance king Frederik II.[48]

Ideas about what was appropriate and how conspicuous consumption should be utilized as a tool of power circulated widely and were shared across courts not just in Italy but throughout Europe. From the late fifteenth century Italy provided a model for all of Europe, to be emulated or rejected, reinterpreted, absorbed, reworked, or transformed.[49] An important concept generated within the courtly environment of Italy was that of *decorum*, the idea of an ideal-type of social behaviours based on good manners and etiquette. A series of humanist writers addressed the issue of decorum and conduct, among them Baldassare Castiglione (1478–1529), the most famous and influential writer on this topic. Castliglione was a member of the court of the Duke of Urbino and acted as a diplomat in the service of the princes of Mantua and the Papal Curia. This first-hand experience allowed him to publish *The Courtier* (1528), a true guide for the perfect male courtier. The book stresses the role of moderation in regulating the appearance of noblemen and their consumption. He says that rulers must be 'generous and splendid in hospitality towards foreigners and ecclesiastics' but at the same time attentive 'to moderate all superfluities, for through the errours that are committed in these matters, small though they seem, cities often come to ruin'.[50] For the courtier, Castiglione emphasized instead the virtue of courage, and the importance of good manners, conversation, and a range of moderate accomplishments that were imitated all over Europe.

A second important concept to be found in Castiglione and later studied by historians is that of the manners encouraged within the courts. Historian Maria Bogucka considers the figure of the courtier, gesture, ritual, and social order from the sixteenth to the eighteenth centuries among the Polish gentry, who developed an elaborate code of behaviour that extended from precedent at table to rules about when to wear a hat or not. The walk of the Renaissance Polish nobleman was slow and full of dignity, and could be recognized by foreigners.[51] Gesture was one central part of the outward expression of the social hierarchy in Italy, France, and Poland, just as in Tudor England.

Sumptuous fashions, textiles, jewellery, and a range of more transient arts set within architectural frameworks reinforced the notion that the ruler's grace and power could not be replicated, but only experienced by his courtiers as a type of radiation. Livery and gifts of fashionable clothes and jewels were central to this civilizing process.[52] Noble bodies were designed and identities shaped through the disciplines of fencing, riding, dance, and ultimately dressing, to become collective mentalities that structured hierarchies of modern European etiquette and behaviour. The historian Peter Burke has usefully described this act of distinction as a task of 'impression management'.[53] He notes the rise of the concept of Renaissance family 'strategies', which included fashion purchase and display. The idea of the 'uniqueness' of an individual, Burke argues, goes hand in hand with a personal style in painting (the artist), the rise of the autobiography, and the first-person address (the humanist).

Jacob Burckhardt, the nineteenth-century Swiss historian who did more than anyone to popularize the notion of a cultural 'rebirth' to describe life in fifteenth-century Italy, created much of his analysis from a study of the incredible public display of this period. Much of this display was ephemeral and survives mainly in written descriptions, along with some prints, drawings, and paintings. The famous festivals and processions of a city such as Venice displayed the fixed dress of the professions, where the relative stability of the dress of the nobles, lawyers, physicians, and merchants was viewed as a proof of the stability of the Republic; and also the luxurious and fashionable clothes of the doge's wife, the dogaressa, which were presented as simultaneously ornamental and delightful.[54] And the scope of aesthetics was understood to be much wider than is generally the case today, so that a metaphysical interest in beauty extended also to the beauty of objects. Yet it was all transitory. According to the sixth-century philosopher Boethius, whose writings were much in vogue in the early modern period: 'The beauty of things is fleet and swift, more fugitive than the passing of flowers in Spring.'[55] There might be a delight in worldly things, which must always perish, at the same time as there must be a profound melancholy and focus upon the transcendental nature of death.

The socialization of manners was predicated on a shared understanding of magnificence and decorum but also a shared visual culture among the European elite. This is particularly noticeable when we consider collecting practices. Literary models were drawn from Aristotle to justify the purchase of objects such as gems, vases, and table services. The purpose of these objects was not to embody the virtue called 'magnificence' but rather to convey artistry, variety, abundance, and decorum.[56] Simply being known as a collector was prestigious, according to this humanist formula. To collect was not simply to accumulate but to generate knowledge and interconnection between things.

LUXURY AT THE COURT OF LOUIS XIV

All this fine clothing, gesture, and comportment needed a stage on which it could be set. The society that established the ultimate stage for luxury consumption was France, even if many of the ideas were originally Italian. The scene was set with the incredible spaces and gardens of Versailles, which has been called 'a hallucinatory statement of power'.[57] Many of the ideas for Versailles came from the mid-seventeenth-century *château* of Vaux-le-Vicomte, about 55 kilometres south-east of Paris. Its lofty spaces of circulation were a huge advance upon French princely Renaissance architecture, which was richly decorated with gilding and painting but had smaller windows and few mirrors. In 1667 Louis XIV left the older palace of the Louvre in central Paris for his rebuilt and much expanded Versailles. A series of victorious campaigns from 1672 gave both funds and impetus to extend the palace. Jules Hardouin Mansart began work in 1678, and by 1684 the Hall of Mirrors was complete (Figure 2.8). As well as being a statement of absolute power and luxury, it was also like a street or road, but one lined with vast mirrors reflecting the light from equally high windows. Cast mirror glass had generally been made by the Italians (Venice had the monopoly), but the French now managed to devise a technique of their own, partly through industrial espionage.

The complexity—both technical and financial—of building and furnishing such an enormous palace should not be forgotten. Seventeenth-century France created from scratch a new luxury sector through the patronage of the court. Royal manufactures—owned by local rulers—had already been present in Italy in the fifteenth and sixteenth centuries, but France established some cutting-edge *manufactures royales* for the benefit not just of the court but also of the state. During the reign of Louis XIV it was an academic artist, Charles Le Brun, who was the principal orchestrator of all these schemes. Jean-Baptiste Colbert (1619–83), France's prime minister, put Le Brun in charge of the most important royal manufacture,

CONVERSATIONS.

Fig. 2.8. *The Galerie des Glaces* (Hall of Mirrors) at the palace of Versailles, with courtiers admiring the decoration. Frontispiece to the first volume of Madeleine de Scudéry's *Conversations nouvelles sur divers sujets* (Paris: Claude Barbin, 1684). Fruit trees can be seen planted in silver urns on either side of enormous consoles held up by putti.

the Gobelins workshops on the left bank of the Seine, in 1667. They manufactured almost everything for the court at the highest technical and artistic standards (Figure 2.9). Le Brun provided the sketches and approved

Fig. 2.9. Tapestry woven in wool and silk, *c.*1670–1700, produced at Les Gobelins.
Designed by Charles Le Brun (1619–90). This tapestry is from a series representing twelve
of Louis XIV's royal residences during different months of the year, with the King shown
hunting with his retinue in the grounds of his *châteaux*. Such tapestries relate to the strong
medieval interest in marking time. The foreground is dominated by a display of abundance, the bounty of nature, and the luxury of court life. The textiles and other precious
objects laid on the balustrade are known to have been drawn from Louis's treasury, and
the animals and birds from his menagerie (private zoo).

designs made by his 250 staff. The aim of the Gobelins workshop under Le Brun was 'to unify all the arts and to establish an ensemble of formulas in which the rules of Absolute Beauty would be fixed forever'.[58]

The Gobelins continued the tradition of royal workshops at the Louvre founded in the early seventeenth century, and they were accompanied by other state-of-the-art manufactures such as Saint-Gobain (est. 1665) for the production of mirrors, and later in the eighteenth century Sèvres (est. 1736) for the production of porcelain. Here artisans worked directly for the Crown and for those who could afford them. These workers had prestige and could engage in innovation and experimentation. Many were foreign and broke all the guild rules; they were, therefore, hated by the competition. Their work showed innovation and richness of craft and materials. In many ways their example set up the pattern of foreign workers coming to a great metropolitan city like Paris and innovating luxuries for the next two centuries.

This was not just luxury and magnificence for the sake of it. The king represented himself through style—architecture, furniture, fashion, and other decorative arts, as much as through his armies and navies: 'The king's objects were the king, the style of these objects belonged to the king's body.'[59] In the case of Louis XIV, his court had to represent the power of the court as 'foreign princes or their ambassadors make inferences about the strength or weaknesses of the kingdom'.[60] Within this model of rule—Absolutism—the king, nation, state, and people were interlinked. The king stood in for the nation, and his things stood in for him. Only certain privileged people had things that resembled his own. The decorative arts had symbolic powers that we barely recall in social life today—for instance, when courtiers bowed in front of the royal *nef*—a shiplike vessel that contained the king's knife, fork, and napkin; and indeed they bowed, whether the king was present or not (Figure 2.10).

France, and Versailles in particular, set a standard for furniture and design of a costly magnificence that few could emulate. Furniture might be made of solid ebony and *pietre dure*, inlaid stones. Chinese porcelain and

Fig. 2.10. Silver, parcel-gilt, chased, cast, engraved, embossed *nef*, produced in Nurem-
berg by Esaias zur Linden, *c.*1609–29. *Nefs* were small ships that served as table and buffet
decoration. They remained popular until the Edwardian period, when they were sometimes converted into vessels for wine bottles. This was not their original function; they had
previously held the knife and napkin of a high-ranking person.

vases complemented the colour schemes, which were tonal, like sophisticated Baroque oil paintings. *Commodes* replaced chests and coffers later in
the reign, and Versailles also had 400 *guéridons*, a French invention that is
an elaborate candlestand. Marquetry, veneers, ivory and dyed horn, gemstones, and *trompe-l'œil* trumped domestic woods. Leather seating was

replaced by fabric and tapestry. The furniture used classical profiles and new decorative motifs such as *chinoiserie* and 'grotesques' of interlaced garlands and figures.

The master cabinetmaker André Charles Boulle integrated metal and sculptural elements including the human figure and marquetry into one piece, as well as popularizing brass laid in tortoiseshell or vice versa. Boulle also invented new furniture forms such as the *commode* (a chest of drawers with a flat top), the *bas d'armoire* (what we might call a wardrobe), and the *bureau plat* (a writing desk with a large flat surface area for papers). Ebony, tortoiseshell, pewter, brass, ivory, horn, boxwood, pear, thuya, stained and natural sycamore, satinwood, beech, amaranth, cedar, walnut, mahogany, and ash were among the materials deployed. Little survives of this splendour—there are only about three of the seventy-six precious cabinets inlaid with stones and lacquers made for Louis XIV known to be in collections today. The incredible woven carpets that were once laid down on the now bare floor of Versailles survive only in fragments.

Following the influx of silver from the South American mines, Louis ordered solid silver furniture to be made. Once again, little survives, but copies with gessoed silver tops can be seen at the great English stately home of Knole in Kent, including a console table, a pair of free-standing *torchères* (stands) for candelabra, and a mirror surround. Paintings by the French artist Alexandre-François Desportes show the silver buffet that was placed around diners. This recalls earlier practices dating back to the medieval period, and it survived as a practice in the dining rooms of the rich until the Aesthetic movement began to declutter the house in the late nineteenth century.

Sumptuary legislation prohibited the use of silver and gilding in furniture or fabric for anyone but the Crown. However, this was luxury that could be easily converted into cash if need arose: in 1689 Louis XIV decreed that all silver was to be melted to finance the war against the League of Augsburg. He melted down rather than sell his furniture. It has been argued that, had he sold his furniture, symbolically he would have sold a measure of his own power. It took six months to melt and yielded 20,000 tons of bullion.

The melting of silver—a practice not at all uncommon for family silverware in the early modern period—allowed the release of resources, but was also a method sometimes used to refashion objects in the latest style. We should not, in fact, think that the category of luxury remained stable or that its material forms went unchanged or were unaffected by fashion. New luxury beverages, for instance, helped pass the time of day at Versailles. Tea, coffee, and chocolate were introduced in the late seventeenth century and then a whole new repertoire of table services came into being, as pewter and pottery are not good for holding hot drinks and they do no permit the colour of the drink to sparkle in the way that transparent porcelain does. Wide-bottomed silver vessels were better at retaining the heat of the tea. Coffee and chocolate also ideally require specially shaped vessels. Horology also improved dramatically: the first practical pendulum for clocks and balance spring for watches were invented in the 1650s–70s and imported from The Hague. Changes in luxury consumption were also present lower down the social scale. The social historian Lawrence Stone, writing on seventeenth-century England, reminds us that the decline of the great funeral, the withdrawal at mealtimes from the great chamber to the private dining room, and the shift from an equestrian cavalcade to the privacy of the coach and sedan chair 'are all symptoms of the same thing', 'a readjustment of values by which emphasis was laid less on publicity and display and numerical quantity and more on privacy and luxury and aesthetic quality'.[61]

THE RENAISSANCE OF LUXURY

The Church and the court were in the later Middle Ages and the early modern period some of the only places where luxury was to be found. Yet, their importance was more than simply performative. Especially in the world of the European courts, luxury was shaped through a series of concepts that ranged from magnificence to splendour, giving a new and important conceptual basis for luxury to thrive. Yet luxury remained divisive and elitist. The luxuries considered in this chapter were within the reach of only a very small fraction of society. Sumptuary laws are symptomatic of the fact that aspiration to luxury spending became widespread, especially in towns and cities, yet the response was unambiguously negative, with legislators trying to limit what they considered as conspicuous expenditure. This axiom was to be challenged in the following centuries and in particular in the eighteenth century—when luxury came to be interpreted not just as a category for the elites but as a motor for the industry and artistry of entire societies.

3

Luxury and the Exotic:

The Appeal of the Orient

In April 2014 a small Ming cup was sold at Sotheby's Hong Kong for an astonishing $36 million, the highest price ever fetched by a Chinese work of art. This sale made worldwide news not just for the record price, but because the cup is only 3.1 inches in diameter and is nicknamed the 'chicken cup' as it represents a rooster and hen with their chicks. Owned by the Philippines-born businessman Stephen Zuellig, the cup was defined by a Hong Kong antique dealer as 'the holy grail of ceramics', one of just nineteen similar cups that 'people, emperors and collectors have always aspired to own'.[1] The rooster and hen are supposed to represent the Emperor and Empress of China and their chicks the Chinese people. Although it is not known who the current owner is, in all likelihood it is one of China's new super-rich. Rather than emperors, today's big players in the Chinese art market are businessmen and women who have made their money from the vertiginous economic success of East Asia since the late 1990s. Mr Zuellig, who in his late nineties decided to part with his large porcelain collection, has spent most of his life developing his father's small Manila-based trading house into the Zuellig Group, the leader in healthcare services and pharmaceuticals in Asia, with an annual turn-over of $12 billion.[2]

The 'chicken cup'—and indeed several other prodigiously expensive Chinese and Asian antiques—have come to challenge the established idea that Western art, and to be more precise modern art, was the pinnacle of collecting, with some of the most expensive objects anyone can purchase. The allure of 'Asian luxury' is something that is rapidly replacing long-established ideas of Asia as the place of cheap mass-produced commodities. Until the late nineteenth century, when figures as different as artists with socialist leanings and connoisseurs began to reassess their products and works of art, China, India, South-East Asia, and to a certain extent even Japan, were considered poor and rather underdeveloped places, whose artistic sensibility was little understood and often derided. It was therefore felt that they could not match or rival the art of the more developed West with its focus on a certain view of the human figure in perspectival space. Yet a history of luxury shows the enduring appeal and fascination that anything Asian had for Europeans. One just has to mention the beautiful Chinese silks worn by kings and high prelates in the Middle Ages or the numerous accounts of the 'riches of Asia' that circulated in early modern Europe. The appeal of the exotic—of the object that came from far away, and as such was different and rare—is something that might be difficult to grasp when everything seems so readily available to us. Yet, in the seventeenth and eighteenth centuries, Asian commodities such as Chinese porcelain and Indian cottons were the luxuries that many aspired to own. These created a taste for Asia, with rich interiors being decorated in Chinese, Indian, or Turkish style. Design and ornament came to be influenced by Asian idioms, and by the late nineteenth century *japonaiserie*, *chinoiserie*, and Moorish style conquered the middle classes, having first been introduced by advanced artists such as Lord Leighton at Leighton House, London, an Aladdin's cave that he had built with old fragments. At the beginning of the twenty-first century, Asia is once again becoming an important place not just for consuming but also for creating new notions of luxury for contemporary consumers.

LUXURIES IN THE ORIENT

Oriental luxuries, because of their rarity, were items of prestige in medieval Europe. This was the case of the silks coming from the Byzantine Empire or from China, the porcelains but also the precious stones, pearls, highly decorated weapons, and carpets from Persia and Turkey, and the other exotic foodstuffs such as raisins, oranges, sugar, and spices that were arriving in Europe in quantity by the eleventh and twelfth centuries.[3] The Orient was imagined as a land of riches, a place of adventure and exoticism. Archbishop Isidore of Seville (560–636 CE), for instance, claimed in his *Etymologies* that pepper was a rare and expensive commodity because the trees on which it grew in India were guarded by poisonous serpents. Historian Paul Friedman observes how 'linking an exotic product with danger appealed to the imagination' and conferred status to commodities from faraway places. So, following Isidore, it was believed that the only way to harvest pepper was to burn the pepper tree to scare off the snakes, thus turning the originally white pepper fruit black.[4]

Oriental luxuries had already been appreciated in classical times by the Roman elites, but in the course of the thirteenth and fourteenth centuries they found renewed publicity in travelogues such as that by the Venetian trader Marco Polo. Polo's journey with his father and uncle from Venice to Mongolia in the late thirteenth century revealed the trade in luxury goods in countries as diverse as Syria and Lesser Armenia, and as far south as the Hindu kingdoms of Ceylon and Sumatra. Without visiting the country, he believed that in Japan gold was used to replace the lead of roofs and that floors were laid with sheets of gold several inches thick. Not all was invented: he reported that, at the port of Layas in Lesser Armenia, the Venetians and Genoese were busy buying up spices and cloth, and in Turkey the Armenians and Greeks lived together to create 'the choicest and most beautiful carpets in the world', adding: 'They also weave silk fabrics of crimson and other colours, of great beauty and richness, and many other kinds of cloth.'[5] In Persia, he observed that the growing of that rare commodity in Europe, cotton, was abundant and that women were 'adept with the needle, embroidering silk of all colours with beasts and birds and many other figures'.[6] On reaching Xanadu, Kublai Khan's summer capital of his Chinese Empire, Marco Polo discovered the emperor's palace to be marble and gilt, wholly 'marvellously embellished and richly adorned'.[7] At one end was a game park where animals were kept to feed falcons. In Cathay he saw 5,000 elephants covered with 'fine cloths', followed by the same number of camels in trappings, also laden with provisions for the feast.

What he described had a profound influence on the European elite's understanding of Asia and their attempts to obtain some of these oriental luxuries for themselves. All this splendour began to be brought back to Europe quite quickly, yet the appeal of the riches of the Orient remained unabated, continuing to thrill and excite European rulers, courtiers, and rich prelates alike. By the seventeenth century, when European kings such as Louis XIV aspired to be as wealthy, cultured, and powerful as their despotic oriental emperor 'cousins', the relevance of Asian luxury re-emerged more strongly than ever. A new series of travelogues composed by merchants, adventurers, and humanists visiting Asia in the sixteenth and seventeenth centuries provided new information and rekindled imaginations. The French physician and traveller François Bernier (1620–88), for instance, provides us with a view of what the Mughal court of the mid-seventeenth century must have looked like. 'Never did I witness a more extraordinary scene,' Bernier recounts.[8] The king was sitting in a robe of flowered satin with silk and gold embroidery 'of the finest texture'. The turban of gold cloth had an aigrette of diamonds 'of an extraordinary size and value' and a large topaz. He wore a pearl necklace and sat on a throne sprinkled with rubies, emeralds, and diamonds.[9]

One object in particular captured the imagination of European readers and rulers alike: the throne of the Mughal Emperor Aurangzeb (Figure 3.1). This was no ordinary throne. It was said to be worth £4.5 million, the

Fig. 3.1. Portrait of Shah Jahan on the Peacock Throne (detail), 386 x 270 mm. Painted in opaque watercolour on paper, *c.*1800.

equivalent of more than 10 per cent of the GDP of England at the time. Another French traveller, the gem merchant Jean-Baptiste Tavernier (1605–89), who had a more professional eye for jewels, calculated that the throne might possibly have been worth three times as much, valuing it at £12 million. But this was no simple extravagance: the throne was the display case of precious stones that over time had been accumulated in the treasury from the spoils of war and the annual presents of lesser rulers to the Mughal Emperors. It was called the 'peacock throne' because it included two peacocks 'covered with jewels and pearls'.[10] Bernier, who was a gossip, could not restrain himself from telling his readers that the throne had been made by a Frenchman 'who, after defrauding several of the Princes of Europe, by means of false gems, which he fabricated with peculiar skill, sought refuge in the Great Mughal's court, where he made his fortune'.[11] Clearly he hinted at the fact that even courtly luxury had its element of risk and that Aurangzeb might have been similarly defrauded by such a rake. We do not know if this was the case.

Bernier, Tavernier, and other travellers to the East Indies were observing the Mughal Empire at the pinnacle of its splendour, especially during the reigns of Akbar (1556–1605), Jahangir (1605–27), and Shah Jahan (1627–58), a period of 'renaissance' when Indian artists and craftsmen combined Hindu, Muslim, and European influences to produce masterpieces in gold, silver and bronze, hardstone, metalwork, ceramics, and textiles.[12] Yet all of this would not endure. The wealth accumulated by the Mughal emperors in the sixteenth and seventeenth centuries became one of the most memorable war booties of all times. In 1739 the Persian emperor Nadir Shah ransacked Delhi and took prisoner the Mughal emperor Muhammad Shah (r. 1719–48). The Persians looted the Mughal treasury estimated to be valued at 800 million rupees (£80 million in eighteenth-century currency and several hundred billion dollars in 2015 money)—such a high sum that Persian subjects were excused from all taxes for three years. The booty included some of the wonders of Asia: the peacock throne (see Figure 3.1), another sixteen thrones, jewelled objects, and the famous Koh-i-Nur diamond. Some of these splendid objects were used by Nadir Shah as presents to the Ottoman and Russian empires and to publicize his exploits. These acts of calculated generosity allowed part of the Mughal treasury to survive in several collections across the world.[13]

DIPLOMACY AND COLLECTING

Sometimes it was not just oriental luxuries that found their way to Europe, but European objects of high-quality manufacture that come into the possession of the rich and powerful rulers of the Orient. One such case is that of the sumptuous crown produced in Venice for the Ottoman emperor Süleyman the Magnificent. This four-tiered tiara no longer survives, but contemporary representations show its elaborate craftsmanship (Figure 3.2). This rather 'over-the top' head ornament—if one is allowed the pun—was notable for its fine workmanship and extraordinary collection of diamonds, pearls, and other precious gems. It was produced by Venetian craftsmen and—prefiguring the luxury industry of modern times—it was a speculation of the goldsmiths of Venice and of several merchants active in Istanbul, who sold it to the Ottoman sultan for the astonishing sum of 116,000 ducats.[14] This was a unique object, not just because of its intrinsic value but also because it was made in the hope of selling it to Süleyman, an emperor who, like all his predecessors, had never worn a crown. Its attraction was the fact that it consisted of four crowns, one more than the Pope's, thus signalling the higher status of the Ottoman ruler over the head of the Christian Church. It also included a pseudo-Roman plume, not dissimilar from those worn by Süleyman's arch-enemy, the Holy Roman emperor Charles V. Extravagance was clearly aimed to flatter the sultan. This was a precious object that was far from functional: Süleyman used it to impress European dignitaries by displaying it, but ironically he probably never wore it, as it was incompatible with the use of the classic Ottoman turban.

Luxuries were the props of ambassadorial relations between different rulers. Splendid gifts were important in particular as part of the reception of Asian and African ambassadors at the courts of several European states in the sixteenth and seventeenth centuries. This was the case of the embassy of the King of Kongo to the Papacy in 1608, followed a year later

SVLIMAN·OTOMAN·REX·TVRC· X·

Fig. 3.2. Portrait of Süleyman the Magnificent, a profile bust wearing an elaborate crown with four tiers of goldwork and pearls. 1535. The crown was made by a group of Venetian goldsmiths and sold in 1532 to the Ottoman emperor Süleyman for 115,000 ducats. The four tiers were intended to represent the four kingdoms over which Süleyman ruled.

by that of Shah Abbas of Persia and the parties from Japan that reached Rome in 1585 and 1615.[15] Each of them brought numerous presents, and they made Asian goods very fashionable among courtiers. The most extravagant of the seventeenth-century embassies was the one sent in 1686 by the King of Siam to Louis XIV of France. It delivered 300 bales of presents, which included Chinese and Japanese vases, thousands of pieces of porcelain, rolls of silk, and hundreds of objects in precious metals. Louis felt obliged to send back a vast embassy with several hundred men and presents worth nearly 200,000 *louis*, which were packed in five ships. They included French silks and velvets, mirrors, thousands of pieces of glass, rich garments, and portraits with diamond frames.[16]

Western luxuries continued to thrill Asian emperors, kings, and princes over the following centuries. A number of European artists sold their services to Middle Eastern, Mughal, and Chinese rulers, churning out works of art that mixed European and Asian aesthetic and artistic conventions. The Mughal emperor Akbar was fond of European atlases, maps, and globes; in fact, his sense of what was valuable in life probably did not differ much from that of any European Renaissance nobleman of the time. The Chinese emperor Qianlong was also an admirer of Western art and employed the Italian Jesuit lay brother Giuseppe Castiglione (1688–1766) as a court painter and designer of the Western-style buildings in the imperial gardens of the Old Summer Palace. Similarly, Shah 'Abbas II (r. 1642–66) of Persia employed at least two Dutch artists at his court, who did not only produce European art but also trained the Emperor in the European techniques of drawing. The Emperor was such an enthusiastic student that he tried to convince Tavernier to produce in goldwork with gem stones some of the drinking vessels and plates that he had designed. As the commission came in at an estimated cost of 200,000 *écus*, Tavernier thought it better politely to turn it down, in fear of never being paid by the whimsical Persian ruler.[17]

Embassies and frequent purchases brought together a variety of exotic and strange artefacts that found pride of place in large and small collections belonging to men of letters, scientists, noblemen, and rulers. For any Renaissance gentleman with cultural aspirations, the ownership of arte-facts from Asia and the Americas was a must. They were to furnish his *studiolo*—literally 'little study'—a small room where learning and business were carried out. The humanist Sabba da Castiglione (1480–1554) comments upon the fact that in these rooms one could find 'all sorts of... new, fantastic, and bizarre but ingenious things from the Levant', including colourful and expensive Turkish carpets (to cover tables), as well as rare things from India and Turkey such as oriental metalwork, knives, and scimitars.[18]

Such collections were often extensive and included a variety of items of different provenance and importance. King Manuel I of Portugal (1469–1521) had a keen interest in Asian objects that included not just rarities and precious things but also animals such as rhinos, elephants, and panthers, while his father kept a camel in his garden at Evora.[19] Rare and beautiful objects from the Orient found pride of place in cabinets of curiosities (*Kunstkammer*) under the category of *artificialia* (manufactured objects), which complemented natural rarities (called instead *naturalia*). Here one would find porcelain and lacquer, but also weapons, utensils, and garments from various parts of the world, rare both because of their provenance, but also in some cases because of their intrinsic value and beauty.

One of the most celebrated cabinets of curiosities belonged to the Habsburg archduke Ferdinand II (1529–95), son of Emperor Ferdinand I and ruler of the region of Tyrol in the Alps from 1564. Famous for secretly marrying a patrician's daughter who was beautiful but deemed to be too low ranking to become the daughter-in-law of the Emperor, Ferdinand spent most of his time collecting armour, memorabilia (items from memorable deeds and events), natural specimens, portraits, and busts, and a variety of exotic artefacts (Figure 3.3). On the outskirts of Innsbruck, he transformed the existing medieval fortress of Ambras into a palace for his vast collection. Here he housed moor masks, Ottoman leather shields,

Fig. 3.3. Scent fountain in the form of a vase, formed of half a Seychelle nut mounted in silver-gilt. Southern Germany, perhaps Augsburg, last quarter of sixteenth century. There are only five extant examples of mounted Seychelles nuts from the late Renaissance; this one belonging to Baron Anselm von Rothschild as a part of his collection formed in Vienna in the nineteenth century. There is a good probability that this magnificent object might have been part of the Archduke Ferdinand II's collection at Ambras Castle in Innsbruck in the late sixteenth century.

cups in rhinoceros horn, splendid specimens of coral and shells arranged in tableaux, ivory and mother-of-pearl items from the Indian subcontinent, scroll painting from China, Japanese armour, examples of *pietra dura* (inlaid hardstone) from Italy, and a variety of other strange items, including baskets from South-East Asia, a beautiful Ottoman turban, a portrait of Dracula, and a 'trap chair' of iron where friends could be tested on how much they could drink. Clearly a collection like this shows how the pursuit of culture was mixed with that of wonder and conviviality.[20]

GLOBAL LUXURY TRADE

On 15 September 1592 the inhabitants of London talked of nothing else than the cargo of a Portuguese carrack that had been seized by English privateers. The vessel carried 900 tons of Asian merchandise worth an astonishing £150,000 (equivalent to $200 million in 2015 money). The cartographer and promoter of exploration Richard Hakluyt was over the moon:

> I cannot but enter into the consideration and acknowledgement of Gods great favor towards our nation, who by putting this purchase into our hands hath manifestly discovered those secret trades & Indian riches, which hitherto lay strangely hidden, and cunningly concealed from us; whereof there was among some few of us some small and unperfect glimpse onely, which now is turned into the broad light of full and perfect knowledge.[21]

He had long professed that Asia was the land of riches and unimaginable luxury and the content of the seized vessel confirmed it. Among the 'principall wares' Hakluyt listed a variety of spices such as pepper, cloves, mace, nutmeg, and cinnamon. There were also silks, damasks, taffetas, and cloth of gold, and, as in Aladdin's cave, one could find 'pearle, muske, civet, and amber-griece' and other wares 'many in number, but lesse in value; as elephants teeth, porcellan vessels of China, coco-nuts, hides, ebenwood as blacke as jet, bedsteds of the same'.[22]

The carrack included also a significant cargo of other textiles such as richly colourful calicoes. There were also canopies, diaper towels, quilts, and 'carpets like those of Turky'.[23] Exotic Asian luxuries were already circulating in Europe in the Middle Ages, but were appreciated mostly in cosmopolitan cities such as Venice and Genoa in Italy or the trading ports of Bruges and Anvers in the North.[24] By the end of the sixteenth century, these new exotic goods had entered into the consciousness of consumers in London and other parts of Europe. A boost to the trade in Asian goods came from the setting-up of trading companies chartered by European governments to rival the state-controlled Portuguese company (Carreira da India) that had traded with both India and the Far East since 1500. By the early years of the seventeenth century the English and Dutch governments had supported the establishment of private (one might say the first joint stock) companies by conferring on them exclusive rights (charters) to trade with Asia: the English East India Company and the Dutch Vereenigde Oost-Indische Compagnie (VOC) were born. They were soon to be joined by other companies such as the French East India Company in the 1660s but also the smaller Swedish, Danish, and Ostend companies.

These companies and private traders operating in the Indian Ocean were responsible for importing into Europe a variety of Asian goods, in particular silks, cottons, and porcelain. In the sixteenth century, porcelain was still within the reach only of princes and the super-rich, who treasured and collected rare pieces coming from China. The porcelain was appreciated because of its translucency and because no one could produce similar objects in Europe. Substitutes could be found in richly decorated majolica—a type of beautifully glazed earthenware that was developed in Italy. But this was no match for the beauty of Chinese porcelain. This is why the rich and powerful Medici family in Florence invested considerable resources in the attempt to establish a court manufacture where porcelain as beautiful as that of China could be made. They succeeded in 1533 in producing the first European porcelain (technically a disappointing imitation of the original) and owned an impressive 373 pieces of what has since been defined as 'Medici porcelain'.[25]

Consequently, during the sixteenth and the early seventeenth centuries, Chinese porcelain remained an expensive rarity within the reach of only a few.[26] Today such pieces are to be seen in many museums in Europe and North America, often mounted in gold or silver. These mounts were added to increase the value of these rare objects, in the same way in which large shells and ostrich eggs were mounted for display (Figure 3.4). Yet the luxurious nature of Chinese porcelain was undermined by the very trade of the European East India companies. By 1615 the Dutch Company was importing 24,000 pieces of Chinese porcelain a year, and this figure had increased to more than 63,000 just five years later. Over the course of the seventeenth and eighteenth centuries pieces of porcelain were traded to Europe in their millions.[27] This does not mean that they completely lost their luxury value, becoming simple commodities, but they certainly became available to much wider strata of society.

One of the most astonishing stories of a luxury that instead turned into a commodity is that of tulips. European expeditions to collect flowers for commercial gain commenced in the sixteenth century; the French explorer and diplomat Pierre Belon travelled to the Levant for this purpose in 1546–8. In the Ottoman Empire, the taste for the tulip was ubiquitous in furnishing and dress fabrics. Many of these textiles were designed for use in palaces, as cushions and as wall hangings and bedcovers, and the textiles also influenced ceramic design. The tulip, which grows wild in eastern Anatolia and the Iranian plateau, was carefully cultivated at the Ottoman court, where an incredible number of bulbs were forced for flower festivals and the palace gardens. This is probably where Louis XIV's chief gardeners got the idea of staging the enormous displays of flowers that changed almost daily at Versailles. Ogier Ghislain de Busbecq, ambassador to Süleyman's court from Ferdinand I of Habsburg, brought bulbs back to Austria, and tulip cultivation

Fig. 3.4. The Howzer cup, hard-paste porcelain with silver-gilt mounts and cover. The cup was produced in China between 1630 and 1650, possibly made as an incense-burner for ritual offerings to the ancestors. It was later mounted in London in the 1660s by the renowned Swiss goldsmith Wolfgang Howzer (d. 1688). It was thus transformed into a luxury cup for display in a private collection and gained a new use.

subsequently spread through the work of Charles de l'Ecluse, professor of Botany at Leiden.[28]

In the early seventeenth century, the Dutch became obsessed by tulips, but also by rare forms of other bulbs and began to speculate on them rather like shares.[29] The cultivation and excitement generated by the tulip, but also the hyacinth and the *Fritillaria* Crown Imperial, indicate the esteem and monetary value of rare flowers; watercolour and printed images of them functioned as sales catalogues. Collectors and patrons travelled between notable botanical centres including Prague, London, Leiden, Brussels, Antwerp, Middleburg, Milan, and Paris to engage with this new science and form of collecting.[30] Paintings of the rare blooms were then commissioned from mainly Dutch and later Franco-Flemish paint-ers, who also worked closely with botanical studies and students. The mimetic transcription of a flower into painting, porcelain, or textile (tapes-try and brocaded or embroidered silks, printed or painted linen) guaran-teed that the elite could view blooms not otherwise available to them, and all the time. The quest for rare garden flowers continued well into the twentieth century. Examples include the writer and gardener Vita Sack-ville West and her husband, Sir Harold Nicolson, who acquired blooms while on a diplomatic posting to Turkey and posted them back to England packed in biscuit tins, and adventurers who travelled to Nepal and the Himalayas to gather rare specimens of the rhodedendra and azaleas that we today would find rather ordinary.[31]

Floral appreciation—integral to medieval and early modern European taste and luxury—extended to Asian textiles.[32] Just as in the Middle Ages richly patterned Asian silks had been an accessory of fashion and splen-dour, so in the seventeenth and eighteenth centuries Indian cottons ful-filled a similar function, though on a much larger scale.[33] The European East India companies imported millions of pieces of Indian cotton textiles a year. Large palampores (hangings of colourful Indian fabrics) were used as bedspreads and valances and were decorated with exotic flowers and birds. These were expensive items, though not as costly as their silk equiva-lents. By the second half of the seventeenth century, however, Indian cot-tons were used for cushions and smaller soft furnishings and soon were donned by both men and women in their apparel.[34] Historians now agree that they were not as cheap as previously thought, but contributed a great deal to the modern phenomenon of fashion.[35] They were richly decorated and could be exposed to light (or washed) without losing much of their beautiful design and intensity of colour. These were not the luxuries of the social elites of Europe. They were for the rising middle classes and even for consumers of more modest means who could now afford to buy a few yards of Asian cloth—at least before their import was banned by many European countries in an attempt to support locally produced textiles.[36]

The European trading companies did not just import porcelain and textiles. Their cargoes also included items of furniture, precious and semi-precious materials and stones, and, much appreciated by Europeans, lacquer. After the direct contact of Portuguese traders with Japan starting in 1543, Japanese lacquer pieces produced in Kyoto and Nagasaki were brought back to Europe as luxurious diplomatic gifts or as liturgical pieces. They could have mother-of-pearl inlay and *maki-e* (gold or silver) decorations.[37] If the Portuguese had sparked a taste for lacquer, supplies of lacquer furniture in Europe increased only after 1600, when lacquered screens, chests, and cabinets made an entrance into elite European houses. The appeal of lacquer was its lustrous, waterproof surfaces, produced using the extract of the *sumac* plant, a subtropical flowering plant to be found in parts of China but not present in Europe.[38] Particularly appreciated were the large folding screens produced in Japan for the European market. These screens were specifically customized to represent daily life scenes and suit European taste and were referred to as *Nambans*, meaning southern barbarians—as the Portuguese were known to the Japanese. They started to be produced in 1591 and often depicted the 'great ships' and the Portuguese in scenes of trade and everyday life, surrounded by African slaves, while Indians and Malay servants paraded their European masters under large parasols.[39] The so-called Coromandel screens were of dark lacquer and often mounted with mother-of-pearl and hardstones; they were the personal favourite decoration luxury of Gabrielle 'Coco' Chanel in the 1930s, who had her apartment in Paris completely covered in them, even cutting holes in them for the electric light switches.[40]

Fig. 3.5. The Mazarin Chest. Wood covered in black lacquer with gold and silver *hiramakie* and *takamakie* lacquer; inlaid with gold, silver, and *shibuichi* alloy, and mother-of-pearl shell; gilded copper fittings. Created in Japan, *c.*1640.

One of the most celebrated lacquered artefacts of the seventeenth century is the so-called Mazarin Chest (Figure 3.5). It is made of wood and covered in black lacquer with gold and silver (*hiramakie* and *takamakie*) lacquer. It was produced in Japan in the 1640s and possibly bought by a servant of the Dutch East India Company. The chest, now at the Victoria and Albert Museum in London, is a typical object produced for the Western market representing scenes from the *Tale of Genji* and the *Tale of the Soga Brothers*, the former being one of the masterpieces of Japanese literature from the eleventh century. Its name derives from the fact that the chest's key bears the coat of arms of the Mazarin-La-Meilleraye family, a branch of the family related to Louis XIV's Chief Minister, Cardinal Mazarin. It was thought to be unique, but in 2013 its companion piece was discovered in France and is now at the Rijksmuseum in Amsterdam.

The Mazarin Chest was given additional lustre by the use of mother-of-pearl shell and gilded copper fittings. Today, in an era of every possible synthetic, it is difficult to appreciate the importance of colour, dyes, and tints to the people of the past. Asian pearls, for instance, held a fascination for Europeans because of their luminousness and tempered opacity. Pearls were used in strings and earrings by women but also as trimming on the sleeves of men's doublets. Sometimes hundreds of them were used on the one garment. Even the restrained Dutch of the seventeenth century appreciated the subtle appearance of pearls, which were often to be seen as women's necklaces or earrings in portraits such as Vermeer's famous *Girl with a Pearl Earring*.[41]

THE LUXURY DEBATE AND POPULUXURIES

Teapot, Ginger Jar and Slave Candlestick by the Dutch painter Pieter van Roestraten is not a traditional masterpiece or a luxury item (Figure 3.6). It was one of the thousands such still lifes that decorated Dutch domestic interiors at the end of the seventeenth century. These types of paintings were commonly referred to as *pronkstilleven*, or 'showy still lives', as they conveyed visually the social aspirations of their owners. They are catalogues of what well-to-do families aspired to possess: English or Dutch silver vases and silver teaspoons, but also new Asian luxuries. The picture includes a lacquer tea caddy, a Chinese blue-and-white teapot and stand, a porcelain teacup, and a porcelain sugar bowl. The English silver-gilt candlestick has a base in the form of a kneeling slave; the slave trade had underpinned much of this global trade since the sixteenth century.

This painting clearly points to what the middle classes aspired to own—a new type of luxury that was no longer restricted to the social elites. Historians see the period between the second half of the seventeenth century and the end of the eighteenth century as one when luxury as we know it was born: a phenomenon that not only interested just the few, but that involved entire societies and that was increasingly connected to taste, fashion, and social and economic competition. As in today's world, the

Fig. 3.6. Pieter van Roestraten (1629–1700), *Teapot, Ginger Jar and Slave Candlestick*, oil painting, London, *c.*1695. Still-life paintings by Dutch artists were new decorative luxuries in Northern Europe in the late seventeenth century. The fact that they were called *pronkstilleven*, meaning 'showy still lives', signalled that not everyone appreciated them.

pervasiveness of luxury (or at least of its pursuit) became a topic of debate and discussion towards the end of the seventeenth century. If luxury was no longer just for the magnificence of kings and queens and their courts, who then was it meant for? And, as Roman authors had asked before, would luxury corrupt the fabric of society, leading to idleness and indolence, or would it foster trade and commerce instead?

These were not rhetorical questions, as luxuries, whether in entertainments, domestic buildings, dress, or furnishings, functioned as potent symbols for the types of social and economic change that modern capitalism enabled. Luxuries in all things represented very different values, which ranged from the positive notion of transformation and liberation to the negative forces of deception and effeminacy, all of which were explored within a range of texts from heavy Enlightenment philosophical tracts to popular broadsheets. If negative views emphasized greed and personal short-term gains from the accumulation of wealth and excess in spending, positive views instead took an approach that went beyond the individual and underlined how luxury allowed the economy to grow, the state to raise taxes, and the power of the nation to triumph.

The Anglo-Dutch philosopher Bernard Mandeville (1670–1733) in his 1714 *Fable of the Bees* passionately argued that luxury was not a vice but a positive force of commerce and prosperity. Without luxury, he claimed, merchants would stop trading and the economy would come to a halt: 'mercers, upholsters, tailors and many others', he said, 'would be starved in half a year's time, if pride and luxury were at once to be banished the nation'.[42] This interpretation of luxury was particularly influential in the way in which David Hume and Adam Smith, two of the most talented thinkers of the century, understood luxury as a force of economic good rather than simply a matter of moral concern.[43]

These changes in attitudes towards luxury were formulated in response to new forms of luxury goods that were more affordable than the traditional luxury of the elites. The economic historian Jan de Vries contrasts the 'old luxury' of royal courts and the European nobility with what he defines as 'new luxury': 'Where the Old Luxury served primarily as a marker, a means of discrimination between people, times and places,' he explains, 'the New Luxury served more to communicate cultural meaning, permitting reciprocal relations—a kind of sociability—among participants to consumption'.[44] What he means is that new forms of luxury goods appeared that were aimed not at achieving grandeur or magnificence, but at satisfying the needs for novelty and delectation of a much wider number of consumers. The eighteenth century brought about a redefinition of luxury. Luxury 'became less a matter of obligations in representing rank, as it had been for the aristocracy, and more a matter of wealth and enjoyment according to the economic means that one had', in the words of the philosopher Olivier Assouly.[45]

Throughout the eighteenth century, luxury goods were copied and recast as *populuxuries* (popular luxuries) or *demiluxe*, which more people could aspire to possess. Clocks, mirrors, and prints were often present in the domestic interiors of artisans and even servants. The same could be said of goods made of more affordable materials such as Sheffield plate rather than sterling silver. English 'flint glass', a type of brilliant crystal produced by the English glassmaker George Ravenscroft in the mid-seventeenth century by using lead, replaced the more expensive and finer Venetian glass. Copies of Asian goods such as Indian cottons, Chinese porcelains, and Japanese lacquer were invented; completely novel goods created by new inventions or the application of new technologies were also introduced in the eighteenth century. These rarely required enormous financial investment, which made it easier for the new popular luxuries to be replaced on a regular basis.[46] They became part of the world of fashion, with their shapes, patterns, and decoration changing regularly and reported in the newly established fashion periodicals, some of which came out monthly. Luxury was no longer about possessing something expensive and unique; it was about owning something *à la mode*. A gown made with the latest chintz pattern or the newest Parisian-styled parasol was a prop for social play and competition. Luxuries did not just have a commercial value here, but through the evolution of fashion came to shape an everyday life crafted by and within shopping, leisure, the sharing of ideas, and polite conversation. They also required the learning of a new set of social conventions. Benjamin Franklin, for instance, sent six coarse diaper breakfast cloths from London to his wife Deborah in the North American colonies in 1758 and explained that 'they are to be spread on the Tea Table, for nobody breakfasts here on the naked Table, but on the Cloth set a large Tea Board with the Cups'.[47]

From the late seventeenth century, invention came to be one of the catalysers of new forms of production and new products.[48] Colour and surface decoration, for instance—which in the pre-modern era had served as the principal markers of status secured by sumptuary laws and the sheer expense of obtaining purple, red, green, and glossy black dyes and intricate designs—were democratized. Francis Dixon of Drumcodan, near Dublin, printed on cotton from copper plates from 1752, producing the first 'linen' for interior decoration.[49] This was about the same time that transfer-printing onto ceramics was developed in England, which enabled the luxurious effects of hand-painting and gilding to be simulated in myriad charming compositions for tableware. More colour and pattern became available within the dwellings of the middling ranks of Western Europe than ever before. The development of new techniques of printing extended from furnishing textiles such as bed and window hangings to cheaper means of producing interior-design elements such as *papier-mâché*, encouraging more experimental and transitory decoration. Wallpaper and hangings began to match from the mid-century.[50] These densely patterned textiles were used both in women's fashions and in the home—another harmonious relationship that we would not expect today, when dresses generally do not match sofas.

The introduction of Indian chintzes, Chinese wallpaper, and their imitations allowed for new colour combinations and effects. *Ancien régime* societies had a sense of colour and chromatic nuance far greater than the vocabulary that exists today. Colours had a range of heraldic, religious, classical, and regional meanings that continued until at least the eighteenth century. In Western European interior design, red represented the colour of fire, Mars, and the Sun. Hence the most elevated forms such as expensive bed hangings and canopies were red, which also happened to be one of the more expensive dyes. Rooms hung in red or green tended to be more important than those hung in blue—the colour for everyday rooms. Black and gold furnishings and forms such as Boulle marquetry suggested the past. Rooms were rarely yellow before the 1740s, but that colour becomes very prominent in rococo fashion in that decade. Green, it has been argued, absorbed less light, was easier to live with, and was also better for displaying pictures.[51] It was the colour of Venus, felicity, and pleasure. Green, a difficult hue to produce, was also a very popular colour for the dress of both men and women in the last third of the eighteenth century, being particularly associated with the foppish dress of macaroni men, who were also described as wearing pea-green, pink, and 'barri' orange. It cannot be a coincidence that this palette was that favoured by the significant neoclassical architect Robert Adam in the last third of the eighteenth century. Fashion of the time was also designed to be seen under candlelight. The light-reflecting details of men's and women's eighteenth-century dress, the fly fringe and lace for women's trimmed gowns, the galloon braid for men's jackets, as well as embroidery for both sexes intertwined with spangles and sequins, make a great deal of sense in the pre-gas and electric world.

To a richly coloured interior, the well-to-do would add other colours, textures, and materials. Foremost among them was porcelain. The secret of hard-paste porcelain was discovered only for Europe in 1709 in Meissen, near Dresden in Germany, although soft-paste imitations had already been produced in Saint Cloud and Rouen in France somewhat earlier. Meissen developed as a state-supported factory for the production of luxury porcelain in high demand across Europe, which replaced the expensive porcelain imported from China.[52] Lacquer, too, came to be imitated in Europe by the late sixteenth century. 'Japanned' tabletops were produced in Venice as early as 1596, and by 1612 lacquer was being imitated in Holland, Augsburg, Nuremburg, and Hamburg.[53] By the 1730s the Martin brothers in Paris had perfected a new recipe for lacquer, the famous *Vernis Martin*, which was more similar to oriental lacquer than anything that had been produced previously. Lacquer had a surge in popularity: from furniture to harpsichords, bedsteads and later buttons, everything could be lacquered (or 'Japanned', as the process was known in Europe), not just in red or black, but also in fashionable shades of green and blue in imitation of Japanese, but also Chinese and Indian, lacquerware.[54]

Some of the key concepts of 'modern luxury' came to be defined in the eighteenth century. One of the most important relates to the fact that luxury goods were no longer necessarily made of inherently valuable materials. Therefore the reputation of the producer—often represented by a name or label—came to assume paramount importance in assessing the value and esteem of a product as a luxury.[55] A series of 'journals' (the equivalent to today's magazines) appeared in the 1760s and 1770s such as *Gallerie des modes*, *The Lady's Magazine*, and the aspirationally entitled *Le Beau Monde*; later also *Ackermann's Repository* and the *Journal für Manufaktur, Fabrik, Handlung und Mode* (Leipzig), which featured real samples of cloth and wallpaper. Advertising became an integral part of the new culture of consumption in the eighteenth century. An example is the trade card (an advertisement to be handed to customers) for Thomas Smith, a mercer in mid-eighteenth-century London, whose shop was to be found at the sign of the 'Indian Queen' in West Smithfield (Figure 3.7). Here he lured his customers through exotic associations, with the Indian queen followed by an attendant who holds a parasol over her, while two boys support her train: marketing was born.

Fig. 3.7. Trade-card of Thomas Smith, mercer at the Indian Queen in West Smithfield, London. *c*.1755. Etching with engraved lettering. The cartouche, containing an Indian queen walking, followed by an attendant who holds a parasol over her, while two boys support her train, conveys the exoticism of the silks and satins sold by this mercer, though he also sold local products such as Norwich 'crapes' and woollens.

ORIENTAL STYLE

The taste for things oriental (and, as we shall see, for things French) was not just a popular phenomenon. The oriental style (Chinese mostly, but also Indian and Japanese) remained popular among the European elites throughout the eighteenth century. Dressing rooms were often the most fantastical space in a wealthy residence, emphasizing the role of fashion in projecting new luxury design ideas. In England in the post-Restoration decades (after 1660), wealthy ladies exhibited a new independence in the design of their dressing rooms or cabinets, which displayed silver-plate novelties in the *chinoiserie* style, porcelain, and Japanese lacquer screens. Novel drinks such as tea, coffee, and chocolate were served in these spaces, which were transitional between public and private, and where the half-dress or *déshabillée* might be worn.

Boudoirs and bedrooms made extensive use of chintz, the printed and painted Indian cotton whose first use was for furnishings in the 1670s and 1680s and which later migrated to clothing. The English East India Company directors called for a new design type as early as 1643 to replace the traditional dark grounds, in order to suit the English, Dutch, and French taste. Indian makers were encouraged to copy English patterns 'in the Chinese mode' with a white or pale background. A famous and fashionable use of chintz in an interior was inside the luxurious Thames riverside villa of David Garrick, the most famous actor of the second half of the eighteenth century. His novel painted furnishings by Thomas Chippendale can be seen today in the Victoria and Albert Museum, alas partly in reproduction.

When visiting one of the many decorative arts museums in Europe or North America or eighteenth-century country houses across Europe, one is struck by the profusion of objects and interior décor bearing a strong Chinese influence. Porcelain helped to create a taste, but Chinese motifs were applied to everything from chairs to tables, chimneypieces, mirrors, clocks, and simple utensils. One of the finest surviving Chinese rococo interiors is that at Claydon House, Buckinghamshire. Even the doorframes as well as an indoor tea pavilion were made to resemble a fantasy Cathay. Gardens were also reshaped in Chinese fashion following more natural lines and including Chinese pagodas and bridges. The house of Confucius, a two-storey octagonal structure built at Kew in *c*.1745, was one of the first of its type in England, followed by similar buildings at Shugborough Park in Staffordshire and at Wotton House in Buckinghamshire.[56]

Not everyone was pleased: exotic visual ideas on bizarre silks, imported tapestries, and Soho tapestry-weavers (Western reproductions) became the target of a backlash against *chinoiseries* led by Archbishop Fénelon in France and Lord Shaftesbury in England early in the eighteenth century. Historian David Porter suggests that both the English and the French theorists 'drew a parallel between the depraved and superficial moral values of the East and perceived on both counts a Chinese threat to established forms of cultural authority at home'.[57] The theoretician Shaftesbury saw 'merit and virtue' in Rome and 'deformity and blemish' in the East: 'Effeminacy pleases me. The Indian figures, the Japan work, the enamel strikes my eye. The luscious colour and glossy paint gain upon my fancy . . . But what ensues? . . . Do I for ever forfeit my good relish?'[58]

Fénelon's and Shaftesbury's sense of stylistic purity was ignored by many of their contemporaries. Development in the art of marquetry—used extensively in furniture and whole rooms for the very rich—goes hand in hand with pictorial fantasies of *chinoiserie* and commercial realities of East–West trade. We see the same taste for the deliberately bizarre and perverse in the contemporary textile designs that simultaneously seduced and repelled the European viewer in the seventeenth and eighteenth centuries. And yet, as luxury fomented criticism, so oriental luxury enraged the most discerning. The taste for the exotic was linked to licentiousness and vice connected with the world of women. For some it posed the threat of a rejection of a male world of scientific order with a new world of disorder and fantasy.[59] Others objected to it simply on artistic grounds. In 1675, for instance, the art theorist Joachim von Sandrart called lacquer this 'miserable painting' and complained of eastern art: 'They present everything as simple, mere outlines with no silhouette, round off nothing but instead coat their things in paint.'[60] Even the popular media of the time were divided about the merits of oriental style, with the *London Chronicle* acidly observing that

> every house of fashion is now crowded with porcelain trees and birds, porcelain men and beasts, cross-legged mandarins and bramins, perpendicular lines and stiff right angles. Every gaudy Chinese crudity whether in colour, form, attitude, or grouping, is adopted into fashionable use, and becomes the standard of taste and elegance.[61]

This type of aesthetic haughtiness was not new. The French playwright Molière could not resist making fun of the 'Asia-mania' that was taking over French society in the 1670s. What had begun as an elite appreciation for the exotic allure of the Orient fast became a passion for the middle classes. These were represented in Molière's *bourgeois gentilhomme*, who provided the title to one of his most famous plays. We find Monsieur Jourdain, the main character, donning a banyan or oriental robe: 'I had this oriental robe made specially for me,' M. Jourdain explains to his music master. 'My tailor told me that people of quality wear these in the morning.' The ridiculous social aspiration of M. Jourdain leads him to welcome his daughter's suitor, thinking that he is a Turkish nobleman rather than a bourgeois. The play concludes with a Turkish ceremony in which M. Jourdain thinks that he is now a member of the Turkish nobility.[62]

Turkey was both repellent and alluring to European sensibility. It was the land of the infidel Turk, but also that of a powerful and rich (though increasingly crumbling) empire. Turkish style was particularly appreciated in dress. Masquerades were popular forms of elite entertainment, especially in the eighteenth century. Here the exotic was presented through the appropriation of Asian costumes. In 1700 the Duke of Chartres gave a

Turkish masquerade complete with dancing girls. At Versailles, too, it was not uncommon during the reign of Louis XIV for the courtiers to dress up in glittering costumes, especially at masked balls. The passion for everything Turkish also included outlandish portraits: in 1755 Madame de Pompadour had herself painted as a sultana by Carl van Loo and, later on, another of Louis XV's mistresses, Madame du Barry, had a painting of herself made in which she was served by eunuchs.

Turqueries, as everything Turkish came to be known, quickly influenced the design of leisure buildings and interiors such as Turkish kiosks and summerhouses. Marie Antoinette was second to none when she decided to have a Turkish boudoir installed at her Fontainebleau residence in 1777.[63] Turkish luxury was associated with sensual pleasure. This was the case of *turquerie*-inspired furniture such as the *divan à la turque*, our present-day couch, which started its life as an exotic luxury. In the early 1740s it was made the protagonist of a salacious oriental novel entitled *Le Sopha* (*The Sofa*) by Crébillon fils, in which the furnishing was witness to libertine acts.[64]

Sexual proclivity and stimulation served also to shape a new product in the late seventeenth century: coffee. A luxury within reach of only the few, coffee was at the time a beverage strongly associated with Turkey. It was very expensive and most commonly drunk at home, not in coffee shops. The print *Homme de qualité buvant du café* (1674), for instance, makes the point that

> It's not enough that I fill myself
> with my country's best foods
> I also demand the coffee of the Levant
> and find excuses for this extravagance.[65]

The problem of coffee (but the same could be said of chocolate and tea) is that it was subject to social inflation as its fashionability spread from the elites to the lower social classes. Coffee, as we have seen, was at the end of the seventeenth century still a luxury, but by the end of the following century had become a common beverage. In 1785 nearly half of all working-class homes in Paris owned a coffee pot.[66]

THE ALLURE OF THE ORIENT IN THE NINETEENTH CENTURY

The taste for things Chinese and things made in the Chinese manner by Europeans was a leitmotif of luxury design. Orientalism was not just the result of a European sense of superiority or, as argued by Edward Said in his famous book *Orientalism* (1978), the creation of an imaginary Orient, often stereotyped and formed via cultural appropriation and misunderstanding (Figure 3.8). Although the power relationships were often uneven, the appreciation of the Orient was also based on an expanding *understanding* of Asia and an appreciation of the riches of the continent's culture, material mastery, and deep past.

The nineteenth-century European taste for Chinese objects was very much formed within a French milieu, although there were other great collectors such as members of the Swedish aristocracy and financial elite. The modern view of Chinese decorative arts was established substantially by the collecting and writings of the Goncourt brothers in nineteenth-century Paris. In the 1870s, the brothers shifted their attention away from the French eighteenth century (they had previously been champions of the rococo) to the Far East. In his diary for 1876, Edmond de Goncourt wrote: 'Since my eyes acquired the habit of living in the colours of the Far East, my eighteenth century has become discoloured. I see it in grey.'[67] The Goncourts' favourite objects were Chinese ceramics. They appreciated the glaze and colour of porcelain above all other features and established a 'visual' system for analysing porcelain vases and other forms that does not make much sense historically but still influences the way we collect and consider these objects.[68] Collectors after the Goncourts preferred multi-colour ceramics, enamelled wares as well as crazed glazes, and special

Fig. 3.8. 'Maison Orientale', poster lithograph from Ernest Maindron's *Les Programmes illustrés des théâtres et des cafés-concerts, menus, cartes d'invitation, petites estampes, etc.* (Paris, 1897). A chic Western woman and gentleman in a summer suit are contrasted with the dark face and traditional dress of an Arab man. The Europeans are intrigued by the goods on sale, but their relationship to them is ambiguous.

effects such as *flambée* and *blanc de chine*.[69] In the words of Edmond de Goncourt:

> Porcelain of China! This porcelain superior to all other porcelain on earth!... This porcelain with an outcome so perfect that the Chinese attributed it to a Spirit of the furnace protecting the firing of the ceramics of which he was fond!... In a word, this earthy material wrought by the hands of a man into an object of light, softly tinged with the glow of a precious stone.[70]

Books, prints, and scholarly catalogues contributed to an understanding of Asian cultures that began to be more truthful to the reality that was under investigation. This was the case with the work of Philipp Franz von Siebold (1796–1866), an eminent *japoniste* whose work included the reproduction of Japanese prints.[71] The famous Impressionist painter Pierre-Auguste Renoir admired Japan over all other artistic nations:

> The Japanese for the time being, or up until now, are the only people to have remained within the sound tradition provided by nature...What's certain is that they're the only people to take the time to find pleasure from their eyes...They go see how birds fly, how fish swim, and have even captured the foam that the sea makes atop its waves, in order to fix them in bronze, on porcelain, and add them even to their unmatched embroidery.[72]

Asia was accorded a new status as an 'authentic' producer of fine and applied art by many advanced parts of French society and collectors in the late nineteenth century. The 'authenticity' of Asian decorative arts and the perceived 'decline' of European taste were mapped on to the notion of alienation and the critique of the machine that had been elaborated by well-known artistic and literary figures such as John Ruskin and William Morris. The Musée Guimet (dedicated to the art of Asia) opened in 1889 at the time of the Paris Universal Exposition, followed by the Musée Cernuschi in 1898. The Musée Enery opened in 1908, also showing Chinese art, although the first large-scale Parisian exhibition of ancient Chinese bronzes was not held until 1934, at the Musée de l'Orangerie.[73]

The taste for anything Japanese or Japanese style developed after the opening of Japan to the West from 1852 to 1854. In Britain, Japanese things became quickly popular with their exposure at the 1862 International Exhibition in London and across the Channel, in France, with the 1867 Exposition Universelle in Paris and the 1873 World Exhibition in Vienna.[74] By 1876, at the time of the International Exhibition in Philadelphia, Japanese style had conquered the taste of the American elites. One of the most famous British designers of the second half of the nineteenth century, Christopher Dresser, was also a *japoniste*.[75] On his way to Japan, he delivered a series of lectures in Philadelphia at the time of the Exhibition promoting Japanese and oriental art as a model for Western decorative arts.[76] Part of the appeal of Japanese art and material culture was its exquisite workmanship as well as its subtle beauty. Sir Rutherford Alcock, in his *Art and Art Industries of Japan*, published in 1878, commented upon the fact that the Japanese artisan 'can give a priceless value to the commonest and least costly materials'.[77] A couple of years later, in 1880, Le Bon Marché, one of the most famous department stores of its day, opened a 'Galerie de la Faïence Japonaise' to sell Japanese ceramics and lacquer of the Edo period (1603–1867).[78]

The playwright and aesthete Oscar Wilde promoted things oriental on his famous lecture tour to the United States and Canada in 1882. He claimed that the simple Chinese cups used by working men in San Francisco were far more beautiful than any of the expensive luxuries handed to him by hostesses, or the thick new vitreous china used in American hotels. A whole array of exotic objects such as Japanese carved *netsukes* (toggles for clothing), lacquered haircombs, snuffboxes, and other practical implements became desirable collectables locked behind glass.[79]

The appreciation of Asian cultures and material culture came at a price. As for the antique, supply was limited and prices increased by the day. In 1883 Philippe Sichel commented about Japanese antiques that they had become 'almost undiscoverable in the country, and those we receive in

Europe are but imitations or new works created for our taste'.[80] It is perhaps because of this combination of scarcity and difference that things
Asian were so potent within the advanced design of the late nineteenth
century. Oriental fine and applied art was a major spur to the lifestyle
movement called Decadence. Decadence was, as the philosopher Roger
Scruton notes in his work on *Beauty*, a 'paradox', as 'it continued to believe
in beauty, while focusing on all the reasons for doubting that beauty is
obtainable outside the realm of art'.[81] The scholar and translator Robert
Baldick provides an excellent summary of Decadence: 'that movement in
France and England characterized by a delight in the perverse and artificial, a craving for new and complex sensations, a desire to extend the
boundaries of emotional and spiritual experience'.[82] Perhaps the most
famous popularizer of Decadence (sometimes more politely called the
Aesthetic Movement) was Oscar Wilde, along with the artist James Abbot
McNeill Whistler.

Apart from sharing the general taste for Japanese *ukiyo-e* prints displaying the luxury of geisha and Edo merchants, and for decorative fans to be
hung on the wall and Chinese blue and white porcelain, the great art nouveau designer-makers such as Emile Gallé (1846–1904) were transfixed by
the small luxuries of China such as glass snuffboxes. These curios, along
with the carved *netsuke* that were used to tie the sash of kimonos, inspired
many of the strange colours, designs, and effects of Art Nouveau glass and
porcelain. Gallé, for example, was inspired by the themes, technical virtu-
osity, and effects of veining found in Chinese glass. These inspired his vege-
table- and animal-like forms, which created an entirely new category of
European glass. The Decadents introduced a contemporary sense of mor-
bidity that had not been present in the Asian originals. Of the glass of
Gallé, the aesthete the Comte de Montesquiou wrote: 'within the molten
glass, a red vein has occasionally run through, like the rosy thread that
recalls the need to triumph, or the necessity of dying'.[83] Gallé and the Parisian
jeweller and glassmaker René Lalique were receptive to both European and

Asian examples of the past, and created new hybrid masterpieces of design that spoke across cultures.

LUXURY AND THE NEW ORIENT

Although we live in a society that greatly values experiences, some materials are still as highly valued as they might have been 1,000 years ago. Many such materials continue to come from Asia. Oud resin, for instance, produced from a parasitical attack on the agar tree, long known in the East, is now a highly fashionable ingredient for Western perfume. Oud costs more than one and half times as much as gold—a kilo is worth around $70,000 in 2015. Tom Ford at Yves Saint Laurent repopularized the musky smell in the 1990s.

As we noted at the beginning of this chapter, the Chinese themselves are now among the most prominent collectors of rare objects and luxuries. Since the early 2010s they have been very interested in stamps. The most valuable Chinese stamp is the 1897 'Red Revenue', which sold for $1.2 million in 2013. Newspaper and magazine stories feature many rather outlandish tales of Chinese luxury: at the moment, for instance, it is apparently very fashionable to have your dog painted by hand to resemble a tiger. This recalls the taste of the Edwardians for keeping absurd pets in the city. Exactly who is buying the hyper-luxuries of the present day is unclear—whether it be the billionaire Chinese or the residents of the Gulf States—as the great couture houses do not release detailed accounts of their sales. In the early twenty-first century the market for Ferrari cars has plateaued in China, the largest market along with the United States, but is rising in Australia, where a surge of property speculation has created a new raft of very rich people.[84]

As well as motor cars, men like buying wristwatches, ironically once the preserve of ladies until airplane pilots required them in the 1920s for ease of access. One of the most important markets in the world for luxury watches is once again China, where they are purchased mainly by men. The heritage but also the ironies of retailing timepieces from Europe to Asia is demonstrated by a visit to the Patek Philippe Museum in Geneva. The museum is presented very much as a museum of horology and various technological and artistic developments in watch-making, but it is also a little jewel box devoted to luxury. The upper floors contain a very extensive collection of Renaissance European enamelled and other timepieces, fine table snuffboxes, as well as the extraordinary pieces sold to the Chinese and Turks in the eighteenth century. Such pieces were generally sold via London. They include clocks, telescopes, fan guards, and perfume bottles. Watches for China were created in incredible forms—peonies or peaches enamelled and inlaid with diamonds to simulate the effect of a Chinese painting—and were generally produced in pairs—yin and yang.

There is a return in the early twenty-first century to the very 'over-the-top' mannerism of eighteenth-century fantasies, whether it be the floral gemstone rings currently retailed by Dior or the re-creations of panther jewels by Cartier. The case of the twenty-seven-storey residence built by India's richest man, Mukesh Ambani, in Mumbai galvanized world attention. With garaging for 168 cars, 3 helipads, 9 elevators, and a dining room that resembles a grand hotel, it is not a subtle space. However, it makes having to visit a hotel redundant for this lucky family, and recalls many of the gestures cultivated by North American plutocrats when the first high-rises of Manhattan were constructed. As the over-the-top 'maximalism' of such structures suggests, today's 'orientalization' or—better to say—'reorientalization' of luxury by rich non-Western consumers is a refusal of the pursuit of the modernist aesthetic paradigm so assiduously cultivated by the likes of Coco Chanel, about which we will read more in the following chapters.

4

Housing Luxury:

From the *Hôtel Particulier* to the Manhattan Cooperatives

Luxury is often associated with fashion and accessories but is also fundamental to many of the greatest schemes of architecture, furnishings, and splendid living. In the nineteenth century, earnest social reformers on the streets of London discovered that the young girls who had fallen into prostitution desired the fine clothes of the ladies they saw walking in the streets, but had little idea that these ladies also had boudoirs, libraries, hothouses, and rich furnishings.[1] There are little luxuries in all aspects of life—from the time and manner of taking meals, to the way in which people sit on chairs. Yet luxury is always time and place specific, and attitudes towards it have changed dramatically across culture and time.

The home, perhaps more than any other space, has long been a site of luxury and display, not visible to all and sometimes even concealed. The invention of free-standing furniture and upholstery in the late sixteenth and seventeenth centuries added the extra premium of comfort.[2] That came at a cost for the wealthy middle classes: by the eighteenth century, the outlay for a fashionable interior was significant. Rich hangings added colour, texture, and decoration. Boulle furniture, precious marquetry, and marble floors became a must for any rich household.

Fig. 4.1. A British lion devouring a French cockerel, carved by Grinling Gibbons above the kitchen court gateway at Blenheim Palace, Oxfordshire. First published in *Country Life*, 20 May 1949.

The size of habitations increased dramatically over time, with rooms becoming more specialized.[3] Country houses in Britain and *châteaux* in France were sometimes as splendid and large as royal palaces. In the early eighteenth century, the Duke of Marlborough's Blenheim Palace was far more magnificent than Kensington Palace, the main British royal residence (Figure 4.1).[4] Size mattered: from the residences of the nineteenth-century *nouveaux riches* to the fabulous houses of the nineteenth-century American tycoons, excess in floorplan meant an equivalent excess in expenditure, not just in furnishing but also for paintings and antiques, as well as an army of servants to manage the household.

LUXURY HOUSING IN THE EIGHTEENTH CENTURY

The cities of Western Europe became more densely populated in the seventeenth century. Different approaches were taken in Paris and London to deal with the resulting shortage of space. In London, the wealthy were prepared to live in grand townhouses that faced directly onto the street.[5] If you were lucky, the exterior and interior might be by a great architect such as William Chambers or Robert Adam, and the staircase and hall ceilings were engineered to create astonishing vistas and effects via cantilevers and landings. Wealthy people enjoyed looking onto squares, which were locked and private, stopping coaches from crossing diagonally, and which provided air and also a pleasant outlook. The very wealthy enjoyed large townhouses set behind walls, and many town-dwellers owned a second villa on the Thames, upstream, where they could pretend to enjoy the sylvan delights of a Roman residence despite the winter weather. Not all dwellings were in the classical style or indeed good taste: the eighteenth-century Prussian travel-writer Johann Wilhelm von Archenholz, noting 'the immense riches possessed by the English', remarked that this enabled 'them to indulge in the most uncommon caprices'.[6] That to build in the gothic mode in the 1790s was almost comical may be gauged from his following comment: 'A wealthy individual, some years since, built a house not far from Hyde-Park, merely to ridicule the gothic style. All that was disagreeable and fantastical in that *taste* was here *caricatured.*'[7]

France developed very different building traditions. In the late seventeenth century Paris expanded dramatically, and courtiers were not keen to spend all their time in the marble grandeur and freezing spaces of the palace of Versailles. Instead they flocked to Paris, with its luxury shopping street the Faubourg Saint-Honoré, and the Faubourg Saint-Antoine, a centre of luxury production outside guild control. The luxury trades and the 'appearance industry' (clothing, wigging, make-up, deportment) were a central feature of the Parisian economy and streetscape.[8] Many new mansions were erected. Residents were not numbered, as the nobles had their crests over their entrances and pediments, and the introduction of street numbering proceeded in an ad hoc manner; this might help to explain the mystery of street numbering that persists in Paris to this day.[9] Some of their mansions, like the hôtel de Soubise (*c.*1730), with its painted monkeys and Chinese-style decoration, are works of art in themselves. Like the English, the French also sometimes built directly onto the street, with barely a pavement between themselves and the road, but the French tended to use the model of a very high front-facing wall and central courtyard, with good acoustic effects. Much later, the very rich of Manhattan would leave their mansions for skyscrapers to avoid the noise from the streets.

Exceptions to the French model of building are also notable, and include the beautiful squares of the Place des Vosges, built in the first years of the seventeenth century, and the Place Vendôme, now the centre of the French luxury industry, but in the eighteenth century the place where aristocrats, merchants, and tax farmers built their sumptuous townhouses. It was at this time that financiers replaced the court as the vanguard and patrons of taste, and the city replaced the rural palace as the centre of pleasure. It was this moneyed class that could afford to build hotels and *châteaux* and collect art.[10]

French society remained extremely hierarchical in the eighteenth century, with its social estates and ranks. For the elites (the nobility, the government officials, and the top rungs of finance), houses were the settings in which hierarchy was materially presented and visually represented.[11] Yet the French elites saw their houses not just as public spaces. It was at this time that the court nobility developed the concept of privacy as a great luxury and architectural innovation. A set of rooms called the *appartement de compagnie* or *de société* provided a semi-public realm distinct from the magnificent ceremonial suite that continued to be built for the very rich.[12] These new private rooms were decorated in what was called at the time either the *petite* (little or charming manner) or the *goût moderne* (modern taste), which later was to be called the 'rococo'.[13]

During the reign of Louis XV, smaller, more private rooms were included in many Parisian townhouses, and easy seating and improved fireplace technology encouraged informality and the search for comfort.[14] Even the King liked to meet his friends in small private spaces, making them coffee after dinner, and his mistress Madame de Pompadour enjoyed an early type of elevator at Versailles.[15] The lucky mistresses and actresses of Paris lived in specially designed villas or apartments that, in the words of the contemporary French writer Louis Petit de Bachaumont, possessed 'insolent luxury'; some even had triumphal arches splayed across their facades.[16] A wealthy man such as Radix de Sainte-Foy, a well-known rake and spendthrift, owned a house in each of Paris and Neuilly, with thirty quality horses to transport him for the city and ten for the country.[17]

From the early years of the eighteenth century the French developed a mode of living that remained remarkably consistent among the very rich across the world until the second half of the twentieth century, when it was finally supplanted by modernism. The private suite was for dining, conversation, reading aloud, musical concerts, and games of various sorts (and new ways of fitting out these intimate but fashionable spaces were required). A salon or sitting room, a purpose-built dining room, and a library appeared as dedicated spaces, each with its own fittings such as marble basins and running water for the dining room. Bathrooms appeared for the first time, although they were quite rare early in the century. The lady of the house had her own boudoir (Figure 4.2) next to her bedroom and the man a study. This was a practical format that was easily transplanted into the luxury 'French flats' or apartments later erected in wealthy cities such as New York.

The new significance of the eighteenth-century dining room meant that it was now often magnificently decorated. For example, in the Parisian house of the famous eighteenth-century Crozat family, the dining room had two marble fountains. After dining, guests retired to take coffee in a cabinet a pale yellow octagonal space decorated with painted flowers from foreign climes that simulated a room outside in a garden.[18]

Mme du Châtel at the Place Vendôme had her own grand *cabinet à la Chinoise* with large panels of black lacquer, each over 6 feet high and set in rococo panelling. Such cabinets often displayed personal rather than public collections of objects. A great variety of built-in libraries and cabinets were developed to hold these often precious collections. New furniture forms to carry and display all these new things were developed, often made by foreign craftsmen in the Faubourg Saint-Antoine; they included the lady's dressing table with adjustable leaves, bedside tables with marble shelves to hold hot drinks at night, women's desks with dainty legs and places to store ink, the *chiffonier* or a chest of drawers with shallow drawers, and the *semainier*, a much higher chest with narrower drawers for storing papers, lace, shells, and the like. Much of this new furniture was mobile—remember that the French for furniture is literally a 'movable' (*meuble*).[19] *Ébénistes* (cabinetmakers) made tables in which, rather than pull out a drawer in an ungainly manner, one pressed a hidden spring mechanism to release the locks. Ormolu-mounted mechanical dice-throwing machines meant that the aristocrats need not exert even their wrists.

For a noble family the gallery was the most prestigious space—this was a male space in that portraits, generally of the male line, were placed there. Crozat had his gallery gilded in 1703, circumventing the slackly enforced sumptuary laws of Louis XIV that stated that only he and the Church could

Fig. 4.2. This little cabinet or chamber was designed by Jean-Simeon Rousseau de la Rottière (1747–1820) in 1778 for a *hôtel particulier* (private residence) in the Marais district of Paris where the de Megret de Sérilly family lived. The de Sérilly family soon faced serious financial difficulties and had to give up the house only six years after the room had been built. The Marquis was guillotined in 1794, and the Marquise escaped the same fate only by claiming that she was pregnant. This photograph shows the range of luxuries enjoyed by an eighteenth-century woman of the upper classes, such as the telescopic porcelain-top work table in the foreground.

own gold and gilded goods. The King expressed disapproval, but Crozat got away with it. The chapel was also a noble prerequisite and was a 'female' space in that it was generally placed near the women's apartments, opening off their rooms. All manner of luxurious silks and sculptures would be offered there to the Virgin and Child in a display that frequently horrified English Protestant visitors. Bathing rooms were placed in odd spots such as near the kitchen, presumably to access the water. It was considered very bourgeois for the husband and wife to share a bedroom, but people had choices, and some of these rich financiers did indeed choose to share their beds with their wives.[20]

French luxury was also connected with eroticism, which is hardly surprising as this had been one of its connotations since the ancient world. All is made clear in this delightful passage from a book by Jean-François de Bastide, *La Petite Maison* (*The Little House*), which published in serial form in 1757 and republished in 1879. Merging two forms, the erotic libertine novella and the architectural treatise, the book presents a progression through the rooms of a charming pavilion as the corollary to a seduction ending in release. Mélite, a virtuous woman, is lured into the 'maison de plaisance' of the Marquis de Trémicour. He takes her on a tour of his 'asylum of love', past girandoles of Sèvres porcelain, silken couches, Boucher paintings, and shimmering and shining surfaces. At the end of the perfumed tour she succumbs to the inevitable:

> Trémicour took her hand, and they entered into a bedroom on the right. In the square-shaped room, a jonquil-colored bed of Peking fabric, brocaded with resplendent hues, lay nestled in a niche, across from one of the windows that over-looked the garden. This room, with chamfered corners graced by mirrors, was crowned by a vaulted ceiling. In the ceiling's center was a circular painting that brought all of Pierre's mastery to the image of Hercules in the arms of Morpheus, awakened by Love. The room's walls were painted a soft yellow; the marqueterie parquet combined amaranath and cedar woods and the marble was a Turkish blue. Lovely bronzes and porcelains were displayed in a studied and orderly manner on the marble-topped

consoles that sat before each of the four mirrors. Elegant furniture of myriad forms resonated the ideas expressed everywhere in the little house, and coerced even the coldest minds to sense something of the voluptuousness it proclaimed. Mélite no longer dared praise anything; she had begun to fear her own emotions.[21]

Mélite then enters an exquisite water closet and descends to the garden, where a fireworks display goes off. Fountains shoot into the air. The rake further leads Mélite into a room solely for the enjoyment of coffee.[22] She is finally seduced in a second boudoir richly furnished with *bergères* (upholstered armchairs), ottomans, *duchesses* (day beds), and *sultanes*, or Turkish-style settees. This reflects the ambience of the supposed hedonism of the courts of Louis XV and Louis XVI: an early nineteenth-century English travel guide claimed that Queen Marie-Antoinette had slept in a suspended bed-basket of roses before the Revolution.[23] Some readers might have believed this to be true.

FURNISHING LUXURIOUS INTERIORS IN THE EIGHTEENTH CENTURY

Furniture is necessarily practical but can also embody aesthetic ideals and convey public or private messages. This was particularly the case with aristocratic furniture with inlaid or mounted arms, or that was made of materials that only the very rich could afford. One of the most etiolated luxuries of the period was the taste for creating elaborate pictorial fantasies in and on the carcass of wooden furniture. Development in the art of marquetry went hand in hand with new knowledge of the artistic production of the East (textiles, lacquer, porcelain, arms, and armour) and the development of the Western taste for *chinoiserie*. East and West Indian trade routes brought new exotic woods to Europe, in France known as 'bois des Îles'— ebony, purple heart, tulipwood, king wood, and bloodwood—making previously unobtainable colours possible: natural purples, reds, blacks, and yellows.[24] The marquetry designs of the highest-style pieces included architectural scenes, scenes from nature, and exotic pieces of *chinoiserie* representing porcelains and flowers.

The French, under the influence once again of refugees and craftsmen from the German lands, developed their own model of inlaid and ormolu (gilded-bronze) furniture that has found favour ever since with the very rich for its luxurious air. French fine furniture of the eighteenth century has a restraint sometimes lacking in German furniture of the period, although such an observation perhaps says as much about our own modern tastes as anything else. The *genre pittoresque* was translated by German designers into a sculptural use of curves and counter-curves. Würzburg and Ansbach were centres of this cabinetmaking, and here the cabinet should be understood as both a piece of furniture and a room. The cabinet was never neutral; it was frequently part of a game, lending itself to flirtation, a site for love tokens and commemoration. Generally the doors would open to reveal some other scenes or vistas concealed within. We are sometimes simultaneously in a jewel box, a cabinet, a garden, or a room.[25]

It is an uphill battle to convince the design-minded consumer today that a fake might be good and appealing. But imitation was not a problem in the eighteenth century. Quite the opposite, in fact: the *ancien régime* viewing public often enjoyed the extra degree of artificiality offered by certain materials and prospects. Marble and wood were of particular interest. Woods were dyed and stained to produce a variety of colours; there were speckled, marbled, and jaspered effects. In a setting such as the grottoes that frequently adorned gardens and villas in the eighteenth century, artificial coral and rocks were often used, even though both were widely available in the natural world. It was believed that certain 'natural' products lacked the beauty—'one might say the desired degree of artificiality—demanded by society for its artistically subterranean environments'.[26] The famous *pietra dura* of the early modern period, the inlaid pictorial stone mosaics, were also prized for their 'ingenious artifice' and the luminescence of their stone. In fact, the materials themselves were sometimes thought to have intrinsic power. This was, for instance, the case with rock crystal, so popular in the ancient world and the Middle Ages, which was believed to have cooling powers.

The role of the *marchand-mercier* was crucial to the luxury economy of eighteenth-century France. The *marchand-mercier* was an elite merchant whose job it was to coordinate the large number of specialist tradesmen who made things in Paris, to create innovations that drove demand, and to maintain and repair the luxury goods once they had been delivered.[27] The most famous such figure was Dominique Daguerre. Some of the most enduring luxury creations of this distinct entrepreneurial group were the ormolu-mounted porcelains from Asia that are so evocative of the rococo era. Expensive imported Chinese and Japanese porcelain vessels and their covers were mounted in gilded bronze or gilded brass, often embellished with elaborate feet or bases. Clocks were built with, for example, a Chinese mandarin, rhinoceros, or elephant in bronze surrounded by porcelain flowers on gilded stalks made by local companies at Sèvres and Vincennes. Such pieces were designed to appeal to the connoisseurs of the time, and the *marchands-merciers* worked hard to emphasize their aesthetic qualities and to match the decorative scheme, including the wall panelling, the carpets, and the chandeliers.[28] This was a potent scheme for a multifaceted, multi-sensory interior decoration that influenced taste in subsequent centuries. It was sometimes even claimed that the French perfumed their paint!

The eighteenth century saw porcelain not just as a luxurious novelty, but as a category of object that signified the connoisseur's discerning taste, which had in all cases to avoid bright colours and decoration.[29] Such objects had particular appeal to the royal mistress Madame de Pompadour (mistress to Louis XV), and they were also regularly given as diplomatic gifts. Pompadour owned decorative articles including artefacts made of lacquer or marquetry as well as myriad porcelains, including twenty-eight rich Sèvres pot-pourri vases to scent the rooms, blue and white as well as pompadour pink porcelain vessels, Vincennes porcelain flowers, and 475 pieces of imported Meissen.[30] Such objects were always among the most expensive objects in the houses of the wealthy, apart from the ormolu-mounted furniture.

Small luxury goods such as candlesticks, lady's mother-of-pearl sewing cases, *étuis* of sharkskin to hold tweezers and scissors for grooming, and novelty animal-form paperweights were made and sold in the luxury shops of the Palais Royal, one of the first purpose-built shopping arcades just inland from the Seine and adjacent to the Tuileries Gardens. Such *bijouterie* or decorative jewellery is still called 'Palais Royal' in the antiques trade, whether it was made there or not. Until the late eighteenth century, the 'old' had little intrinsic value whatsoever to buyers, other than to slightly eccentric antiquarian collectors like Horace Walpole.[31] Second-hand objects were, however, remounted with new bronze borders and mounts from time to time, even for royalty—hence the importance of the *marchands-merciers* with taste.

Refinement was a result of specialization of production and the development of newly specialized craftspeople in the luxury trades. The *menuisiers* were frame-makers, craftspeople and technicians at the forefront of structural design for furniture. They helped develop a whole new repertoire of furniture that has perhaps never been equalled for its variety and comfort until the experiments of Charles and Ray Eames with modern materials and forms in the post-war period. Myriad new chair types were introduced in the eighteenth century, from the *bergère* (armchair) to the *chaise-longue* or *duchesse*, and the *duchesse brisée* (comprising a separate but coordinated armchair and long stool).[32] The *ébénistes* were a specialist guild who worked on the design and the surfaces of furniture, as well as coordinating construction. They were not just makers, but finishers, and this is a distinction that has continued until today in the French luxury tradition of furniture-making. Another guild provided the gilt mounts, while yet another built compartments for travelling bureaux and trunks, fitting out the drawers and compartments with often elaborately edged padded silks (known as *passementerie*). The finest upholstery was of tapestry made at Beauvais or Gobelins, followed by furnishing silks such as brocades, and then by inlaid leathers.[33]

Many of the masterpieces of French furniture were made in the Faubourg Saint-Antoine, the specific area of Paris where thousands of workers found employment outside the jurisdiction of the guilds and normal rules of apprenticeship. Labour was more sharply divided by task than in the guilds. Here a sideboard could be made by one man, but more often it was the product of one large diversified workshop. The area was largely peopled by foreigners and migrants from the country. By 1791 there were 8,000 workers in furnishing trades; 4,500 lived in the *faubourg*, which must have been like a luxury compound. Comparisons with the official guild were not favourable to the latter, which had only 895 masters; 200 were cabinetmakers (*ebenistes*), and 100 were chair-makers.[34]

LUXURY AND THE LEGACY OF FRENCH TASTE

'Things French' fascinated the rest of the world in the eighteenth century and continued to be seen as the apogee of luxury over the following centuries. French words related to fashionability that were incorporated into English included: *etiquette* 1750; *fête* 1754; *rouge* 1753; *ennui* (boredom) 1758; *monde* (society) 1765; *chignon* (upwards hair-knot) 1783; and *bandeau* (head-band) 1790. The great styles of furniture and furnishing, such as Louis XV and Louis XVI, were named retrospectively in the nineteenth century.

The revolution meant a temporary end to luxury consumption in France. The French nobility either fled to England or fell victim to the guillotine. Their wonderful townhouses, palaces, and castles were ransacked and their contents destroyed, stolen, or confiscated by the revolutionary government. Yet this presented an unforeseen opportunity for eighteenth-century French furniture and artefacts of the highest quality to be bought up relatively

Fig. 4.3. Blue Velvet Room, Carlton House, London. The room is richly furnished with English and French neoclassical furniture and a woven fitted carpet, then a new vogue. The hangings are of rich contrasting silk.

cheaply by foreign nobles and the very rich. For instance, the Prince Regent, later George IV, bought furniture and decorative arts from a series of auctions following the French Revolution for the lavish decoration of his now demolished Carlton House (Figure 4.3) and also the Brighton Pavilion.[35] The rise of the taste for things French was not always so appreciated and became more pronounced only in the last third of the nineteenth century. The social and cultural historian Peter Mandler, in his work on the English country house, notes that nineteenth-century visitors did not like the luxury and extravagance of Chatsworth, which was found to be too French and too elaborate.[36]

From the 1870s taste changed. Wealthy collectors such as the banker Mayer Amschel de Rothschild began to collect French furniture voraciously for his massive Joseph Paxton-designed 'Jacobethan' pile, Mentmore (near Aylesbury in Buckinghamshire), the contents of which were dispersed at auction in 1977. Before the sale of Mentmore, Eva, Lady Rosebery, was asked the locations of the kitchens, to which she replied that she had never been there.[37] Here the luxury was so great that 'at Mentmore even the washing facilities in the guest bathrooms were provided by Louis XV or XVI commodes whose marble tops had been pierced and fitted with basins and taps'.[38] The taste for things foreign did not just extend to the French, but included objects made from amber, ivory, rock crystal, and enamels from the Renaissance, the finest German Baroque cabinetmaking; arms and armour; and seventeenth-century table-caskets from Augsburg and Antwerp. Gold boxes and paintings by the great masters covered all surfaces and walls. Old things (not antiques but of the previous century) were now more appreciated than ever before.

The most famous British collection of French luxuries was formed by the illegitimate son of the 4th Marquess of Hertford, Sir Richard Wallace, who was raised in Paris. In 1870 Richard Wallace inherited from his father one of the most exquisite small bijou *châteaux* in France, the Bagatelle near Paris, and he began to add to the significant collection of French furnishings and paintings by masters such as Greuze, Boucher, and Fragonard assembled by his father there from the 1830s. Originally housed in Paris and then on temporary display in London, the collection was left to the British nation by Sir Richard's widow, Lady Wallace, in 1897. It may now be seen in a large nineteenth-century London townhouse, Hertford House, known as the Wallace Collection, in London.[39] It includes the famous nineteenth-century copy of Louis XV's desk for his study at Versailles by the great cabinetmaker Jean-François Oeben, and finished by the royal cabinetmaker Jean-Henri Riesener in 1769, featuring a built-in clock and gods and goddesses of plenty supporting the roll top. The desk cost Louis nearly 63,000 livres, or about $3 million in 2015 money, making it the most expensive piece of furniture ever commissioned.[40]

The auction of the French crown jewels by the Third Republic in May 1887 included some of the surviving gems that had belonged to Louis XVI's wife, Marie Antoinette. It also included many of Napoleon's gifts to Josephine mounted by the jeweller Bapst, and many of the jewels that had belonged to Napoleon III's empress, Eugénie, as well as treasures from the reign of Charles X (1824–30). The auction was an international sensation, with Tiffany & Co. of New York purchasing the best diamonds and one-third of the gems for approximately $12 million in 2015 money.[41] Buyers came from all over Europe, from Turkey, Egypt, Tunis, and Havana, indicating the global spread of wealth at this time.[42] The French had cleverly put them all on display first in the Universal Exhibition of 1878, at which time they received extensive media attention via line engravings and photography. Nearly all the gems were reset by the buyers in newly fashionable styles. Some of these dazzling crown jewels (including the diadem of Empress Eugénie) have been reacquired in recent years by the French state, and they now reside in a special case at the Musée des Art décoratifs in the Musée du Louvre, a few hundred metres from where the Empress once wore them in her apartments at the Tuileries.

By this time, French taste had become a 'must have' also in the United States. Francophilia set the tenor for the luxury of the American gilded age and for much of the subsequent century. The term 'gilded age' refers to the novel by Mark Twain and Charles Dudley Warner entitled *The Gilded Age: A Tale of Today* (1873), a satire of greed and corruption in post-Civil War America. While the very rich were acquiring genuine French furnishings for their new villas, even at this date a great many new pastiches in the French manner were created for them, and their freshness probably was a part of their appeal; the Vanderbilt mansion in New York contained many such ormolu-mounted items, including a Louis XV-style inkwell for important correspondence.

The American passion for things French continued well into the twentieth century. Millionaire businesswoman, philanthropist, and connoisseur

Mrs Marjorie Merriweather Post, for instance, started to acquire her massive collection in the years following the Russian Revolution of 1917, when it was possible to obtain great French furniture with royal provenance, as well as the exquisite neoclassical Russian furniture dispersed by the Soviets in a series of famous sales from the 1930s. It is somewhat paradoxical to think that two of the major revolutions of modern times have contributed so much to shape luxury consumption and taste, with France at the top of the pile. This inspired generations of Americans to buy into French culture—quite literally. The prominent New York socialite Caroline Astor (1830–1908) spent up to five months a year in France, had an apartment on the Champs Elysées, and collected French paintings by the likes of the famed 'Carolus-Duran', the society portraitist.[43] A visit to Paris continues to be one of the 'must-do' things for middle-class tourists today. The city has retained its allure as a centre of art, luxury, and gastronomy, despite the growing incursion of the English language, the global food revolution, and globalized shopping. It is now a favourite destination, along with Italy, for the new middle class of China.

THE NOUVEAUX RICHES AND THE 'DOLLAR PRINCESSES'

By the mid-nineteenth century, wealth from new industries created enormous fortunes at a time when taxation and labour costs were low. Large cities in North America, Australia, and South America still had enough space to enable very large townhouses to be built, and a country residence was also *de rigueur* for the rich. As has been well documented, the claim that nineteenth-century mansions lacked conveniences is largely a myth. Indeed, a great deal of technology was commissioned for renovations and new residences in this period. Arundel Castle in Sussex, rebuilt in the 1850s, had electricity, eight bathrooms, and sixty-five water closets, as well as hydraulic service lifts. Technology at this date was also much more expensive than the fittings—a complete inversion of twentieth-century economics, notes journalist Michael Hall in his fine work on the Victorian country house. At Arundel Castle, the chimney piece by the sculptor Thomas Earp cost £150 and the electric system cost £28,652.[44] Service wings grew much larger in this period and appear to have been a status symbol. They were also increasingly demanded by the servants, who were coming to expect better working conditions away from basements, and who moved around for work more than contemporary television drama might suggest.[45]

Much of this luxury was selected and directed by men. The wife of Lord Coleridge noted 'my husband tells me he worships the ground I tread on, but I am never allowed to choose the carpets'.[46] High society nonetheless valued the contribution of witty and urbane women, even sometimes actresses and opera singers, and was also opening up to foreigners and those of different cultural and religious backgrounds. In the last third of the nineteenth century, England was notable for greater social mixing even at the level of the court than in many other parts of Europe. This was an important era for Jewish integration in England, and King Edward VII has been praised as one of the first monarchs who would not countenance anti-Semitic behaviour. He embraced the invitations of his wealthy Jewish advisers such as Sir Ernst Cassell, accepting them as 'leaders of society' for the first time.[47] He was also regularly entertained by some of the richest Jewish banking and industrial families such as the Rothschilds. This was widely reported in the press.

One of the most extraordinary of all nineteenth-century houses is Waddesdon Manor in Buckinghamshire, one of the Rothschild family's residences, built in a hybrid French Renaissance *château* style in the 1870s and 1880s. Designed by the famed French architect Gabriel-Hippolyte Destailleur, it incorporated every conceivable luxury and novelty, including aviaries of delicate gilded metal, and the finest collections of French, Islamic, and oriental antiques. In Figure 4.4, we see Waddesdon and its encrusted stone ornament readied for the summer season with canvas awnings and

Fig. 4.4. The garden front of Waddesdon Manor, which overlooks a formal parterre. The house was designed by Gabriel-Hippolyte Destailleur for Baron Ferdinand de Rothschild and built in 1874–83. Photographed but not published by *Country Life* in 1902.

newly established flower beddings in the extravagant Victorian taste. The first design proved too small for the needs of entertaining, and it was extended soon after completion.

Waddesdon Manor was built, in a place where there had been no house at all, by Ferdinand de Rothschild, one of the first generation in his family who did not work at the family bank. His life was one of luxury and pleasure, and his residence was one of the favourite visiting spots of the gourmand and sybarite Edward VII. Guests could take a private steam launch to Ferdinand's sister's house at Eythrope; transportation for the very rich, from private boats to Pullman cars, was always an essential ingredient of superior living. (Surveys around 1900 in England debated whether 'public transport' was a 'luxury' for the working classes; the conclusion was that it was a luxury, not a necessity—and that the quarter of the population living in poverty had the means only to walk to work, not to be transported there.[48]) Guests at Waddesdon were accommodated in great comfort, as if they were guests in one of London's or New York's luxury hotels.[49] The luxury at Waddesdon was so great that the hearth rugs to protect the carpets from cinders were cut out of the original *savonnerie* (royal French tapestry works) stool covers from the chapel at Versailles.[50] Its dining room, which appears to be painted in trompe l'œil, is actually made out of solid veneers of marble interspersed with large wall mirrors surmounted by paintings all designed by Nicolas Pineal (1732–33) (which were taken from a Paris *hôtel particulier*), and the room was also furnished with Beauvais tapestries from eighteenth-century France, and Louis XV-style chairs softly covered in modern buttoned upholstery (Figure 4.5). The enormous marble putti who carry the candelabra beside the chimneypiece find their echo in the so-called beach houses of the Vanderbilts in North America. As in many nineteenth-century mansions, the decoration and fittings at Waddesdon harked back to the royal courts of the previous centuries (particularly those of pre-revolutionary France). For example, the billiard room contained an enormous sixteenth-century French stone mantle with classical motifs that was flanked by a pair of caryatids with large projecting breasts. It referred directly to the court of François I, King of France from 1515 to 1547.

The French *château* style was the sign of the wealthiest and most luxurious approach to domestic architecture. But mansions of extreme detail and luxury such as this were nevertheless often written off by snobs as *nouveau riche*. In the words of the impressionist artist Auguste Renoir, writing in his journal:

> A gentleman who only recently has come into money wishes to have a castle. He inquires what style is the most in vogue. It turns out to be Louis XIII. Fine, let's go for it. Naturally, he can easily find an architect to make him fake

Fig. 4.5. The dining room at Waddesdon Manor, which is lined with marble and hung with a series of Beauvais tapestries after Boucher. The mirror frames, designed by Nicholas Pineau in 1732–3, are from the Paris home of the duc de Villas. First published *Country Life*, 20 December 1902.

Louis XIII. Who's to blame? It's society, then, that must be addressed, and must elevate his taste . . . To have a beautiful palace you must be worthy of it, otherwise you can address yourself to anyone at all and you'll have nothing. The artists, knowing how empty you are, won't dare to be personal.[51]

Despite Renoir's melancholy regarding the state of contemporary taste, many such palaces were constructed around the world. This model was used extensively in cities such as New York and even by the sea—at the Vanderbilts' 'Marble House' (1888–92) and 'The Breakers' (completed 1895) in Newport, where the bronze chairs in the 'red marble dining-room...required a footman's help to get them near the table'.[52] As with Waddesdon, many of these urban dwellings incorporated references to the great luxury courts of the past. For example, the Vanderbilt townhouse in New York was described by Consuelo Vanderbilt, the unhappily married 9th Duchess of Marlborough, as having held a dining room that was

> enormous and had at one end twin Renaissance mantlepieces and on one side a huge stained-glass window, depicting the Field of the Cloth of Gold on which the Kings of England and France were surrounded with their knights, all not more magnificently arrayed than the ladies a-glitter with jewels seated on high-backed tapestry chairs behind which stood footmen in knee-breeches.[53]

The surrounding rooms were in the 'Louis' style and held furniture with a royal provenance to Marie Antoinette. Among the great New York society hostesses there was considerable waspishness attached to this agenda concerning purported accuracy. Mrs Stuyvesant Fish, famous for her harsh words, once remarked to a hostess who was proudly showing her a 'Louis Quinze salon' in her residence: 'And what makes you think so?'.

A part of the Arts and Crafts reaction to French cosmopolitanism was its hostility to continental luxury—when Eaton Place in London was rebuilt in the nineteenth century it was described in Badecker as a place to please even those who 'have little taste for the triumphs of modern luxury'.[54] Philip Webb's exquisite design for the country villa Standen was reported, according to Michael Hall, as a 'reaction against the luxury and conspicuous expenditure so evident in English society at the end of the century'.[55] Standen, in West Sussex, was built in 1892–94 as his family's country residence by a London solicitor, James Beale. It was designed in its entirety by

Philip Webb, one of William Morris's close friends.[56] Not a modest house, it has twenty-one bedrooms, two porcelain and nickel bathrooms, and seven modern lavatories. Fine wooden details, asymmetry, and a shift away from densely hung walls characterized this style. The wardrobes were fitted rather than free-standing (which was unusual for the time); radiator shelves kept food warm outside the dining room and the electric lights were *repoussé* metal sunflower-shaped sconces. Like many wealthy families of the time, the Beales purchased a motor car at the turn of the century; the head coachman was sent to be retrained at the Rolls Royce Chauffeur School. His other job was to wind the clocks once a week.[57]

All this building, rebuilding, and refitting did not come cheaply. Indeed, they required resources held only by wealthy Americans—the richest people in the world at the time. Clare Booth Luce, a wealthy ambassadress and society figure, formerly married to Henry R. C. Luce, chairman of *Time-Life* publishing house, once said: 'In America money is a thing less valued in the spending than in the earning. It is less a symbol of luxury than of "success", less of corruption than of virtue.'[58] The famed inventor of beauty creams, Helena Rubinstein (Russian born, living in outback Australia for a short time before making her fortune in New York), had this to say about collecting: 'Quality's nice, but quantity makes a show.'[59] While Americans were good at making money, they seemed to need Europeans to spend it quickly. The raft of rich American women who began to marry into the European aristocracy in the late nineteenth century were known as 'dollar princesses'.[60] The term came from a popular song 'we are the dollar princesses'. The British aristocracy were, of course, in turn marrying into this American wealth. The fictional Lady Grantham from the TV series *Downton Abbey* is now one of the world's most famous 'dollar princesses'. Generally their fathers had become immensely rich through business after the American Civil War and still felt shunned by the first families of Manhattan, the many Dutch-origin dynasties such as the Astors, the Stuyvesants, and the like. They included such famous figures as Consuelo Vanderbilt (who married the Duke of Marlborough, becoming the Duchess, and lived at Blenheim Palace until her divorce); Mary Leiter, daughter of the founders of Marshall Fields Stores (who became first Lady Curzon and later Vicereine of India); and Anna Gould (who married—and later divorced—the French aristocrat Boniface de Castellane). May Goelet, daughter of a real-estate tycoon, had a mother who famously gave out silver Tiffany party favours to the hundreds of guests who attended her balls. May married the 8th Duke of Roxburghe in 1903 and brought a dowry of $20 million to Floors Castle, her husband's hereditary seat, which she decorated in a comfortable, understated French style that one could easily still live in today.[61]

The arrival of a number of wealthy American heiresses coincided with a series of challenges to the British aristocracy: between 1890 and 1910 a series of legislative and social changes occurred, including reform of local government, the access of industrialists to the peerage, the Liberal attack on the House of Lords, the introduction of death duties, and the threat of land tax.[62] The Asquith Budget of 1912 proposed to increase income tax and estate duties, much to the fury of the House of Lords; it was at first defeated but later passed after tumult.[63] 'The Great Unrest' or the Great Strike of 1912 further unsettled those with means, and the sinking of the 'unsinkable' luxury liner *Titanic* that year, with so many English and American plutocrats losing their lives, has often been seen as a metaphor for the end of a whole world before the catastrophe of world war in 1914.[64]

The American fortunes enabled the ancient piles of noblemen to be restored and elaborate new residences to be erected, and the newly arrived women injected a certain American vigour into social life. Many of them, including Lady Randolph Churchill (née 'Jennie' Jerome and mother of Winston Churchill), were more actively interested in up-to-date interior decoration than their British sisters.[65] So many wealthy women arrived that a magazine *Titled American* was published. Not all the lavish spending undertaken by some of their husbands was welcomed. Sometimes the male partners spent so much of the family's money that the newly acquired American relatives felt they had to intervene. For instance, Boni de Castellane, the French Belle Époque taste-maker and trend-setter, held legendary fabulous parties, featuring nine miles of specially commissioned red carpets, gardens in which Nubian men in turbans walked jaguars and panthers, and precious antiques and art works in abundance. Boni's father-in-law once innocently enquired why Boni was purchasing so many 'second-hand' objects from the eighteenth century. Boni explained in his memoir: 'I preferred to exist in a dream world of past splendour, pretty women and interesting people.'[66]

AMERICAN OPULENCE

During the nineteenth century, wealth was predominantly generated in new occupations, professions, and industries, and in the financial sector of the economy. Even if they were rejected by older members of a snobbish society such as that of Manhattan (with its '400' list of people 'worthy' of being received), the so-called plutocrats—a word coined in the seventeenth century but only used widely in the late nineteenth—could easily find a place in high society. Yet even new money was aware that power (or at least prestige) was based on the ownership of vast estates.[67] One might even say that the greatest luxury in late nineteenth-century England was, in fact, land. Land is often considered an investment, rather than a luxury, but, at the turn of the century, the acquisition of vast estates was more the paraphernalia of status than anything else. This is because the return on land was between 2 and 2½ per cent per annum, while bank interest was 3–4 per cent.[68] If land itself was a luxury, then we should consider the incredible houses built in the second half of the nineteenth century an 'exuberant pleasure'.[69] Whether they patronized an architect, an artist, or an electrical engineer, male patrons delighted in commissioning the latest and the greatest. Novelty was embraced. The variety, size, and ingenuity of the late nineteenth-century dwellings in Britain and the Empire have never been equalled and, despite the enormous number of demolitions in the twentieth century, most cities in Britain and many of the dominions retain some evidence of this building mania. For example, the first house in the world to be lit by incandescent light in the world was the English country house Cragside in Northumberland, in 1880.

Craftsmen from many countries were hired to build and furnish great houses across Britain, which along with France was a centre of finance, learning, and art and considered a most desirable destination from which to conduct business. Men who relocated from other countries to live in Britain included the German-born Sir Julius Wernher (1850–1912), one of the so-called Randlords from South Africa who had made a fortune in diamond and other mineral exploration. In the 1890s he refurnished his London residence, Bath House in Piccadilly (previously owned by Mr Baring of Baring's Bank), and in 1903 he bought and furnished the eighteenth-century Robert Adam-designed Luton Hoo in Bedfordshire (since 2007 a Luxury Hotel and Spa), with an enormous collection of medieval ivory and parcel-gilt treasures, old masters, and French eighteenth-century furniture. The taste was *le goût Ritz* (Ritz Hotel taste), and in fact Wernher was part of the syndicate that had backed the Swiss hotelier César Ritz in creating that London landmark of luxury accommodation.[70] The interior of Luton Hoo was redesigned by Mewès, the very architect of the London Ritz, and it was later described by the architectural expert Ernst Pevsner as 'Beaux Arts at its most convincing and indeed most splendid'.[71] Wernher's wealth was so great that at his death in 1912 his estate of £11.5 million was the largest ever recorded in England.[72]

Despite the glamour of nineteenth-century London and Paris, the money was and still is in North America. The word *millionaire* was coined in 1843 upon the death of the New York tobacco magnate Pierre Lorillard. Later on, one had to be a billionaire in order to aspire to the pantheon of genuine riches: in 1982 there were twelve billionaires in the United States alone.[73] The figures have risen dramatically since then. By 2014 Russia had 111 billionaires, China had 152, and the United States had 492.[74]

Wealth is not just concentrated in the hands of the few; wealthy people like to live close to each other. One of the greatest concentrations of wealth in the world today is the area of real estate known as the Upper East Side, New York, specifically Fifth Avenue from 59th Street to 96th Street. Most of these buildings are known as cooperatives, and they can exclude any applicant. Cooperatives were invented in 1879 as a new way of dealing with the looming housing crisis in densely populated Manhattan. They were the idea of Philip Hubert, and were called either 'French flats' or 'Parisian buildings'. The ideas behind the early ones were partly utopian, and they were popular with artists and their followers. The first so-called French flat was built by Rutherford Stuyvesant in 1869 at 142 East 18th Street. They were all rentals and contained the Otis elevator, invented in 1853. C. K. G. Billings, who hosted the famous 'horseback' party at which men in dinner suits ate their meal astride horses, was one of the first residents at such a building at 820 Fifth Avenue. By 1885 there were 300 apartment buildings in New York. Five thousand were constructed in the first ten years of the twentieth century.[75]

The urban issue in Manhattan was a shortage of land and the rising cost of that land. The last free-standing great Fifth Avenue residence was built in 1918 by the banker Otto Kahn (covered in imported French limestone, no less) and the last extant one was the home of one of the heirs to the Stuyvesant fortune, until his death in 1949. Gertrude Vanderbilt had said that 'it takes three generations to wash off oil and two to exterminate the smell of hogs'.[76] But the walls of a *château*-style townhouse apparently helped a great deal. When the great mansions disappeared, an increasingly large number of rich and newly rich moved into the so-called Park Avenue cooperatives.[77] Yet exclusivity has been retained through the opaque method of selective access. The boards of the cooperatives can and regularly do summarily exclude applicants, no matter their wealth.[78] One famous heiress once tried unsuccessfully to sue a cooperative that was apparently not impressed that she was unmarried and felt she was too close to the 'garmentos' (people in the clothing business). Today, most of this luxury property is managed by a handful of brokers, who bring 'pre-qualified' buyers in to look. Some applicants even have to provide copies of their cheque-account statements, which reveal shopping habits and other private details to the cooperative's membership committee. One might well ask why wealthy New Yorkers came to live in these relatively low-ceiling spaces and why they put up with this ritual abuse.

In the late nineteenth century, an alternative to living in an apartment was to rent rooms for an extended period of time in one of the extraordinarily stylish Manhattan hotels. The famous Chelsea Hotel, for instance, was built in 1884. Most striking in the New York building scape was the Ansonia Hotel (Figure 4.6). Popular with the theatre and entertainment crowd, it cost $6 million to construct and opened in 1904. Here was every luxury: there were 1,400 rooms and 340 suites in its 17 storeys, 70,000 electric lights, 400 baths, and 600 toilets. More than 125 miles of pipes carried messages in pneumatic tubes. There was hot, cold, and also iced water on offer. In summer, freezing brine was pumped through the walls to cool the building. Each suite had mahogany doors, and a selection of furnishings was possible. Most striking was the inventory of linen. Every suite had eighteen face and bath towels, and a set of eighteen table linens, which were changed three times a day, along with the soap and stationery. There was a fully working farm on the rooftop to supply fresh eggs and milk for the residents. The Ansonia had the world's largest indoor swimming pool—which became the famous gay bathhouse the Continental Baths when the hotel later declined.[79] Before the London Ritz opened in 1906, boasting a bathroom per room, these were incredible levels of luxury.[80]

Some well-to-do people resorted to much more extreme measures. This was the case for the apartment built in 1926 as the residence of Mrs E. F. (Edward Francis) Hutton, at 2 East 92nd Street, Manhattan. Its owner was Marjorie Merriweather Post Close, the Postum Cereal Company (later General Foods) heiress. Her company owned such iconic brands as Jell-O,

Fig. 4.6. The Ansonia Hotel, 2109 Broadway, between West 73rd and 74th Streets, New York, opened 1904. This is the view at the intersection of Amsterdam Avenue, photograph 1905. The design of the hotel was lavish but also eccentric. Live seals played in the foyer in the fountain and there was a farm on the roof to supply fresh milk and eggs. Famous people like the Ziegfelds of the Ziegfeld Follies lived there.

Birdseye, and Maxwell House, proving that to get rich, you sell to the poor. Post Close (at that date still Mrs E. F. Hutton) inherited in 1914, when she was just 27. In 1924 Post decided to demolish her New York mansion, because of the increasing noise of the New York streets. She asked the architect Rouse and Goldstone to re-create parts of her mansion in a triplex at the top of a fourteen-storey apartment. It was the largest apartment in New York and described as the most luxurious in the city when completed in 1926. The family had their own entrance, separate from the one used to welcome the hundreds of people who came for balls and dinners. The dwelling had seventeen bathrooms, cold storage for furs and flowers, and a room for storage of large ballgowns. The library panelling came from the demolition, as she had requested (Figure 4.7). The room was symmetrical and included fine classical detailing. Furniture was mainly French. Shaded electric lights, gilt-bronze sconces, a large Persian carpet, and a matching clock and barometer filled out the opulent scheme. The rooms resembled many others of the period, and without the portraits of the owners it would be hard to say that the room was very individualistic. When the lease expired on this building in 1941, it remained empty, as no one else could afford to take it. Notwithstanding such extravagance, Mrs Post was a generous woman with strong philanthropic tendencies and fed thousands of people in New York during the Great Depression.

This might appear a distant world, but it is not as far distant as we might think. In 2014, Christie's New York held a most curious auction, the estate of the late Huguette M. Clark, who had died in 2011 at the age of 104. Huguette, with her charming French name, was the much-loved daughter of the man considered the richest man in the Unites States in the late nineteenth century, William Andrews Clark. Having made his fortune from prospecting, cattle, and railroads, he removed himself from Montana to New York, where he commissioned one of the finest mansions in the city at the time, a *château*-style 121-room house on Fifth Avenue with 41 baths and 4 art galleries. Like the Post mansion, it was later demolished, as it was

Fig. 4.7. Library in the Residence of Mrs E. F. (Edward Francis) Hutton, 2 East 92nd Street, New York. Gelatin silver print, unbound photograph album created c.1915–30, photograph c.1926. This was the penthouse apartment of the famous American business-woman and philanthropist later known as Marjorie Merriweather Post.

thought too excessive for anyone else to reside in. Much of Clark's significant art collection and even parts of its French wall panelling are now in the Corcoran Gallery, Washington, DC. After the death of her father in 1919, the unmarried Huguette and her mother moved to three separate apartments and 42 rooms over several floors at 907 Fifth Avenue. Later she checked herself into private hospitals that she endowed, and lived there in complete seclusion from 1991, having not been seen by the general public since the 1940s. Perhaps privacy is sometimes the greatest luxury.[81]

Huguette's mother, Anna, who might have afforded anything in the world, selected for her Manhattan residence an interior and contents that were mainly French but with some English materials, the latter including Jacobean and eighteenth-century furniture that evoked a sense of the English country house. She also owned one of the finest sets of lacquered *chinoiserie* 'magot' figurative clocks known to have survived from the 1740s, the definitive product of the *marchands-merciers* of eighteenth-century Paris. Her bedroom and boudoir furnishings were completely French, with silk satin upholstery, of the mid-eighteenth-century rococo style, covered in gilded mounts and brimming with pictorial inlay. But, rather than original antiques, she ordered contemporary copies of these items, produced by the greatest furniture-makers of the late nineteenth century such as Maison Krieger, and incorporating new innovations such as pivoting mirrors.[82]

Huguette had all this bedroom furniture later copied by the best French craftsmen in the 1990s, in order to live among it once again, possibly after the 'originals' had been sold. Huguette was musical, well read, and educated. Copies of first editions by writers such as Charles Dickens and Charles Baudelaire were in the library. What were Huguette and her mother trying to evoke in the decoration of their houses? They were picturing the urbanity of eighteenth-century Paris, the delicacy of the Enlightenment *mondaine*, the sociability of a society that lived for appearances but that also expected erudition. Paris of the mid-eighteenth century supplied one of the most elegant templates for sophisticated living, dining, and sleeping that there has ever been, and the super-wealthy of the New World always understood that fact. It is sad to think that Huguette enjoyed all her luxury in private, along with her very large collection of dolls.

From the eighteenth century and throughout the nineteenth century, French taste was key in shaping luxury living. The sumptuous urban space of the *hôtel particulier* was replicated in the different cities of Western Europe and in the Americas; it was scaled up to shape *château*-style country houses in England and scaled down to suit more modest flats. Architecture and interior decoration are often forgotten in the long history of luxury. It is erroneously assumed that they belong to the history of the applied and decorative arts, and it is sometimes overlooked that interiors—their comforts, their furnishings, textiles, technologies, and curious objects—were and remain some of the major items of expenditure for poor and rich alike.

A great deal of money was required to cultivate taste, to purchase expensive objects, and to outdo the neighbours. In the late nineteenth century, such levels of spending were showing strains at the bank, most obviously for the English nobility. Rich Americans, by contrast, seemed to have endless resources, although over time few wanted to maintain enormous houses in places like Manhattan where land was extremely expensive. They moved instead into more comfortable apartments, though we should not think that these were in any sense similar to what today we call an apartment or flat. They were really little mansions in the sky. Americans also went to the rescue of the penniless but titled British and European continental aristocracy, bankrolling the extensive building projects and furnishing endeavours of their daughters' new husbands. American money certainly gave a new lease of life to Old World luxury in this period. And, as we will see in the next chapter, it was American money that was partly responsible for the apotheosis of a new and rather whimsical form of luxury in the years to come, between the end of the nineteenth century and the Second World War.

5

Luxury and Decadence at the Turn of the Twentieth Century

We live in a very anodyne world. Eccentricity is not well regarded. Women no longer walk black pigs with gilded trotters in Hyde Park nor do men dye their doves rainbow colours for house parties. We no longer recline in circular beds covered in pink ostrich feather fronds. Why was such luxury created and who was it for? This chapter charts the rise of forms of luxuries that emphasized the importance of the senses. We go back to the people here, as a history of a changing concept can be tracked only by examining what people at the time considered to be 'luxurious', and why. Architecture, furniture and interior decoration, clothing and accessories, gems and jewels, fur and precious silks are all props in what we might define as 'the social life' of a concept, to paraphrase a well-known cultural anthropologist.[1] But next to a list of objects is also a list of people engaged in conspicuous consumption, in collecting or simply 'living the life' of luxury. They range from Renaissance courtiers to eighteenth-century *salonniers*. For the years of the Belle Époque, the 'beautiful era' that was swept away with the devastation of the Great War, the key figures would include American heiresses and decayed noblemen, the emerging glamorous Hollywood stars, and the rich plutocrats who prefigured the 'jet set' of a later period.

LUXURIOUS LIVING

Between the end of the nineteenth century and the Second World War, luxury was widely reported and commented upon in diaries and memoirs. It often concerned the senses and was therefore partly ephemeral. For example, the rooms in which the Prince of Wales, 'Bertie', later King Edward VII, made love were sprayed with perfumes before the arrival of the amorous royal.[2] The house parties about which so much was written were characterized by excessive meals of great refinement, elaborate decorations, and characteristics that we still associate with the finest luxury hotels today—for an Edwardian visitor, the height of luxury was the Asprey pen for ladies on every desk, the posies and flowers that they might choose to match their evening toilette, the soft lighting, and the hangings around the bed. For an American such as the actress, interior decorator, and socialite Elsie de Wolfe, a private telephone beside the bed was already a requirement in 1913.[3]

Notable social climbers such as 'Mrs Ronnie' (Dame Margaret Greville) made the pursuit of luxury their *raison d'être*. She remodelled her Regency-period residence near London, Polesden Lacey, from 1906 with the explicit aim of dazzling royalty and to rival the riches of the maharajas from India who were taking London society by storm. The design duo Mewès and Davis, who had just finished the interior decoration of the London Ritz Hotel in the fashionable white-and-gilt Louis XVI style, worked on her house. In addition, she employed a great many servants, including the best French chef, M. Delachaume, who would cook eight courses for a shooting party. In the words of her biographer, 'afternoon tea consisted of delicious home-made cakes, exquisite sandwiches, and for King Edward, his favourite snack, lobster salad' (other hostesses knew that he expected a whole cold chicken in his bedroom in case he became hungry at night).[4] At houses such as this, footmen were considered vastly superior to parlour maids, who were considered distinctly 'middle class'. When the First World

War broke out, Lady Sackville, of the great medieval house Knole, wrote to Lord Kitchener asking if her footmen, carpenters, and other male estate workers could be excused from war service: 'I must say that I never thought that I would see parlour-maids at Knole . . . instead of liveries and . . . powdered hair.'[5]

Mrs Greville's taste could be said to epitomize Edwardian luxury. Her writing desk was covered with Chinese vases; Fabergé decorations in the fashionable form of pets and animals from Queen Alexandra's zoo at Sandringham (which had first been commissioned by the King); inlaid silver and tortoiseshell writing accoutrements; seals and bell pushes. It was one of the few places that the austere Queen Mary would attend informally for afternoon tea with barely any notice, where she was served in the dedicated tea room that was fitted out like a boudoir with eighteenth-century French painted panels, tapestry-covered Louis XVI chairs and Sheraton caned furnishings, flowers, and palms. The society figure Beverly Nicols recalled 'Maggie's (another of Mrs Greville's nicknames) terrific teas with great Georgian teapots, and Indian and China, and muffins and cream cakes and silver kettles sending up their steam'.[6] The taking of tea was one of the great social rituals of the period, and crossed all classes from poor to rich (Figure 5.1). Mrs Greville also enjoyed the eccentricities of her superior male servants; she retained an infamous butler who was often drunk; the famous story goes that once, at dinner, Mrs Greville wrote him a note stating 'You are drunk, Leave the room at once', which he proceeded to pass to one of the principal male guests on a silver salver. Mrs Greville spent her last days in a lavish suite at the Dorchester, a concrete new build of 1931 with seaweed- and cork-lined rooms to dull all sound, seeing out the bombs and the war. She retained a butler and footmen at the hotel and wore her famous emeralds and a swathe of other jewels daily, despite the crashing and the chaos outside.[7] Edwardian luxury died with her generation.

In the Edwardian period, only married women were permitted to take their breakfast in bed; for everyone else it was bad form and also slightly

Fig. 5.1. Notman Studio, 'Miss Evans and Friends', 1887. These ladies were from wealthy Montreal families, and they are posing for tea with delicate china vessels in the studio of the Scottish–Canadian photographer William Notman. The photographer evoked the mood of contemporary paintings by artists such as Tissot and Alfred Stevens, and the women wear rich dresses with *cuirasse* bodices in the manner of the couturier Worth. Ostrich feather fans and artificial flowers are pinned to their dresses, in an exuberant display of rather smug luxury.

effeminate. These days the habit is associated with a good time in a luxury hotel. Luxury for well-to-do women in the past was often about the fitting-out of the personal bedroom—Marjorie Merriweather Post's bedroom in the 1920s featured a Chinese embroidered satin hanging, cut and trimmed with fur, as a bedcover; Edwina Mountbatten had a pink satin and ostrich feather bedspread in the inter war years; and Diana Mitford wrote lovingly of her white satin bedroom—at a time when coal dust remained a major hazard when keeping things clean. Elsie de Wolfe provided much of the taste and repertoire of these luxurious bedrooms, which were generally furnished either in a reproduction style such as English Sheraton or Louis XVI, or in art deco. They included soft lampshades for the new electric lighting, often converted from Chinese and Delft vases. De Wolfe had gleaned many of her ideas from the aesthete American architect–decorator Ogden Codman and the writer Edith Wharton, who co-published *The Decoration of Houses* in 1897. Elsie did not approve of the taste for silver-plated beds, which she described in 1913 as 'this newest object of bad taste. It is a little too much.'[8]

Bathrooms can also be turned into works of art, and enormous amounts of money are currently expended upon them. There is a stereotype that the British always had poor or inadequate bathrooms compared to the Americans, but this is not really fair. The British created components of plumbing that were considered the wonder of Europe and were described not simply as proof of an advanced civilization but as tantamount to 'racial superiority' by the German commentator Hermann Muthesisus in his widely read three-volume report and subsequent book *Das Englische Haus* (1904–5). Men enjoyed taking showers, rather than baths. The shower at Ardkinglas featured wave and spray controls (Figure 5.2). The house was built in 1906–7 for wealthy arms-dealer Sir Andrew Noble to designs by Sir Robert Lorimer.

Well-to-do ladies frequently had bathrooms of great luxury in the Edwardian period, when a purpose-built plumbed room came to be the expected thing, even for the working classes, if they were lucky enough to live in a contemporary housing scheme. With the influence of art deco, bathrooms became little things of beauty, such as the 1930s bathroom shown in Figure 5.3, which was in Belgrave Square, one of the most fashionable squares in London. The design is very 'Hollywood' in matched and veined marble with etched mirrors and recessed lighting, and appears to include a steam or Turkish bath to the left of the tub. Such baths were a great favourite of the Prince of Wales, briefly Edward VIII and then Duke of Windsor. Men could take such baths in the luxury Turkish-style *hamaans*

Fig. 5.2. A shower at Ardkinglas, Argyll, United Kingdom; fitted in 1906, it features wave and spray controls. The house was completed in 1907 for the armaments dealer Sir Andrew Noble to designs by Sir Robert Lorimer. The house remains in the family. Published in *Country Life*, 29 September 2010.

Fig. 5.3. A modern bathroom at 11a Belgrave Square, London, *c.*1944. To the left there appears to be a Turkish bath for the man of the house. The carpets are modern Chinese.

of the nineteenth century that were adjacent to the gentleman's shopping area of Jermyn Street. Here they might also gain a Japanese-style tattoo on their back or shoulder—something that was popular with European male royals (though very discreet, of course).[9] The Prince was not permitted one.

The King's sister Princess Mary, who married Harry Lascelles, 6th Earl of Harewood, in 1922 and lived at the beautiful eighteenth-century house Harewood, had an exquisite boudoir designed for her by Sir Herbert Baker, Edwin Lutyens's chief assistant, and a recessed bath fitted with silver taps. But even the princess's bathroom was perhaps no match for that of the plutocrat Mrs Horace E. (Anna Thomson) Dodge (1871–1970), whose car fortune enabled her to commission in the early 1930s a complete version of the eighteenth-century French pavilion 'Le Petit Trianon', called 'Rose Terrace', at Grosse Pointe outside Detroit, designed by the architect Horace Trumbauer. Alas, it has now been demolished. Mrs Dodge sold her late husband's car operations in 1925 for what was at the time the largest transaction in American corporate history, an astonishing $146 million. This enabled her to build what is considered the finest and also the last great French-inspired private residence, before the Second World War rendered such residences (and the staff that they required) impossible. The famous dealer Joseph Duveen was actively involved in the creation of this luxurious residence, supplying her with paintings by Thomas Gainsborough and Joshua Reynolds, as he did also for the Fricks, Huntingtons, and other American multimillionaires. Rose Terrace, lived in for only three months of the year, included a truly exquisite gilt-bronze appointed bathroom by the French–American decorators L. Alavoine and Company. Rather like the *marchands-merciers* of eighteenth-century Paris, this high-society firm both fitted out rooms in exquisite taste but also maintained the furnishings, and closed and opened the residences for their owners, including Mrs Dodge.

There are other luxuries of this period that might surprise us today, which were commented upon in private both by members of the British royal family, particularly Her Majesty Queen Elizabeth the Queen Mother

(1900–2002), and also by the photographer and aesthete Cecil Beaton. Such figures, from very different social backgrounds but enjoying the same sense of *joie de vivre*, nearly always describe in their diaries the experience of a house party or dinner in terms of the following luxuries: the quality of the flowers, food and wine, and towels and soaps. There are frequent descriptions in both their travel notes concerning the enormous amount and variety of bathroom linen available in the great private homes of the United States: 'millions of towels, large, medium, small, tiny, face flannels, in great profusion', as the Queen Mother wrote in 1954.[10] Linen was quite a concern to people in the recent past; when the Queen Mother had become engaged in the 1920s, Mrs Greville offered to gift £1,500 worth of linen for the trousseau. The then Duchess of York wrote: 'Whoever is buying it for us must remember that we are not millionaires (what ho!) and don't you think £1,000 ought to do it?'[11] In the 1920s £1,000 could buy a comfortable detached house in the London suburbs.

The private 'care of the self' clearly mattered a great deal. Elsie de Wolfe used the word 'luxury' only very sparingly in her book *The House in Good Taste* (1913), but when she did use the term it applied to women and to the 'lots of little dodges' for

> the dressing room of the person who wants comfort and can have luxury. There is the hot-water-towel rack, which is connected with the hot-water system of the house . . . Another modern luxury is a wall cabinet fitted with glass shelves for one's bottles and sponges and powders. There seems to be no end to the little luxuries that are devised for the person who makes a proper toilet. Who can blame them for loving the business of making themselves attractive, when everyone offers encouragement?[12]

Such small luxuries continue to structure the way in which traditional luxury hotels operate; the great innovation of the owner of the first Four Seasons Hotel in the 1970s was to give the ladies hair shampoo in small bottles, which was considered astonishing at the time (it saved them having to pack them and it rendered 'dressing cases' redundant).

Fig. 5.4. Lucien Lelong, 'Robin-hood' silver and mink-covered lipstick, 1935–42, mink fur and metal tube with cardboard box, 2013.975.2AB. This was a prototype, along with several covered in faux jewels, that represents true 'over-the-top' luxury between the wars.

Some luxury was never seen in public. But details from the lifestyle of the Duke and Duchess of Windsor provide a great many examples from the late 1930s to the 1960s. Friend Diana Mosley (one of the Mitford sisters) wrote: 'Their perfectionism [is] apparent everywhere, their elaborate food—melon with a tomato ice in it, eggs with crab sauce.'[13] The Duchess owned mink garters to wear under her skirts, many jewels held secret inscriptions from the Duke, and jewelled compacts or *minaudières* invented in the 1930s by Van Cleef and Arpels held pop-up mirrors and compartments for powder and rouge. Lucien Lelong designed a mink-covered lipstick prototype that was not put into production (Figure 5.4). Its extreme luxury would have been absurd for anyone except, perhaps, the Duchess.

A ROOM IS A MOOD

The complete lifestyle notion of Terence Conran in the 1960s, Laura Ashley in the 1970s, and Ralph Lauren in the 1980s, in which fashion clothing, furnishings, upholstery, and homewares were selected and coordinated by a design team, was imagined much earlier. In the 1880s and 1890s new taste-makers became interested in the 'associative' aspects of symbolism. The famous aesthete, the impeccably dressed Comte Robert de Montesquiou-Fézénsac, announced that a room is a 'mood'.[14] Oscar Wilde knew this notorious figure, a poet and *bon vivant* who provided the decadent character 'Charlus' for Marcel Proust. At his house, the Pavillon Montesquiou, in the town of Versailles, perfumes of different scents were pumped into the rooms and the famous gilded tortoise wandered across rooms filled with Japanese artefacts (the author Vita Sackville West's mother also had a live tortoise in England at this time with her monogram inlaid in diamonds on its shell). The dwelling included a sledge on a white bearskin and glass cases for his silk socks, as well as church furniture.[15] The bedroom of the Comte, illustrated in *La Revue illustrée* in August 1894, included a Chinese carved bed and a *portière* curtain with a motif of a large Japanese iris, in the manner of the rich Lyons silks popular for well-to-do ladies' evening dresses in the nineteenth century.[16]

The English-speaking world was uncomfortable about aesthetic and literary decadence, and their version of *fin-de-siècle* taste tended to be more geometric and restrained. Think, for instance, of the designs of Charles Rennie Mackintosh, in comparison to the more extreme forms of interior decoration designed by an artist such as Gustav Klimt. Vienna was a great centre of design incubation in all areas of design, from furniture and ceramics to women's bags and dresses, in a geometric manner with highly bold colours and strong black outlines that has resonance with the later art deco. From 1911 the Wiener Werkstätte ran a dress workshop within its tailor department, and Klimt also designed dresses. More commercial and long-lasting models of art nouveau taste were created by Liberty's of London, which opened in 1875 to retail an entire lifestyle based on *japonisme*. Other decorative innovators of the time such as Henry Van de Velde and Josef Hoffman proposed completely integrated interiors in which the works of art were embedded into the very structure of the rooms, and the women who populated them (often the artists' wives) in turn looked like the paintings.

A highly developed and new sensitivity to colour, form, and texture was apparent in the work of such figures, who were also often involved with stage and costume design. More *avant-garde* design was created within the Bloomsbury circle. Roger Fry's Omega Workshop produced and sold designs for clothing and furnishing textiles influenced by Cubist and Futurist art, as well as Primitivism and the colour schemes and athletic eroticism of the *Ballets Russes*. This circle also understood that money alone could not buy taste. A humble kitchen colander, for instance, could be painted and hung to create an elegant ad hoc chandelier, as in the farmhouse owned by members of the Bloomsbury group at Charleston, near Brighton.

The first figures to call themselves 'interior designers' transferred the promotional and personalized techniques of mid-nineteenth-century couturiers such as Charles Frederick Worth to the field of interior decoration. The American Elsie de Wolfe (later Lady Mendl) was first an actress noted for wearing lavish contemporary fashions on the stage in the 1880s, but in 1905 announced her services as an interior designer in New York. If ever a woman embraced luxury it was Elsie. She deployed the home as a female space in which women might refashion themselves from the restrictive spirit of their Victorian mothers; indeed, she was a suffragette supporter and perhaps the first woman who made a million dollars from a personal business that she had not inherited. Surrounded by mirrors, light open spaces, and delicate French eighteenth-century furniture, she promoted a new type of modernity that did not reject traditional languages of design. De Wolfe exhibited a type of hyper-femininity, with the house, clothes by leading designers such as Elsa Schiaparelli and Coco Chanel, hairstyle and facelift so perfect that it verged on the parodic. Her white satin and feather dresses found a corollary in the plate-glass and mirrored interiors that she popularized. Her visit to Bombay (a city described by *Vogue* as a cross between 'Nice and Miami') and her rapturous account of Indian elephants' jewels were reported by the magazine in December 1938.[17] Elsie lived her life as a work of art and dressed to suit the changing moods of fashion and interior decoration. Her parties were notorious, including her second Circus Ball of 1939, just before the war, held at her villa 'Trianon' (not the real Petit Trianon) near Versailles. A firm worked for three days to set up the night lighting.[18] Rare white horses were imported specially from Finland and women wore enormous plumed headdresses.[19] The ideas were formed in close collaboration with her many designer friends, creative personalities such as Schiaparelli, and contemporary interior and furniture designers such as Jean-Michel Frank and Emilio Terry. Similar balls were also held by plutocrat South Americans such as the Lopez-Willshaws and the Marquis de Cuevas, in the gilded years before the Second World War. Many of these entertainments had historical themes, such as the Racine ball and the Louis-Philippe ball of 1939, and all required incredible sets and costumes, vast amounts of white lilies, and a great deal of champagne. The striking effects of the great couturiers of the day, such as Jeanne Lanvin, who could fashion a dress from ribbons pleated and stitched on to gauze, turned women into mobile works of art. Just as today, one can buy the ideas of others to create one's own personal 'experience culture' if one is sufficiently rich.

Fashion designers had already set the stage as brilliant publicists much earlier, in the years before the First World War. Paul Poiret flew his models to North America and Vienna for fashion parades, hosted the most lavish fancy-dress balls in Paris, and commissioned a series of avant-garde architects to design his salon and residence. This notion of the celebrity designer, famed for extravagant living and familiarity with avant-garde circles, in time became associated with other fields such as interior design, undoubtedly inspiring people like Elsie de Wolfe in their own ruthless self-promotion and high living.[20]

DRESSING UP

The costume ball was in fact one of the most popular pastimes in the Victorian and Edwardian period. It was popular with all classes, as many levels of improvisation were possible. But for the rich it offered the chance really to flaunt wealth without limit. A series of grand New York balls in the late nineteenth century was widely reported in the press because of their incredible opulence. The first was the 1883 Alva and William K. Vanderbilt ball, followed by the Bradley Martin Ball of 1897. The latter cost so much and caused such a scandal that its host was forced to go abroad. Banks of orchids and roses were arranged for the guests, who arrived in allegorical gowns designed by the famous couturier Charles Frederick Worth (1826–95). Some were dressed as goddesses, others as men and women from famous paintings. One was even dressed as 'electricity'.

The last such American ball was hosted by James Hazen Hyde in 1905. He was accused of using funds from his Equitable Life Assurance Company, and such lavish balls ceased as a result.[21] Across the Atlantic, the greatest costume ball was the Devonshire House Ball held in 1897 to mark Queen Victoria's diamond jubilee. The theme on that occasion was 'great courts of the past'. About 200 of the guests were photographed under electric light by the society photographers Lafayette and Bassano, and the images demonstrate the astonishing wealth of the period, with women such as Mrs Paget having her real gems mounted like costume jewels in her Cleopatra headdress. The Romanovs held similar balls in Russia, and they were particular favourites in France during the Second Empire. There are echoes of these great *fin-de-siècle* balls in the staging of Truman Capote's famous Black and White Ball of 1966 at the Plaza Hotel, when it was said

Fig. 5.5. Notman Studio, 'Miss Fraser, Montreal, QC, 1897', or 'Woman with Parasol', Montreal, 1897. Notman used state-of-the-art camera technology to create crisp effects such as this; his work won prizes around the world. He captures the strength of the sitter's face contrasted with a wide variety of materials from the organdy parasol to the embroidered blouse and artificial flowers on the hat.

that those not invited had to fly to distant points of the United States to pretend that they had not been available. At this ball women wore beautiful contemporary evening gowns, not costumes, and both men and women sported amusing masks, many of great whimsy.[22] Lee Radziwill (Jackie Kennedy's sister) could boast that her 'spiral silver sequin dress was made by Mila Schön, who came from Milan to London several times for fittings, as well as to oversee the mask'.[23]

The social codes of the nineteenth century demanded different garments for day and evening for both men and women who wished to be socially active, and for women the code extended to numerous changes throughout the day and into the early evening (Figure 5.5). The most popular couturier of the gilded years of the last third of the nineteenth century was undoubtedly Charles Frederick Worth. Worth's couture house opened in Paris's rue de la Paix in 1858. Worth is claimed to have said of his American clients: 'They have faith, figures, and francs.'[24] As well as designing for the dollar princesses, he dressed the imperial circle around Napoleon III and his empress, Eugénie, as well as the Parisian demi-monde of actresses and courtesans. Like Christian Dior in the 1950s, who worked closely with the major textile manufacturer Boussac, Worth commissioned special textiles from Lyons silk designers that were impossible for others to emulate. Women knew who had the originals.

Descriptions of the mid-nineteenth-century clothes of affluent women are very much about the effects of colours, textures, and the folds of the fabric. The trimmings and linings of the clothes of the second half of the nineteenth century have probably never been equalled: rare birds' feathers that appear to be like fur, crystals and semi-precious jewels, and extraordinary *passementerie* (decorative trimming) that links the dresses to the high style in furnishings. Worth's archive, now in the Victoria and Albert Museum in London, includes clothes of an almost modernist geometrical cut for their day, with incredible lace and appliqué.[25] Among the most embellished garments were the *visites* or paletots, bustled jackets that ended just below the waist that were worn only outside in the afternoon, as well as the floor-length evening capes to be worn after dinner or the opera. Luxurious textiles, elaborate embroideries, and linings of fur continued to dominate the highest level of haute couture for women, until the 1960s rendered such effects and materials old fashioned. Although there was an attempt to revive this luxury at the house of Lacroix in the early 1990s, the revival never really caught on, and the fashion house ceased operations.

Many Worth customers bought their Paris millinery at Madame Virot, his neighbouring business; she was famous for taxidermy and rare materials. Figure 5.6 shows an example from the period by Madame Heitz-Boyer of Paris, with a small fox head peeping out from among the silk velvet, lace,

Fig. 5.6. Toque (hat), label 'Mme Heitz-Boyer', Paris, 1890s, taxidermy, fox fur, silk charmeuse, silk velvet, lace, and glass beads. Milliners were known as the 'queens of fashion' in nineteenth-century France. The more successful among them were able to command very high prices for their novelties, which went in and out of fashion very quickly. Coco Chanel began her life as a milliner, which required little capital and space to set up.

and glass. Men, too, could enjoy luxurious hand-crafted fashion accessories, which were often novelties for the hot months of summer. A Paris-made silk waistcoat by Carette, a business in the fashionable Boulevard Haussmann, is hand-painted with hydrangeas, a fashionable flower of the 1890s; the waistcoat is signed and dated '1904' in ink, most likely by the finisher (Figure 5.7).

Such clothes demanded appropriate jewels and accessories, which were worn by both men and women, although by this date men wore fewer rings and their jewels were more subtle. Before the commercial cultivation of pearls started in 1916, pearls were among the most valued type of jewel and were frequently matched with the flash of diamonds. The New York jeweller Jacob Dreicer is said to have sold a rope of pearls in the 1890s for $1.5 million.[26] A panoply of accessories for women—parasols, canes, lorgnettes, opera glasses, handbags, and binoculars–contributed to the splendour of dressing. Fans were obligatory for grand ladies, such as the *point-de-gauze* lace example by Dumoret of Paris shown in Figure 5.8, with its fine mother-of-pearl guard carved with artfully sculpted naked ladies, and the owner's first name set in diamonds: Phébé (in fact, Phoebe) Apperson Hearst. It retains its duck-egg blue silk-covered box: the packaging of luxury goods has and always remains vital to their allure. The Impressionist painter Pierre-Auguste Renoir had begun his career painting fans; it was a major part of the French luxury trades. Renoir was born into the working class, but he derided the materialism of his age. Like the Goncourt brothers, he advocated a return to the 'haut luxe' that had characterized France before the Revolution. In terms of official culture, the *Union Centrale des Beaux-Arts appliqués à l'industrie* was encouraged by the prime minister of the day, Léon Gambetta, to lobby for a decorative arts museum in Paris (realized in 1894) and to shift the emphasis of French design away from the industrial and back towards the decorative. This, it was felt, would allow for a return of the decorative arts to the former aristocratic level, and the production of those high-quality products that had made France's

Fig. 5.7 (a and b). Man's vest (summer waistcoat) and handwritten label: 'Carette, 121 Boulevard Haussmann, Mr. Margeurette, Date, 23 Février 1904, no. 350', hand-painted silk depicting blue hydrangeas and stems. Summer fashion for wealthy men in the nineteenth century was light, often white with contrasting and playful effects, such as this painted floral waistcoat. Its boned construction shaped the form of the male body.

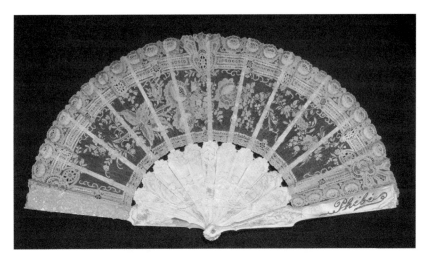

Fig. 5.8. Fan by Felix Alexandre, retailed by Dumoret, Paris, 1870–5, initialled 'Phébé' [Phoebe Hearst], carved mother-of-pearl, silk *point de gauze* lace and diamonds with silk-covered box. Phoebe Hearst (1842–1919) was an American feminist and philanthropist. The family money came from newspapers. She sponsored expeditions and education.

international reputation.[27] Another such effort, this time with anti-Semitic overtones, was made in the 1920s by Chanel's friend Iribe, as we shall see.

The American riches of this period were far from secret. Some plutocrats published their own collections, such as *Mr Vanderbilt's House and Collection* (1883–4) and *Artistic Houses* (1883–4). New media and technology developed hand in hand; the invention of flashlights that neither smelt, nor emitted smoke, facilitated the first precise photographs of interiors, which were widely published. *Cosmopolitan*, *Munsey's Magazine*, *Collier's*, and *McClure's* were established between 1886 and 1893. The New York publisher Condé Nast purchased *Vogue* in 1905 and dramatically improved the quality of film technology and printing, building his own printing plant in the 1920s, emphasizing colour, and adding other periodicals to his stable such as *Vogue Pattern Book*, *Vanity Fair*, *House & Garden*, *The American Golfer*, and *Glamour of Hollywood* (later *Glamour*).[28] Although the word 'luxury' does not appear as frequently as one might imagine in such magazines, all manner of luxuries were laid out there by advertisers and feature writers.

The search for fine gems was the apogee of a taste that had commenced in the mid- to late eighteenth century. Wealthy women could wear their jewels in profusion at any time of day. Favourite items included tiaras (not to be worn in restaurants, only in private houses), bracelets (known as 'service stripes' by British women in the 1930s and 1940s), rings, dog collars of pearls and gems, brooches, corsage ornaments (that covered the breast), and earrings and earclips (popular in the 1930s and 1940s). It was a period when women were laden with jewels for dinner: Kenneth Clark, the art historian, noted in his diary of a New York party in 1930 that the women 'even brought pieces of jewellery in their hands and laid them down on the dinner table. This could have happened in the Middle Ages.'[29] The millionaire Mrs Greville, friend of the Duke and Duchess of York, loved her jewels, owning pieces that could be traced back to Marie Antoinette and Napoleon's first wife, the Empress Josephine. The Queen Mother inherited key pieces of jewellery from Mrs Greville, a friend from the time she was still Duchess of York, but, as Elizabeth wrote in her diaries, she did not wear the lavish Cartier and Boucheron pieces until 1947, so as to not appear 'out of sync' with the austerity movement immediately after the war. She was very practical about conspicuous luxury, writing in 1934—probably of the Great Depression—that 'a few years ago people were embarrassed and unhappy if they glimpsed a diamond or ate quails in company, which was a shame as it had no reaction to one's misery at the poverty and sadness of the people of this country'.[30] This is an important point. Profligate luxury naturally often risks looking out of step with public morals and public mores.

DEPARTMENT STORES AND OUTFITTERS

The decline of the department store around the world as the principal point for the purchase of luxuries is remarkable. Until the 1990s, very few luxuries were sold outside the department stores in a typical town or small city. Yet the department store has reinvented itself as a place of spectacle and whimsy—consider the Pradasphere held at Harrods in 2013, and in many smaller cities it continues to occupy an important place in the consumer mentality. For example, both Stockmann in Helsinki and NK (Nordiska Kompaniet) in Stockholm have very large subterranean food halls. Here you will find the very best meat, the *pâté de foie*, the Duchy of Cornwall biscuits, the teabags by Fauchon. In other countries such as Australia and the United Kingdom, luxury food, wines, flowers, and accessories are sold in every affluent suburb, in smaller branded boutiques or privately owned shops. This has spelt the decline of the many department stores that once existed—for instance, David Jones in Sydney, Australia, which made luxury its speciality for 100 years but no longer enjoys the same prestige or exclusive access to many luxury products. The 'revolution of the domestic economy', as the historian Charles Wilson put it in 1965, has been going on for some time, particularly in the growing market for items such as food, drugs, books, newspapers, and cosmetics. Wilson described the incredible transformation of the Britain of the Crystal Palace era (1851) to the Edwardian period, and a veritable explosion of shopping; from 1,500 general or 'specialized multiple grocers' in England in 1880, to '11,645 such stores in 1900. Specialised multiple grocers likes Liptons or Home and Colonial, shoe shops like Freeman Hardy & Willis, chemists like Boots (with 150 shops by 1900), tailors like Hepworths, newspaper and book stores like W.H. Smith and scores of others transformed the retail scene.'[31]

Sports and commercialized leisure also provided new 'little luxuries' at a time when a holiday was still a great rarity for the poorer working classes, who might instead have a dance once a year, but were beginning to go on day trips to the beaches. Wilson goes on to make an important point concerning relative living standards for the United Kingdom—a nation where minor luxuries were now available to the many for the first time: 'Each called for capital, labour, enterprise, ingenuity to supply the needs of an urban people living at standards which most believed were higher and all agreed were different.'[32] A good example of such a new luxury is chocolate. In the nineteenth century, confectionary was sugar, not chocolate, based, the latter being a luxury, but chocolate began to replace sugar-based sweets (candies, toffees, drops, boiled sweets, and so on) after about 1900.[33]

The consumption of foods is obviously always relative, both between cultures and over time, although it has become more globally homogenous in recent years. British soldiers serving in the Second World War had been amazed by the food and also the luxurious leisure and bathing facilities on American wartime bases; they were astonished to see 'unlimited supplies of steak, chops, chicken and ice cream', when they had only tinned food.[34] Chicken was a great luxury until the post-war period; in 1950 it comprised 1 per cent of the total meat consumed in Britain.[35] After the war, British entrepreneurs made study tours of chicken farms in the United States and began to breed new birds, made use of pharmaceuticals and steroids to hasten growing, moved away from flock to shed farming, and implemented the complex plant that was required to eliminate the bacteria that easily attends chicken carcasses; this normally meant the installation of freezing plants. The frozen chicken subsequently made its appearance, and no longer appeared just at weddings and Christmas. By 1980 fresh chicken made up one-quarter of total market share of meat consumption in Britain.[36]

Health, too, is connected to the debate about luxury. In the late Victorian period, attending the doctor and displaying the associated medicines in the front room of a British working-class dwelling was an important aspect of respectability, indeed a sign of luxury expenditure. Similarly, insurance certificates against unemployment and illness were also displayed in working-class parlours and front rooms, in what the historian Paul Johnson calls 'working-class conspicuous consumption'.[37] For these people, basic healthcare was a form of luxury, something to be proudly displayed to the world. One person's basic necessity is another person's luxury.

ORCHIDELIRIUM

Flowers grown out of season are clearly superfluous to necessity, but the pleasure they have given people since the ancient world suggests that the delight in them might be near universal. The presence of a good florist in a hotel and flowers in the room is still considered an important indicator of a hotel's quality, although the presence of myriad flowers has been diminishing in recent years in all but five- or six-star hotels. Fresh flowers are generally included in the tiny lavatory of a business-class airline today (orchids for Thai International Airways and gerberas for the Scandinavian Airline System), and sometimes also attached to the seats of First Class.

The association between flowers and luxury goes far back in time and includes, as we have seen, pastimes such as gardening, the importation of rare blooms from distant shores, and phenomena such as the seventeenth-century 'tulipmania'. In the past, flowers were one of the most important attributes of magnificent living for royals and good living for others. Flowers are often mentioned in accounts of high society in the late nineteenth century. Consuelo Vanderbilt wrote: 'When I think of spring it is Paris, with its sweet scents of budding chestnut trees and flowering lilac, and of the lilies the hawkers vend in the streets, those sprigs of *muguet* one wears on the first of May.'[38] Queen Alexandra had 300–400 flower vases changed every day at Marlborough House, her large residence adjacent to Buckingham Palace, in addition to 'the magnificent Kentia palms in every room'.[39] In very old age, in 1989, the Queen Mother wrote a letter in which she recalled her youth: 'I remember dancing with a nice young American at Lady Powis' ball in Berkeley Square (aged 17) and the amazement and thrill when the next day a huge bunch of red roses arrived! In those days flowers were very rare!'[40] She was clearly very excited to have received a bunch of roses out of season. Diana Cooper, visiting the Queen Mother's private apartments in 1948, mentions great 'bathtub' sized vases of flowers, including what she describes as obscene pink ones with male stamens.

This taste was founded in the *fin-de-siècle* pan-European taste for palm-filled winter gardens, from Nice to Stockholm, and for cut flowers and even fruits out of season that had to be continually forced. There were 100 florist's shops in St Petersburg before the Revolution of 1917, run mainly by foreigners, who satisfied the Russian aristocracy's love for fresh flowers by importing them on an express train from Nice. Queen Alexandra electrified her showcases of artificial Fabergé flowers at Sandringham and turned the lights on as an entertainment for her guests.[41]

Many great houses offered flowers to both male and female guests several times a day from the breakfast trays to posies and corsages: 'fresh flowers just had to be there ... There was never a dead flower. It was as if flowers, for them, lived for ever. It was part of the magic of their lives,' stated the head gardener of a large country house.[42] Queen Alexandra received gifts of flower baskets (generally roses, but long carnations arranged in sun bursts were also very fashionable) 12 feet by 8 feet high, soon to be the stuff of Hollywood movies. At fashionable London balls in 1915 (the 'dances of death', when young men serving in the forces had some last hours of pleasure), banks of orchids and sweet-smelling stephanotis were replaced with wild flowers at dawn, when the breakfast course was served.[43] Flowers were a must in society wedding celebrations and were often used in abundance on the stage (Figure 5.9). Apart from fragrant hothouse flowers out of season, the most sought-after blooms were orchids. Orchids were first propagated commercially in England in 1812, and their propagation increased from the 1830s. The passion for orchids was known as 'orchidelirium': commercial expeditions were launched to Java to collect them, and a single rare, blue vanda orchid was sold by the Veitch nursery in England in the 1830s for the incredible sum of £300.[44] They remained one of the most expensive floral commodities until the 1990s, continuing to be 'seen as the badge of wealth and refinement and worldliness'.[45] Ziegler tells us: 'In 1899 a New York florist claimed that floral expenditure (in terms of flower stems sold) had increased one hundred times over the previous five years.'[46]

Fig. 5.9. 'The wedding party standing in the Rosenblatt residence at 55 East 92nd Street, 1903'. This image depicts the love of kentia and other palms and trailing florist's flowers that were used to decorate the grand balls and weddings at the end of the nineteenth century. The bridesmaids all held fans at this wedding, which were probably gifts for the occasion, and the men have removed their top hats, which they carry in other photographs of the event.

Flowers remained an important attribute of women's dress, worn fresh at the wrist in the nineteenth century and as artificial ornaments on hats and at the chest until the counter-cultural politics of the 1960s rendered them old-fashioned. The flower was once the most important motif woven, embroidered, or printed on women's garments, although many women today dislike wearing such patterns because of their over-feminized connotations. Contemporary designers have attempted to promote floral patterns of late, but to little avail with their women customers around the world, at least when it comes to business and everyday attire.[47] Receiving flowers is no longer such a surprising luxury. They are commercial global products, hybridized and farmed in developing countries and cheaply priced for the high street.[48] Nonetheless, to receive a bunch of roses still commands a respect that plays on older understandings of luxury and sensuality, as they cannot last more than a few days and their beauty fades as one looks.

LAST DECADENCE: CAFÉ SOCIETY

The great fashion designers such as Elsa Schiaparelli and the interior designer Jean-Michel Frank worked at the centre of the so-called Café Society of the inter-war years. Paris was the natural home of this grouping, which was based more around money and talent than birth, but which at the same time included quite large numbers of titled aristocrats. It was a society that frequented the resort towns of the south of France (going by the overnight first-class *train bleu* from Paris), New York, Miami, and South America. Paris had been an exciting, louche, and daring place since the nineteenth century. Drug-taking, gourmandize, and eroticism were a part of its appeal. On her visit there in 1924, the young Duchess of York wrote that she went to the

> Casino de Paris, where for the first time in my life I saw ladies with *very* little on ... a dance hall full of doped Russians & Argentines, & then to a tiny place where we drank off a coffin, surrounded by skeletons & exchanging very vulgar badinage with a man carrying a huge Bone ... & then to a tiny place with several Negroes with delicious voices ...[49]

Needless to say, she did not return to such places when she became Queen of England.

Café Society included the global members of a deracinated aristocracy: exiled Russians, cosmopolitan Indian princes with money to burn, British Lords and Ladies. It also included many of the super-rich South Americans such as the Patinos, who made Paris their second home, or the incredibly wealthy dilettante collector the Comte de Beistegui, a Mexican whose family had returned to France in the nineteenth century after the fall of

Emperor Maximilian. Quite a lot of nastiness was directed at the South Americans within this group, just as there is media interest and discrimination concerning the wealthy Chinese and Russians today. One anecdote notes that the South Americans visiting the United States called the St Regis New York the *Sawn Raygee*; and that Chilean women squashed their dresses deliberately to pretend that they had bought and packed them in Paris.[50] Café Society was also louche, with its lesbian major-domo (Elsa Maxwell, the first gossip columnist and party-giver of her type), its pretty 'joy boys', its quirky artists, and its other *demi-mondaine* inhabitants. It quickly turned into 'Nescafé Society', as Loelia Westminster put it. It was a gay way of life based on long transatlantic voyages, regular sea holidays, stays in exclusive resorts from the Greenbier in the United States to the great South American hotels (some designed by Jean-Michel Frank's Argentine company 'COMTE'), and multiple residences. Although the rich still try to live in this way, they are no longer such a coherent group, and they no longer dictate the *ne plus ultra* of luxury for all in the way they once did.

The Duchess of Windsor was one such well-known member of Café Society, and much reported in women's magazines by editors such as Diana Vreeland at American *Vogue*.[51] It is believed that Vreeland had sold Wallis Simpson, as she was then called, the luxury *negligées* that she wore to meet the Prince of Wales, when in the 1930s Vreeland had a small shop in London, with nuns making up fine copies of French lingerie. The Duke and Duchess of Windsor were one of the most famous and photographed couples in the world from the late 1930s to the 1960s and if anyone embodied twentieth-century luxury, it was they (Figure 5.10).[52] The Prince gave up his throne in 1937 to marry this twice-divorced American who dressed smartly but was not generally considered attractive by the conventions of the time. Instead, she was *soignée*: beautifully dressed and famed as a hostess and party-giver. In the early 1950s the couple moved to Paris, where they lived in a grace-and-favour villa gifted by the French government for the duration of their lives. The Duchess set out to create a small court

Fig. 5.10. The Duke and Duchess of Windsor relaxing, 20 May 1950, White Sulphur Springs, West Virginia, USA. The Windsors were household names around the world from the late 1930s to the 1960s. With no formal social role to fulful after the Adbication (1937), their life consisted of travelling from one luxury home, spa, or resort to another, according to the seasons. In that sense, they replicated the passage of the nineteenth-century elites from city to country to beach resort, which was such a part of the mentality of passing time. The travel was not rushed, but a part of the luxury experience, whether it be by train, limousine, or ocean-liner. Here they are watching polo near the famous Greenbier Hotel.

to compensate her husband for what he had lost, to divert him and pleasure him.

The Villa Windsor, as it was called, stood on the edge of Paris in the Bois de Boulogne, where the fine ladies of the nineteenth century had once driven in their carriages. It was but a ten-minute drive to the Place Vendôme and the Avenue Montaigne, where the Duchess shopped for her haute couture dresses by Elsa Schiaparelli, Mainbocher, Christian Dior, and later Marc Bohan for Dior. The Duke had good access to Cartier, where he was one of the best customers, ordering incredible bespoke modern jewellery for the Duchess on an annual basis. The Windsor residence was decorated by Maison Jansen, the interior-design firm, in a style that was redolent of the 1930s. Walls were stippled to resemble coloured marbles, a silver and blue carpet was woven with Prince of Wales feathers for the salon, which featured paintings of the Royal family, and fine French furniture and silvered *torchères* were installed on custom-made white and silver *boiserie* panelling, which was unkindly described by *Country Life* magazine as 'grand hotel' (Figure 5.11).[53] Concealed perfume-burners and banks of fresh flowers created a sensual ambience, and it was said that the Duchess's night lighting was the best in Paris. Upstairs was a great deal of private luxury, including one of the great twentieth-century bathrooms, designed by Jansen for the Prince, in grey-veined marble with stainless-steel mirrored doors, pivoting mirrors, and appliquéd brick-red curtains (Figure 5.12).

The Duchess's bathroom had a *trompe l'œil* candy-striped *tôle* (metal) tented canopy over her bathtub and frescoes of great whimsy by the well-known decorative painter Dimitri Bouchène, who also worked as a fashion illustrator. The couple spent part of the year in the United States, always travelling across the Atlantic by ocean liner in the best suite, and staying in New York in a set of rooms permanently decorated for them at the Waldorf Astoria Hotel. In Palm Beach they stayed at the local millionaires' residences. They were accompanied by servants, dogs, and so much luggage that numerous carts were required. They often travelled on a private train

Fig. 5.11. Salon of the Duke and Duchess of Windsor, decoration by the firm of Jansen, c.1953, 4, route du Champs d'Entraînement, Paris; illustrated John Cornforth, 'The Duke and Duchess of Windsor's House in Paris', *Country Life*, 1987. The salon incorporated a painting of the Duke's mother, Queen Mary, and a custom-made pale blue and silver low-weave carpet with Prince of Wales feathers. The sofas are post-war upholstery with cushions depicting seashells. The room had lost its grandest eighteenth-century French furnishings at the time this photograph was taken (following the death of the Duchess), and the chandelier is a replacement.

Fig. 5.12. Bathroom of the Duke of Windsor, decoration by Jansen, c.1953, 4, route du Champs d'Entraînement, Paris; illustrated John Cornforth, 'The Duke and Duchess of Windsor's House in Paris', *Country Life*, 1987. The Duke's exquisite bathroom, decorated with framed prints of regimental dress, in its snappy red and white decoration, has a military but also rather melancholy air. The weighing machine is American, and the tubular steel chairs are British. The couple's bathrooms were almost as large as their bedrooms and more elaborately decorated, and were planned to allow them to inspect their appearance from all angles. The decorator was Stéphane Boudin of the firm called Jansen, who later worked for Jacqueline Kennedy.

provided by a friend, the rail tycoon Robert R. Young, who also owned the luxury Greenbier Hotel, West Virginia, where they enjoyed staying.

The Windsor possessions were auctioned after their death, revealing the great luxury in which they had lived. Their dogs ate from silver-plated bowls (not silver, as was sometimes claimed). The couple slept in crested *crêpe de chine* sheets, their clothing was monogrammed and of the highest craftsmanship, and there was so much of it that the Duke had his own swatch book and filing system to manage it all.[54] As for the Duchess, her silk velvet and crocodile shoes and dozens of handbags carried her mono-gram, sometimes overlaid with carved jades and semi-precious stones, even though it had never been authorized by Buckingham Palace. Her other possessions were the quintessence of what was soon to appear a rather old-fashioned kind of luxury: a zebra-skin case for sunglasses, a *pochette* made from ocelot fur, a delicate marabou feather evening cape by Chanel, a range of other rare furs, and a mink evening bag. For better or for worse, the 'space age' of the 1960s would soon replace many of these perhaps now rather quaint-looking objects of desire with plastics and other cheaper man-made materials.

6

Between False Poverty and
Old Opulence:

Luxury Society in the Twentieth Century

How one should spend one's money is clearly a matter of debate and personal opinion, and throughout the twentieth century different extremes were promoted by taste-makers as to how to pursue a beautiful life. The scale of the issue is not insignificant. By the end of the century there were more than 250 billionaires worldwide, with an estimated 6.5 million millionaires in the United States alone. *Millionaires* magazine had to add the subtitle 'Opulence' at this point. All these millionaires and billionaires have to make decisions as to how to spend their money. And now as in the past, they have a great many choices to make. From the 1920s onwards, luxury become more than a practice for a relatively small elite. This, however, entailed a redefinition of luxury away from mere decadence and whimsicality to sometimes more obscure and recherché choices.

Throughout the twentieth century, luxury thrived on a set of contradictions—for instance, between revealing versus concealing wealth, between knowledge and erudition versus vulgarity and crassness, and, most of all, between opulence and understatement. Privacy became an end in itself, and was assiduously cultivated by the likes of actress Greta Garbo, former US First Lady Jacqueline Kennedy Onassis, and the philanthropist–gardener

Mr Paul 'Bunny' (Rachel Lowe Lambert) Mellon. Yet, in spite of their reclusiveness, theirs was not the entirely understated luxury that the couturier Coco Chanel and other minimalist architects and designers argued 'true luxury' ought to be. Luxury in the twentieth century also had to concede to publicity: in the image- and media-saturated world that came to embody the century, it was virtually impossible to keep one's home and appearance completely away from the camera lens or the pen of the gossip columnist.

The luxury of the few came to be the aspiration of the many through Hollywood films, the pages of fashion and lifestyle magazines, and the many reports on the lives of the rich and famous that enthralled the general public. The cultural historian Stephen Gundle has argued that the act of 'being seen', either framed by the camera lens or witnessed in movement, was a fundamentally necessary component of 'glamour' in this period: 'The type of personality who was glamorous was generally available to the public and, for commercial or professional reasons, regarded this availability as an important part of their being.'[1]

THE DEATH OF OLD LUXURY: COCO CHANEL

The First World War brought with it the death of millions of young men, the disruption of succession in the great landed estates, and the destruction of huge swathes of Europe. A certain cultural pessimism also set in, as well as modernist aesthetics that rejected the lavishness and historicism of the Belle Époque. Luxury underwent a redefinition, losing much of its former opulence. But can luxury be 'poor'? Modernist ideas minted in the first part of the twentieth century argued for a notion of luxury that transcended intrinsic value. In the interwar years, a new generation of designers, from Coco Chanel for fashion to Jean-Michel Frank for furnishing, turned their backs on the ostentatious exoticism and orientalism of *fin-de-siècle* and 'robber-baron' taste and reinvented the notion of luxury. The 1920s revelled in living for the moment and focused more on 'experience

Fig. 6.1. *Frauen in Ballkleidern* (*Women in Ballgowns*), *c.*1925. Fur-trimmed capes with velvet linings, ostrich-feather fans, tulle, and lavish embroidery, contrasted with flesh-coloured short dresses that emphasize the body, are cleverly conveyed by the illustrator.

culture', in the form of sex, sport, and travel, and fast-changing fashion (Figure 6.1).

The person who most contributed to redefining luxury in the first half of the twentieth century was the famous Gabrielle 'Coco' Chanel. We associate Chanel with the term *chic*, although this was not her invention. Théophile Gautier, the French journalist and literary critic, used the term as early as 1864, calling it 'a dreadful and bizarre word of modern fabrica-tion'.[2] With Chanel, *chic* came to mean an approach to style that was not simply dependent upon money, although money always helps. This explains her use of simple materials, muted colours, and rigid lines. She claimed that she was not interested in diamonds and pearls—most of hers were in fact fine fakes crafted by the jeweller Verdura. Although known as a *couturière*, Chanel made her fortune from the sale of Chanel Number 5, a very expensive perfume made with the rarest luxury ingredients from the south of France but with the novelty of adding synthetic ingredients. It was first released in 1922 in its medicinal-looking bottle, stripped of all historical association.[3] Chanel was not the sole author of these ideas regarding a luxurious simplicity. Clearly associated with wider aesthetic minimalism, they appear also in the popular writings of decorator Elsie de Wolfe, who wrote in 1913 that 'the woman who wears paste jewels is not so conspicuously wrong as the woman who plasters herself with too many real jewels at the wrong time'.[4]

Chanel had much to say about the relationship of taste and luxury as she aged. Paul Morand's *L'Allure de Chanel* (1976) was the product of an important dialogue between the author and Chanel after the Second World War, which was intended to provide the basis for her memoirs. In this caustic little book Chanel reveals how she saw the years just before the First World War, as did many others, as the watershed that extinguished luxury as people knew it:

> When I went to the races, I would never have thought that I was witnessing the death of luxury, the passing of the nineteenth century, the end of an era. An age of magnificence, but of decadence, the last reflections of a baroque style in which the ornate had killed off the figure, in which over-embellishment had stifled the body's architecture, just as parasites smother trees in tropical forests. Woman was no more than a pretext for riches, for lace, for sable, for chinchilla, for materials that were too precious. Compli-cated patterns, an excess of lace, of embroidery, of gauze, of flounces and over-layers had transformed what women were into a monument of belated

and flamboyant art…There were parasols, aviaries and greenhouses in gardens. The uncommon had become the normal; wealth was as ordinary as poverty.[5]

Chanel was revolted by the approach to luxury connected with the vibrant *Ballets Russes* of the early 1910s and the associated fashions, perfumes, and household products retailed most notably by the fashion designer Paul Poiret: 'The Ballets Russes were stage décor, not couture. I remember only too well saying to someone sitting beside me: "These colours are impossible. These women, I'm bloody well going to dress them in black."'[6] She pursued an equally novel approach to her residence:

> I had the first carpets dyed beige. It reminded me of the soil. All the furnishings immediately became beige. Until the day came when the interior designers begged for mercy. 'Try white satin,' I told them. 'What a good idea!' And their designs were shrouded in snow, just as Mrs Somerset Maugham's shop in London became buried in naïve innocence and white satin. Lacquerware, Chinese blues and whites, expensively designed rice papers, English silverware, white flowers in vases…Eccentricity was dying out; I hope, what's more, that I helped kill it off. Paul Poiret, a most inventive couturier, dressed women in costumes…the most modest tea party looked like something from the Baghdad of the Caliphs.[7]

Chanel was not alone in arguing that luxury was in need of a redefinition. One of her great loves was the French illustrator and entrepreneur Paul Iribe, who designed the famous art deco style 'Iribe rose' that came to define art deco luxury goods. Iribe was also behind an intriguing publication, the *Défense du luxe* (1932). The *Défense du luxe* was a printed manifesto maintaining that France remained the centre of luxury, and it was also an attack on aesthetic modernism of the type never embraced by Chanel, tubular steel rather than the carved wooden chairs that she favoured, concrete rather than stone buildings, and also much contemporary art practice. Iribe criticized everyone from Le Corbusier to Pablo Picasso. Point two of the *Défense* went thus:

We have given up our French stone in favour of cement.

We have given up our French architecture in favour of Germany.

We have given up our French furniture in favour of a cube.

We have given up our French wood in favour of laminated materials.

We have given up our French bronze in favour of Krupp steel and aluminium.

We have given up our French furnishing fabric in favour of wicker and Duco.

We have given up our French rugs in favour of rubber.

We have given up our French fashion in favour of uniforms.

We have given up our French jewellery in favour of *gris-gris*.

We have given up our French fabrics in favour of uniform colours.

We have given up our French hat in favour of a cask.

We have given up our French embroideries and artificial flowers in favour of nothing at all.

We have given up our French champagne and great wines in favour of the cocktail.

We have given up everything that we produce in favour of what we do not produce at all.

We have—act of terrible treason—forsaken our French workman who has never forsaken us. We have forgotten that his science both precise and French was transmitted to him from father to son, in what is a great tradition, and that this worker, debased to the sordid needs to which our feebleness pushed him, cannot be replaced with anything else in the world.

This is an act of treason and the worst commercial sin that one can commit; we have forgotten a basic truth that a French product is sold worldwide because it is French, but that an 'international' product can be sold in the world only through levels of commercial and industrial competition that we can neither comprehend nor understand.

We have forsaken exceptional exclusivity to accept price competition![8]

There is a lot going on in this passage, with its anti-American, anti-German, anti-global stance and with its rhetoric of the passing-down of craft skills from father to son that the great houses continue today to propagate as an ideal. The *Défense* also had anti-Semitic and anti-cosmopolitan overtones, suggesting that an international conspiracy was attempting to drive away the old value system that had created France as the pinnacle of luxury taste and style.[9] Aristocracy and a 'pure' French race were required, Iribe argued, in order for luxury manufacturing to continue. Luxury was also closely connected in his mind with the world of women consumers. This was all a little ironic, given that his lover Chanel earned a living from selling licensed copies of her dresses in North America. Chanel's designs, nonetheless, in their focus on craftsmanship, taste, and elite luxury (they were extremely expensive), were both a reaction to the state of affairs that Iribe posited and also a confirmation that Paris remained the centre of luxury. Chanel's own anti-Semitism, not uncommon for high-society elites of the time, came to stand as a dark shadow over the subtlety of her designs later in life.

The style of the late 1920s and the 1930s was instead the result of the staging of one of the greatest twentieth-century design fairs, the so-called Art Deco Exposition of 1925. Actually entitled the *Exposition des Arts décoratifs et industriels modernes*—the term 'art deco' was coined by dealers only in the 1960s—the exposition redefined cars, ocean-liners, interior design, dress, and fashion goods. It had been planned before the First World War broke out and was designed to ensure that Frenchness remained synonymous with luxury goods. Particularly notable were the schemes by *ensemblier* and furniture-designer Jacques-Emile Ruhlmann. He designed the furnishings for the mock pavilions such as the 'Residence of a Collector', 'Residence of an Ambassador' (French, of course), and a Pavilion of Sèvres Porcelain. The most costly and recherché material was used to create his furnishings, such as *galuchat* (stingray), with inlays of silver, ivory, and ebony. The furniture forms themselves owed a great deal to the neo-classical taste of the late eighteenth century, updated for a new time with cubist overtones. The forms themselves were not modern but from the eighteenth century—an array of *bergères*, *secrétaires*, sleigh beds, *commodes*, and *consoles*. They suggested an unchanging world, in which women reclined on circular beds with matching Aubusson carpets—a new generation of Madame Récamiers.

The art deco manner was truly global. It spread almost immediately via travelling architects, magazine culture, black-and-white film sets, and samples sent to department stores around the world. The French government was extremely proactive, sending out exhibitions from the exposition of 1925 to other countries, such as Japan in 1928. Tokyo was being rebuilt at this time after the Great Kanto earthquake of 1923. The country was very receptive to the new tastes in design, the American architect Frank Lloyd Wright's organic and crystalline Imperial Hotel having survived the earthquake. The Japanese architect Junpei Nakamura created lavish staterooms for Japanese ocean-liners in the art deco style. The new style was always likely to find a receptive audience there, as the French version had a sparseness and sense of line that suited Japanese aesthetics. And, by the same token, French reviews of the Japanese pavilion of 1925 were equally favourable, stating that 'the Japanese, enamoured of fine materials and refined work, have created a charming work, displaying in the *Cours-de-la-reine* a pavilion at once both modern and traditional'.[10]

In 1933 the Japanese Prince Asaka employed French decorator Henri Rapin to build a palatial Tokyo interior for him with glass fittings by René Lalique and bronzes by the sculptor Blanchot; Eaton's department store in Toronto, Canada, was also redesigned around this time, with a fashion floor in high French style. Business records of the time show that the wealthy of Toronto spent thousands of dollars a week on interior decoration there.[11] Resorts and holiday villas from Sydney to Singapore incorporated art deco flourishes as a sign of leisure, luxury, and modernity. The French Embassy in Tokyo provided Ruhlmann with one of his last commissions in the early 1930s.[12] The French-inflected art deco manner relies on pale colours, linear outlines, and tonal effects (rather than the more colourful American jazz style of the 1920s). It is still used today for the design of the luxury hotels of the Peninsula Group, with hotels in Hong Kong, Bangkok, Tokyo (from 2014), and Paris, where 1930s cars and modern limousines in green-painted livery are parked outside.

MINIMALIST LUXURY

Coco Chanel's equivalent in the art of interior design was the short-lived but brilliant Jean-Michel Frank (1895–1941). As his work suggested, minimalism is not simply a matter of an editorial eye and an ability to edit. Our own age does not particularly prize the furniture-maker or the collector, the *ensemblier* who builds a home in layered stages. We are meant to hold our lives on digital devices, and our clothes, dishes, and furniture are meant to be about fashion and are simply disposable. There is a perception that the middle-class antiques trade has been largely destroyed around the world; the prices for so-called brown furniture have collapsed, and a huge generational shift has taken place in terms of consumption. It is because the whole ethos that sustained that particular approach to filling a space has been superseded. The *ensemblier* approach survives as an older and often a queer affectation and is fast being extinguished, with the recent deaths of figures such as the decorator Albert Hadley, and the New York queens of style Nan Kempner and Brooke Astor.

Minimalism in terms of interior decoration is not the same thing as having neither ideas nor objects (the sculptor Donald Judd's 1960s New York studio is a brilliant example of a truly thoughtful minimalism). Frank was not really a 'minimalist'. Frank's disciplined and elegantly severe design of interiors and furniture for the transatlantic elites of the 1930s navigated between the poles of post-Bauhaus austerity and neo-Baroque opulence (Figure 6.2). Unlike the art deco of the era, Frank's work redefined ideas of style and luxury. His use of modest materials—straw, leather (albeit super-fine and by Hermès), parchment, rope, plaster—made into objects and transformed into exclusive actions and works of style suggested that the ideas and concepts of the designer and the choices of the client were more important than older notions of luxury and exclusivity. Similar experimentation with 'poor' materials was also present in fashion in the 1930s, as in the case of shoe-designer Salvatore Ferragamo's use of straw and candy wrappers in response to a lack

Fig. 6.2. Jean-Michel Frank, dressing table probably made for the Sans Souci Palace, Buenos Aires, c.1931–2. Silvered bronze and mirror. This was part of a commission for the Sans Souci Palace, a mini Versailles conceived by society architect René Sergent in 1912, and completed in 1916. As Frank had never used mirror glass before, this was probably a special order, and an allusion to the Hall of Mirrors at Versailles. The firm who made it up for Frank in Argentina was called 'COMTE Ltde'.

of precious materials.[13] An example of Frank's great ability to use relatively worthless materials is a cabinet made of gypsum, which sold at a Paris auction in 2014 for a record price of €3.67 million (Figure 6.3).

Frank's design ethic had a global reach. He executed schemes in South and North America, and supplied many North American interior decorators as

Fig. 6.3. Jean-Michel Frank, designer, a gypsum and patinated bronze cabinet, c.1935, 109 x 75.5 x 22 cm, first exhibited in the Galérie d'Art et Industrie, *Formes d'aujourd'hui* exhibition, Paris, 1936. Sold at Sotheby's Paris, *Félix Marcilhac. Collection Privée*, March 2014, Lot 63, for €3,681,500 (estimate €400,000–600,000), a record price for Frank. The refinement of this piece lies in the contrast of the fairly worthless material, gypsum, and the abstracted form set up by the bronze framework.

well as designing the famous Rockefeller apartment in New York.[14] Frank worked in collaboration with some of the great artists of his era: Christian Bérard, Jean Cocteau, Alberto and Diego Giacometti, Elsa Schiaparelli, Serge Roche, and Emilio Terry. All these figures contributed to the image of French luxury as playful and modern while also paying homage to the neoclassical tradition. On one occasion, he designed a set of garden furniture for the villa La Armonia in the south of France, to be upholstered in a fabric of multi-coloured lozenge shapes, in the same proportion and tones as Picasso's series of harlequins, saying to the wealthy patroness: 'I want my lovely seats, when seen from far across the lawns of La Armonia, to look like Picasso's harlequins reclining.'[15] To the great patrons of the day, the visual arts were a part of *l'art de vivre*, and artists tended to retain their predominance.

Although Frank's work was for an exclusive elite, his aesthetic was much more widespread and had portability into upper-middle-class taste, particularly through the styling industries and retailing. Elements of his style and also that of Elsa Schiaparelli's extreme fashions appear in the kitsch and hilarious George Cukor-directed film *The Women* (1939), which featured hyperbolic luxuries from a transparent glass bathtub for the scarlet woman (Joan Crawford) to bathe in, to white satin bedrooms for the good girls. Frank's approach to design, with its sparse aesthetic and fresh approach to furniture design (frequently collaborations with artists such as Giacometti), was disseminated in aspects of the work of prominent decorators, including the later years of Elsie de Wolfe, as well as Syrie Maugham, Eleanor Brown, and Frances Elkins (the latter being his agent in the USA).[16] He did much to popularize a pickled, blonde look for interiors that was the exact opposite of the dense Victorian aesthetic of the past.

Frank was in fact co-opting the 'chic of poverty', which had already been suggested in the deceptively simple clothing designed by Chanel. As the society photographer and designer Cecil Beaton noted in his 1954 book *The Glass of Fashion*, Frank 'invented new surfaces and fabrics, tables made of parchment, banquettes upholstered in sackcloth... even encouraging people to sit on leather floor cushions'.[17] Unlike the work of Cecil Beaton, or of artists such as Rex Whistler or Oliver Messel, Frank's theatricality and sense of luxury never became saccharine, nor was his approach especially camp. The discipline and restraint in his work avoided that charge. It was perhaps for this reason that Frank was asked to design major schemes of luxurious interior decoration for figures such as Nelson Rockefeller: gilded sofas of an unusual form merged with plaster *consoles* against walls and major works of art by Matisse and Picasso. This formula is the type of juxtaposition that has returned with a vengeance for the super-rich and is much in evidence in the interior decoration of the Candy Brothers and at luxury fairs such as Masterpiece London, which operates as a tie-in with the prominent 100-year-old art and antiques collectors' magazine *Apollo*.

The legacy of Frank is important. In the post-war period, luxury was reconceptualized; it was neither opulent in a traditional sense nor did it necessarily use overt historical references. The modern masters designed and taught quite the opposite. This is exemplified by the designs of an architect like Philip C. Johnson. His Glass House at New Canaan, Connecticut (1949), was built primarily for him to entertain in. Of its design, his biographer has said: 'The Glass House was so spare in form that it gave little outward hint of the amount of labor that went into it.'[18] Johnson rarely slept there, and the food came from the local caterer, heated up on a simple stove that was covered by day with a wooden flap. Luxury was expressed in the inordinate attention to detail, from the steel-framed structure itself, to the placement of the circular ashtray—everyone of course still smoked—to the circular leather-clad bathroom. A number of little follies—including a writing room and his own subterranean pink silk sleeping chamber—completed the estate.

Around this time Johnson built for Mrs John D. (Blanchette) Rockefeller III (with a small part of her oil money) a beautiful little modern guesthouse at 242 East 52nd Street, designed in 1949–50. Here she served her receptions and teas surrounded by modern sculpture, in rooms almost bereft of furnishings. The luxury was in the space and the peace, with the steel-framed fenestration providing the visual rhythm of the rooms with their own internal courtyard.[19] In a much-copied design, Johnson created a sleeping chamber across this courtyard reached by 'three small islands of stone' set in a reflecting pond.[20] The house was gifted to the Museum of Modern Art in 1958 and later resold. The property was listed by Christie's at an estimated $5 million in 2000.

The Second World War was a watershed for both pockets and tastes, and no more villas on the scale and magnificence of Mrs Horace E. Dodge's Rose Terrace were ever built again. Indeed, many such houses were demolished. Entertaining in an Edwardian manner was now considered old-fashioned, and fewer formal rooms were to appear again, with the exception of separate dining rooms, which persisted into the twenty-first century when they were vanquished by the taste for open-plan living and the integration of expensive kitchens. There were always exceptions, such as John Paul Getty, who built a private museum in the form of a Herculaneum villa. But even Queen Elizabeth II and Prince Philip requested that the architect Sir Hugh Casson and designer John Wright should provide the royal yacht *Britannia* with simple blonde sycamore furniture with Bakelite handles, anglepoise lamps, plain fitted carpets, and Edouardo Paolozzi-designed abstract textiles.

Luxury became more subdued and restrained and had to confront the fact that social conditions had changed. When Mies van der Rohe designed Farnsworth House in rural Illinois for Dr Edith Farnsworth in the late 1940s, people were shocked that a woman (a professional doctor) would live in a 'glass house' by herself.[21]

LUXURY LIVES: TRAVEL AND NEW TECHNOLOGIES

Part of the success of minimalism and mid-century design as new forms of luxury can be explained by social changes and a rebuttal of traditional forms of Edwardian opulence, increasingly seen during the twentieth century as both undemocratic (as if luxury is ever anything else) and unproductive. Social changes in both American and European societies and a move towards a dream of democratic equality (characterized by progressive policies and social welfare) made pre-war luxury unappealing, unpleasant, and for some plainly wrong. The period from the 1940s to the early 1980s is one in which luxury was definitely out of fashion, and those who still wished to practise it (as many indeed did) had to do so with great care, even surreptitiously. The fact that discussions of luxury fell off the radar did not, of course, necessarily mean that luxury was 'retreating' in any way. Quite the opposite: one can chart the ways in which luxury rejuvenated itself, and in fact in the period leading up to the 1980s acquired many of the features that have allowed the twenty-first-century luxury industry to emerge. These transformations are particularly evident in the areas of travel, the diffusion of sartorial fashions, and the application of new technologies.

Before the Second World War, long-distance travel was still the luxury of the elite. The 1920s and early 1930s were the heydays of the great luxury ocean-liners. One of the best examples was the SS *Normandie*, launched in 1935, whose interiors were the wonder of the world. The liner was decorated in the art deco manner, with bronze doors and bas-reliefs, glass ceilings and pillars by Lalique and *églomisé* (reverse glass-painted) panels by Jean Dupas, silver by Christofle, blonde pianos by Louis Süe, and mural paintings and tapestries in a genteel modern style by the greatest artists working in the art deco style. Its glass dining hall was hailed as the last Hall of Mirrors. Yet it also incorporated the latest technology: the large unobstructed public spaces were possible because of the funnel intakes running up the walls, a great innovation at the time (Figure 6.4).

Stars of the screen and stage such as Marlene Dietrich and footloose aristocrats such as the Duke and Duchess of Windsor mingled with American

Fig. 6.4. *History of Navigation*, mural by Jean Theodore Dupas (1882–1964), 1934. Glass, paint, gold, silver, palladium leaf. Overall: H. 245, W. 348¾ inches (622.3 x 885.8 cm). Dupas was a French painter trained in the classical manner, later becoming notable for his work in the French art deco style. In the early 1930s he and the glass master Charles Champigneulle created four murals for the ocean-liner SS *Normandie*, launched in 1935. This panel was for one corner of the first-class salon. It depicts a fanciful scene of the history of ocean-going mixed in with mythical sea creatures. The reverse painted glass technique is a particularly luxurious effect that was used in the eighteenth century—for example, at the restaurant Grand Véfour in Paris—and continues to be used by skilled decorators at the top of the market.

millionaires such as Jimmie Donohue and his bejewelled mother, the Woolworth's heirs. Dinner aboard ship demanded a full panoply of evening wear in satin, lace, or velvet, full-length white gloves for women, sets of matching gemstones, and sometimes even tiaras or at least jewelled headpieces. Marlene Dietrich, for instance, travelled on the liners regularly, 'with or without lovers, with male lovers, with female lovers, with male and female lovers', as

Fig. 6.5. Evening jacket, Travis Banton and Howard Greer, for Marlene Dietrich, silk crêpe, gold metallic thread, glass rhinestone and seed beads and gelatin sequins, 1938–40. Clothes such as this were designed to look as good in black and white as in colour; the garment is in a striking red, purple, and blue. This jacket is believed to have been made for Dietrich's personal wardrobe.

the complete records of her secretarial correspondence now housed at the Museum für Film und Fernsehen in Berlin reveal.[22] The types of clothes worn on board are well represented by one of her beautiful jewelled jackets, an evening top that revealed her fine figure but embellished her at the same time. Such garments were designed for the stars by brilliant costume designers, such as Adrian and his contemporaries, to look equally good in black and white photography and film (Figure 6.5). The effect of such

clothing, jewels, lacquered hairdressing, and painted nails created an alluring type of glamour that has never been equalled.

Yet this was a world that the Second World War killed off once and for
all. In the late 1940s and early 1950s liners remained an important way to
travel in comfort, but their luxury was altogether different and catered for
larger audiences. An example might be an ocean-liner like the SS *Canberra*
(from 1961), whose interior was directed by architect Sir Hugh Casson, in
which a simple sculptural staircase, modern Danish-style chairs, and dramatic lighting established the space of a luxury dining room for its own
time (Figure 6.6). *Canberra* incorporated large amounts of plastic and

Fig. 6.6. 'Luxurious *Canberra*: The First-Class Lounge', *Supplement to the Illustrated
London News*, 1960. Known as 'Tomorrow's Ship Today', SS *Canberra* operated from 1961
for P&O's service Australia to the United Kingdom. The interior design was overseen by
architect Sir Hugh Casson, who was also the preferred designer for Queen Elizabeth II and
Prince Philip. Thoroughly 1960s, the ship was one of the first to make a virtue out of plastic, which was used as a laminate in the first-class cabins. The copy accompanying this text
notes that 'the international design of *Canberra* marks a new era in ocean travel' and that
the most striking feature of the first-class lounge 'is the angular ceiling of glittering metal
facets. The curving walls enclose the sit-up bar, which is a new feature for P&O Liners. The
chairs are of glass reinforced plastic.'

'Formica' for the first time as a luxury material. From Helsinki to Sydney, modern architects and designers created a new, simpler format for a more democratic luxury in spaces such as hotels, cinemas, restaurants, coffee houses, outdoor bars, music halls, and department stores. Modern lighting, often concealed, novel rubber materials for flooring, etched glass, comfortable tubular steel chairs, laminated woods and striking veneers, fitted carpets, escalators for department stores, and good heating and cooling systems defined the new approach. These design ideals had been formulated decades earlier by the great modernists, often working in harsh European climates and adjusting to new materials such as steel and power such as electricity. For an architect such as Alvar Aalto in the 1920s and 1930s, it was just as important to design a sanitarium very carefully as it was a private residence. Aalto's designs used the latest technology and often featured large windows to take maximum advantage of the available perspectives and views. Space, light, and air were becoming the new luxuries that mark contemporary design today.

The decline of ocean-liner travel in the 1950s and the introduction and popularity of the safe and quiet Boeing 707 (introduced in 1958) meant a whole raft of luggage types such as trunks and heavy suitcases were no longer suitable or even possible. Clothing, luggage, and accessories lightened up. Even if a chef served a joint of meat on a trolley in first class, no one could pretend that the interior of a jet liner was like a restaurant. Women and men alike needed more comfortable but decent clothes for this type of travel, and informality—jeans, cashmere sweaters, sunglasses, and blazers—proliferated. Jackie Kennedy's security guard recounted that she enjoyed sleeping across the seats when she was given a whole row in the front of a plane, and of course she enjoyed arriving somewhere much faster.[23]

The late Duchess of Devonshire was related by marriage to the Kennedys.[24] In 1963 the Duchess described in a letter the effect of flying: 'We got a lift off the Prime Minister who had chartered a Boeing 707 . . . 150 empty seats behind . . .'. She was returning with sadness from the funeral after

John F. Kennedy's assassination. Her point was that the whole plane had been provided for such an exclusively small group of people: the Duchess and her husband, along with the Duke of Edinburgh, a number of high-ranking officials, and a couple of secretarial staff and detectives.[25] The unexpected privacy and space, once again, were key to the recollection, just as they were in advertisements for luxury air travel of the period (Figure 6.7). This sense of private space is what the premium airlines now emulate, with the introduction for the first time in May 2014 on Etihad Airways of 'The Residence', a completely private three-room cabin on board the A380, with its own bed, living, and shower rooms. This product outdid similar offerings called 'Suites', introduced by several airlines in 2014, which did not offer Etihad's private shower or a butler trained by the Savoy in London. The approximate price of a return flight Sydney–London in this manner was $60,000 in 2014, ten times the cost of a Business Class ticket and several times more than the cost of conventional First Class. Although contemporary marketing panders to the general public's love of small luxuries, 'meta-luxury' as it has been called is still palpable in the travel industry.

Comfort of course relates to luxury, and being at ease might be an aspect of luxury, but comfort is also socially generated and conditioned. Full-length fur coats were essential fashion accessories for both well-off men and women until the 1920s, as cars could not be heated (the early models were completely open) and steam or hot-water central heating was not widespread outside the United States until the 1920s or later. By the 1930s cars had also achieved new levels of comfort. Commodious interiors and more space for fitted luggage (to be stored within the very structure of the car) allowed for leisure travel. In this period the car became a potent symbol of design and 'streamlined luxury', and car interiors sometimes even matched lady's dresses (Figure 6.8). Cars were extremely expensive, and only later did they become a mass means of transport in the United States in the 1940s and in Europe in the 1950s and 1960s. For example, in Austria

Fig. 6.7. 'The Luxury of Gracious Living is Reflected on the Monarch', late 1950s advertisement of the company BOAC. BOAC (British Overseas Airways Corporation) was established in 1940 and operated until it was merged with British Airways in 1974. The overnight flight from New York to London promised 'the comfortable privacy of your own foam-soft sleeper berth' with 'lavish dinners sparkling with select wines and served graciously from silver carts'. There was a lower deck cocktail lounge and the option of sleeper berths.

Fig. 6.8. Image from the German magazine *Sport im Bild*, 1933. The illustrator uses a cubist language to capture the metallic modernity of the luxury car. The smart chauffeur would have been wearing a form of livery, or uniform. Trunks were held in the compartment at the rear of the vehicle.

in 1930 there was one car for every 376 inhabitants. As a historian of the car notes: 'The 1930s marks a time of transition in which the automobile starts to change from being a curiosity to providing competition for the railway and from being a plaything of the rich to an item of daily use for broader sections of the population.'[26]

Comfort also extended to interiors. Air-conditioning, which became widespread in both commercial and domestic environments in the USA, Asia, and Australia after the 1950s, rendered certain 'colonial' modes of dress such as the linen and safari suit redundant. Not all luxuries are welcome; the Queen Mother reported to the Queen that Princess Margaret, unused to air-conditioning, complained, as she often did in private, about the 'cold in her sleeping cabin' and 'coughing rather ostentaciosuly [*sic.*]' on the train laid on for her and her mother when they visited Southern Rhodesia on a tour in 1953.[27]

The twentieth century also saw a return to more sober materials and restrained shapes for the ultra-rich. More than in previous centuries, the novelty of new materials that imitated older, more established, and more expensive ones reached new heights. In 1943 the British design critic John Gloag praised the imaginative potential of plastics but feared that they would 'create a new rococo period' marked by extravagance, excess, and ornament. The use of plastic, he argued, was an act in which 'the artificial becomes the real'.[28] To a modernist this was a great lure, but if faux-luxury was created from a plastic masquerade, then mass world corruption might ensue. Roland Barthes, in that prose of his that manages to be bald and poetic at the same time, wrote of plastic: 'it is the first magical substance which consents to be prosaic...The hierarchy of substances is abolished. A single one replaces them all: the whole world can be plasticized, and even life itself since, we are told, they are beginning to make plastic aortas.'[29] In the words of one commentator, 'plastic becomes the site of an apocalyptic cultural battle'.[30]

From Bakelite to rayon, most of the synthetic materials made in large numbers especially in the United States, were ersatz and surrogate. Materials such as Formica laminates, used widely in the auto and aircraft interiors and as the light casings of communication devices, imitated materials from the natural world such as timber and marbles. Yet few of these imitations exactly resembled what they copied. As the historian of modern plastics Jeffrey Meikle notes of the post-war materials, the 'more novel an object's form became, the more artificial and thus totally controlled it seemed'. The vast majority of plastic mouldings were meant to simulate wood:

> Too smooth and uniform to be products of the same natural processes that yielded wood's irregular growth, pattern, and texture, they too suggested an unprecedented act of instantaneous transformation...When viewed on a surface of polished black Formica, on the other hand, they seem to

emerge smoothly, without interruption, almost naturally, as artificial flora of the "fourth kingdom" of chemical synthesis.[31]

Plastic jewellery, handbags, ladies' shoes, and even flowers might be a new type of luxury for an aspirational bourgeoisie, as was so wickedly pointed out in the 1958 film by Jacques Tati, *Mon Oncle*. We are a very long way here from that Louis XV inlaid purple-wood table purchased by Mrs Dodge.

Luxury in the twentieth century might be expressed in different ways, in the smooth industrial design of a new refrigerator by Raymond Loewy, a Western Electric telephone with its light streamlined design, or a fibre-glass chair by Charles Eames. In the post-war period people enjoyed the over-the-top designs of Morris Lapidus. His Fontainebleau Hotel (opened 1954) was considered one of the most luxurious hotels in the world, but it had none of the gilded woods, bronze stairs, or silvered mirrors associated with 'le goût ritz'. Instead it was conceived as a modernist set: 'If you create the stage setting and it's grand, everyone who enters will play their part,' Lapidus remarked.[32] The semicircular multi-storey hotel had enormous public spaces with recessed lighting and sparse walls, very large bedrooms fitted out with Venetian or modified Louis-style chairs and bedheads, and the famous cantilevered 'staircase to nowhere', which floated in the air above a painted mural and marble basins (Figure 6.9). Much of the aesthetic derives from post-war Italian schemes by designers such as Fornasetti and Giò Ponti, which playfully referred to the classical period while using modern materials and spindly forms. Other ideas were undoubtedly derived from one of the first so-called lady decorators, the American Dorothy Draper, who from the 1930s until the 1960s designed hotels in both North and South America, featuring dramatic hallways with black and white floors, oversized furnishings, and enormous lamps (including that favourite of the Windsors, the Greenbrier Hotel in West Virginia, which Draper redecorated in 1946). Such designs did not let guests forget that they were in a hotel, and not a domestic space. They were also reminiscent of the public spaces of the ocean-liners, which were, by the 1970s,

Fig. 6.9. Stairs of the Fontainebleau Hotel, Miami Beach, Florida, by architect Morris Lapidus.

becoming unfashionable as a means of travel. People revelled in Lapidus' novel use of lighting, plastic, potted plants, and contrasting colours and theatricality. It was the type of design that would inspire Robert Venturi and Denise Scott Brown to write *Learning from Las Vegas* (1972), a work that embraced the kitsch styles of casinos and the facadism of many rural towns and cities across North America.

LUXURY, CELEBRITY, AND THE NEW MEDIA

Part of the global success of luxury in the twentieth century was its ready availability on magazine pages showing rich interiors, their owners, and lifestyles. Magazines—but also movies—made ideas concerning luxury democratic, in particular from the mid-twentieth century when colour photography became more widespread. *Vogue* perhaps more than any other magazine in the world embodies such dynamics. Founded in 1892 as a society weekly in New York, *Vogue* was purchased by the publisher Condé Nast in 1909. The Condé Nast headquarters were subdued and elegant, with antique furnishings and a servants' zone. Nast wanted his stable of magazines to reflect the connections between contemporary fashion, writing, and ideas, and therein lay *Vogue*'s novelty. Its formidable 'lady editors' included Edna Chase, then Carmel Snow, followed by Diana Vreeland (Mrs T. Reed Vreeland).

Lifestyle recording was common in the late-nineteenth- and early twentieth-century illustrated periodical press after new flash photography had been invented. Yet the real shift came when a new emphasis upon modernist elegance and refined integration of word and image was promoted by *Vogue*, as well as other magazines such as *Harper's Bazaar*. Its main creator was Diana Vreeland, who set the model for what later became the powerful 'Lady of Fashion'. Today this is the role of Anna Wintour, editor of *Vogue* since 1988, but in the post-war period Vreeland became the very first editor of a fashion magazine to be popular with the masses. Born in Paris, she favoured the dresses of Coco Chanel in her youth. Because of her striking personal style she was spotted as a potential magazine writer, joining *Harper's Bazaar* in 1936, moving to the position of fashion editor there from 1939. She worked extensively with the fashion photographer Louise Dahl-Wolfe, with whom Vreeland acted as stylist and created various *mis-en-scènes* that developed a particularly dynamic and American vision of fashion and style.[33] Vreeland finally became editor-in-chief of American *Vogue* in 1963; she was fired in 1971.

Vreeland was well known for her series of columns 'Why don't you?', which appeared in *Harper's Bazaar* from March 1936. The most infamous is 'Why don't you ... rinse your blond child's hair in dead champagne to keep it gold, as they do in France?' Others include 'Why don't you ... order Schiaparelli's cellophane belt with your name and telephone number on it?' and 'Why don't you ... have a private staircase from your bedroom to the library with a needlework carpet with notes of music worked on each step—the whole spelling your favourite tune?' She was quickly satirized, but her concern was fantasy and her milieu was in part Surrealist. '"Why don't you?" was a thing of fashion and fantasy, on the wing…It wasn't writing, it was just ideas. It was me, insisting on people using their imaginations, insisting on a certain idea of luxury.'[34] Indeed with Vreeland luxury came to be part of the fantasy of millions of American housewives, and a few men, too.

Diana Vreeland appears to have been responsible for a new type of editorial format at American *Vogue* in which the highest-quality colour photography fused with lifestyle. Vreeland's innovation was a new layout with text and image arranged in a dynamic manner with photographs of different sizes, sometimes not much larger than a large stamp, and other times doublebled for maximum impact. The images and texts were republished on high-quality paper in 1963 as *Vogue's Book of Houses, Gardens, People*.[35] Vreeland favoured women and men who lived in some splendour, although she did also shoot the bohemian house of Truman Capote and several space-age interiors. Vreeland was also interested in style icons such as the Standard Oil heiress Millicent Rogers, who in the 1940s took native American lovers at her compound in New Mexico, wore clothes by 'America's First Couturier' Charles James, and had a fondness for wearing antique Navajo bracelets, gold she had crafted herself to look 'pre-Columbian', and stars that turned out to be Russian military orders.[36] The surrealist fashion designer Elsa Schiaparelli said of her: 'If she had not been so terribly rich, she might, with her vast talent and unlimited generosity, have become a great artist.'[37]

Film, too, had a powerful impact on luxury throughout the twentieth century. Celebrity was devoured by the press and by its millions of readers. One of the most potent means of learning about new tastes, attitudes, and fashions was by going to the movies. Australians were the biggest movie-goers in the world *per capita*, going to the movies every week. Nineteen-thirties movies presented the lives of the rich on the big screen, and department stores encouraged the links by creating commercial tie-ins to the clothes worn by cinema stars. This was not always considered good taste. For example, looking today at magazine culture of the 1920s and 1930s, one would assume that the lure of Hollywood was universally lauded. This was not the case. It was certainly true that cinema became very important in spreading fashion ideas: the up-market David Jones department store in Sydney, for instance, had a whole section devoted to its 'Cinema Fashion Shop' on the second floor of the store, selling copies of stars' clothes. Yet cinema images were not always approved of; the more expensive woman's magazine *Home* disparagingly called them 'lower class' and 'tasteless'.[38]

Those who did not have to go to the movies for fashion inspiration sometimes appeared rather indignant. The far-too-often pungent Cecil Beaton was rather critical of the infamous American silent movie star Mae West. Of her apartment, he said:

> everything was off-white, cream and pale yellow. Such a riot of bad taste as you could not imagine to be taken seriously...the piano was painted white with painted 18th century scenes adorning the sides, a naked lady being admired by a monkey as she lay back on drapery and cushions, was the centrepiece of one wall. On the piano was a white ostrich feather fan, heart-shaped pink, rose-adorned boxes of chocolate, nothing inside but the discarded brown paper. A box of Kleenex was enclosed in a silver bead box...She was rigged up in the highest possible fantasy of taste...the mirrors reflected the figure standing as she wished to be presented, a trunk of artifice, a tall, svelte woman, who had with ostrich feathers, stoles, fur, high hair created her own silhouette.

Beaton might have not approved, but this was very much the style that Hollywood stars promoted, both on and off stage, with great effect among the masses.

In the post-war period, Hollywood stardom presented a more restrained view of luxury. It promoted traditional views of fashion with bustles, petticoats, and crinolines in what has been seen as a 'fully fledged emulation of the rococo' that reassured people in the post-war period that tradition had not been erased.[39] Such fashions were promoted in the films of the

1950s, many of which took co-joined luxury and femininity as their themes—notably Hitchcock's *To Catch a Thief* (1955), with the ice cool Grace Kelly. It must be remembered that Princess Grace of Monaco's wedding dress was made by an American wardrobe designer, Helen Rose of MGM studios, and that the whole event, including Grace's arrival by yacht and the courtly greeting offshore with Prince Rainier, was stage-managed by Hollywood, carefully designed to be viewed in black and white on television sets around the world.

Hollywood—not always appreciated for its self-humour—sometimes used luxury as a theme of parody in the 1950s. Movies such as *Gentlemen Prefer Blondes*, one of the great hits of 1953 and starring Marilyn Monroe, presented all the caricatures of luxury consumption that we so much enjoy chuckling over today. A blonde and a brunette from Little Rock seek their fortune and affirm it through diamonds. What the movie did not make so apparent was that the ladies in this film are really prostitutes. The film is based on the novel by Anita Loos, entitled *'Gentlemen Prefer Blondes': The Illuminating Diary of a Professional Lady*, first published in 1925. Set in New York, Paris, London, and Vienna, it is the story of a group of flappers out to get rich and help themselves to a few of life's luxuries. The irony, of course, is that the girls are in fact themselves the luxuries for their male admirers.

All the themes presented in the Hollywood movie are set out in the line drawings and chapter titles that accompanied the original work: 'Kissing your hand may make you feel very good but a diamond bracelet lasts forever' (Figure 6.10); 'Fate keeps on happening'; 'Paris is devine [*sic*.]'; 'Brains are really everything'. The girls are seeing a 'button king' manufacturer and an aristocrat. They attend the Trocadero and receive orchids, as well as 'a nice string of pearls' and a 'diamond pin'.[40] They are taken on a transatlantic crossing: 'the steward said as soon as he saw Dorothy and I that he would have quite a heavy run on vases.'[41] Of course, they stay at the Ritz: 'When a girl can sit in a delightful bar and have delicious champagne

Fig. 6.10. 'Kissing your hand may make you feel very good but a diamond bracelet lasts forever', frontispiece, Anita Loos, *'Gentlemen Prefer Blondes': The Illuminating Diary of a Professional Lady*, intimately illustrated by Ralph Barton (London: Brentano's Ltd; New York: Boni & Liveright, Inc., New York, 1926).

cocktails and look at all the important French people in Paris, I think it is devine [*sic*.]'[42] More flowers arrive: 'Sir Francis Beekman sent me 10 pounds worth of orchids every day while we were in London.'[43] Such camp eccentricity had become the butt of comedy by the 1950s. Eccentricity,

Fig. 6.11. Weegee (Arthur Fellig), 'The Critic', 22 November 1943, gelatin silver print, 25.7 x 32.9 cm. Mrs George Washington Kavanaugh and Lady Decies were attending the Metropolitan Opera, New York. Austrian-born photographer Weegee posed this image, in which a drunken woman brought to the scene from a dive at the Bowery was propelled into the path of the two *grande-dames* in their heavy make-up, ermine coats, *bandeau* tiaras, *sautoir* necklaces, multiple diamond bracelets, and an enormous orchid corsage. Weegee originally called the photograph 'The Fashionable People', and it exists in numerous versions, including this cropped one, which cuts out the rest of the crowd. It was published in *Life* Magazine, 6 December 1943.

unusual posing, too many hot-house flowers, extreme fashions, and jewellery were becoming old-fashioned, even comical (Figure 6.11). As we have seen, modernism promised a new and more rational future. Women might not need to dream about fur coats and silk slips anymore; there were nylon ones available and the heating was better anyway. A new view of luxury was around the corner.

THE NEW OLD: JET SET AND THE LADIES WHO LAUNCHED

On the opposite coast of America, the seaboard where much of the old money (a relative concept in the United States) resided, the post-war period created a rather different view from the West coast Hollywood popular version of cinematic luxury. Truman Capote made the notion of the 'ladies who lunch' infamous, which led to his own notorious social unravelling.[44] His unfinished novel *Answered Prayers*, published as *La Côte Basque 1965* in instalments in *Esquire* magazine in 1976, centred around an exclusive Manhattan restaurant and the conversation and appearance of Lady Ina Coolbirth, a thinly disguised portrait of the 1950s New York socialite and fashion icon Slim Keith, co-mingled with vignettes of Jackie Kennedy and her sister Lee. The forty-page plot unfolds, taking about the same length of time as an afternoon lunch, full of word pictures of the mainly women diners: 'A redhead dressed in black; black hat with a veil trim, a black Mainbocher suit, black crocodile purse, crocodile shoes.'[45] The air is thick with luxury.

The image of sartorial and domestic simplicity promoted by Hollywood at this time did not wash with all the 'ladies who lunched'—the wives of the rich and powerful American elites. Francophiles Jackie Kennedy and her sister Lee lived in beautiful but relatively simple apartments in New York. Lee, like Princess Radziwill, had previously commissioned for her London and country houses the great Italian decorator Renzo Mongiardino to create striking murals and wall hangings in which Sicilian peasant scarves were glued and lacquered to the walls. He then worked with her on her striking Manhattan apartment, which featured (among other things) crimson walls. Alongside the sense of 'boho chic' were always fine French furnishings.[46] Classical busts, eighteenth-century ormolu clocks, and candlestands mixed it up with cheap wicker baskets and tourist discoveries such as beads and polished stones. The mark of a sophisticate was to add some contemporary art, as Lee did with her Francis Bacon *Man in a Cage*.

The new luxury of the East Coast American elites of the 1960s was neither popular nor purist in quite the way Coco Chanel had stipulated. Indeed, even Coco by this time did not disdain the past and had moved into the Paris Ritz surrounded by eighteenth-century French furniture and rich textiles. Francophilia in high-style American living was given the stamp of approval by no less than the First Lady, Jackie Kennedy. She brought over the French firm of Jansen to fix up parts of the White House in 1960, and her personal decorator was 'Sister' Parish (Mrs Henry Parish III), who preferred continental to English furnishings and created for Jackie her first home when her husband was a senator.[47] Jackie's best friends were the tasteful wives of multimillionaires such as 'Bunny' (Mrs Paul) Mellon and Jayne Wrightsman. The latter had, with her husband's oil money and full support, created in the 1950s and 1960s the finest collection of French furniture in the United States, and built up an art collection including paintings by the French baroque painter Georges de la Tour and the elusive Johannes Vermeer for their many private residences, much of which was subsequently gifted to the Metropolitan Museum of Art, New York. The Wrightsman Galleries were decorated, of course, by Jansen. Jokes continue to be told about *Tous les Louis* and *Louis the hooey* to describe the general taste for the *grand siècle* of France that is still particularly loved by rich Americans, despite the fact there was nothing democratic about the taste.

In the 1960s and 1970s, despite the rise of clubbing culture, cocaine use, and countercultural movements, many of the *mondaine* members of the international jet set clung on to an old-fashioned pleasure in conventional luxuries. There was a certain return to the Edwardian period, an era of sensuality and experience culture. The beautiful people loved going to Studio 54 in their fine evening dresses by Yves Saint Laurent; as Diana Vreeland said in an interview in old age: 'I wanted to get where the action was.' The big difference from her going to a club in the 1930s was that as much cocaine as champagne was now likely to be consumed in the dark sections of the club. The pop artist Andy Warhol, a fixture at Studio 54, might have appeared to be very bohemian, but he was wearing real art deco women's jewels and bracelets under his Brooks Brothers shirts, and he threw the gems that he had bought from second-hand dealers on to the canopy of his four-poster bed every evening (they were found there after his death). War-hol loved collecting everything, from 1950s cookie jars to fine Federal fur-niture; all of it was dispersed for vast sums after his untimely death. There was a little bit of the kleptomaniac about a character like Warhol. He had a full set of cutlery that he had taken from Concorde, an aircraft that had only one class—first. Truman Capote also loved stealing souvenirs from hotels. In the auction catalogue dispersing his property we find a large col-lection of hotel silverplate from Claridge's, the Hotel Bristol in Paris, and the Four Seasons in London. He stole keys from the Connaught Hotel Lon-don, the Fairmont Hotel San Francisco, the Hyatt House Hotel Los Ange-les, and the Navarro in New York City. What he was stealing was a little piece of luxury to take back to his New York apartment in Brooklyn and later the UN Tower. His apartment, photographed for American *Vogue* by Horst P. Horst in the early 1960s, contained many items of little to no value. Victorian rosewood sofas then out of fashion, metal trivets that had once stood in fireplaces, old French metal milk pails used as waste-paper bas-kets, a Victorian velvet cocaine case given by Andy Warhol, an old flower tub used as an ice bucket. The overall effect was considered worth reporting at length in American *Vogue*. But what was going on here?

THE REAGAN YEARS AND THE END OF AN ERA

The 1980s marked a crisis for style, aesthetics, and taste in twentieth-century life. Dissatisfaction with modernist design and poorly considered urbanism and housing schemes saw the rise of a new historicism from the late 1970s. Prince Charles made a rare statement of dissent by a British royal for the times and opined that contemporary architecture was ugly; that really made the news, as members of the royal family do not usually make controversial comments. Charles favoured the designs of architect Quinlan Terry, who created well-proportioned and thoughtful buildings that were nonetheless pastiches of Georgian architecture. All around the world, from Chelsea in London to the suburbs of Sydney, developers began to build low-ceilinged air-conditioned flats and townhouses, complete with garaging for cars, that pretended they were from the eighteenth century. Cable television and a proliferation of homeware, decorating, and 'shelter' magazines popularized the look, which demanded a full panoply of antiques to go with the house. Women's fashion was also retrospective, with a very American style echoing the glamour of the 1930s. Shoulder pads, peplum skirts, taffeta ballgowns, and lace day dresses all made an appearance once again. These were the Reagan and Thatcher years.

The 1980s also saw a reaction against plastic, foam, and fibreglass. Instead, the 'English Country House' look took the world by storm. It had been presaged by the dress and textile designs of Laura Ashley, but combined with the new wealth of the 'yuppie' class (young upwardly mobile professionals) suddenly everyone wanted festoon curtains, English chintz, and masses of ornaments. It was a very 'feminine' period in terms of style, the era of the Sloane Ranger, girls with pearls, and ironic features about debutantes in *Tatler* magazine. Antiques of all descriptions reached prices that they had probably not seen since the late nineteenth century. It was the heyday of luxury decorating magazines such as *Architectural Digest*, which began to feature the homes of the rich and famous, often saying so on their covers. Robin Leach's corny but very watchable *Lifestyles of the Rich and Famous* launched on television in 1984 and ran for ten years; it was the first such reality TV show. There were also large markets for the finest avant-garde jewellery, hand-made punk clothes, cutting-edge art, customized craft-ware, vintage cars, fine wine at auction, and custom-guitars.

Yet the 1980s are unlikely to be remembered in the future as an age of luxurious good taste, although they were years of great fun. One of the most intriguing scandals of the Reagan Presidency (1981–9) was his wife's response to living in the White House. Some people were clearly out to get these former Hollywood stars, and Nancy Reagan's redecoration of their private rooms and her commissioning of a new White House dinner service caused a scandal. The White House, the palace of the people, has always been a problem for those who live in it, as its fittings are often old-fashioned and sometimes inadequate. Although there were numerous dinner services that had been commissioned for different administrations—the tradition extends back to a Paris delivery of 1817—Nancy Reagan felt that the supply was too small, and she ordered one for her own era. Lady Bird Johnson had previously ordered a service for 140 guests, but Nancy Reagan ordered one of 19 pieces each for 220, which came to a grand total of 4,370 pieces of American-made Lenox ivory china with a grand red band and etched gold borders and crest. Although it was paid for by a foundation, its cost of nearly $210,000 caused quite a fuss.

The redecoration of the Reagans' private rooms was undertaken by Ted Graber, a society decorator from Beverly Hills who had trained under Billy Haines, the incredibly good-looking gay movie star of the silent era who became one of the first Hollywood decorators. The bedroom was papered in a newly blocked Chinese wallpaper with birds and bamboo by the American firm Gracie, and the furniture was mainly antique, with a Chippendale gold mirror. Another sitting room had extremely pretty *strié* painted green walls and gilt furniture in an Upper East Side taste. It was a typical scheme for a wealthy transatlantic woman of her generation; aspects of it resembled *Dynasty* (interestingly enough, the 'good' female character in *Dynasty*, Krystle Carrington, had a traditional bedroom quite similar to Nancy's, whereas the 'evil' Alexis Colby, played by Joan Collins, lived in a sexy silver and white modernist apartment with purple highlights).

Nancy Reagan's scheme was unkindly, if trenchantly, attacked by the American decorative arts scholar Debra Silverman, who, in her clever and cutting book *Selling Culture* (1986), claimed that the Reagans and their best friends the Bloomingdales, the department-store owners and inventors of the Diner's Card, were trying to identify themselves with *ancien régime* splendour at the expense of traditional democratic American virtues and values.[48]

Europe arguably produced some more enlightened forms of luxury at this time, perhaps best exemplified by Karl Lagerfeld. 'Kaiser Karl' is certainly a man who understands luxury, history, and time, and his large collections of finest quality furnishings are proof that luxury can be expressed in different ways. Lagerfeld was an early adapter of the approach to historical interiors promoted by the scholar Mario Praz, who studied watercolours and paintings in order to understand the past.[49] One of Lagerfeld's residences, in Rome, was an exercise in the chaste taste for things Biedemeier, which became fashionable at this time. Lagerfeld quickly moved on. He first acquired a beautiful Belle Époque Louis XVI-style villa near Monaco, which he filled with Memphis postmodern design. He then created a large Paris *hôtel particulier*, which appeared inside as if Marie Antoinette and friends had just left the room. The contents were sold by Christie's Monaco in 2000.

DISPERSAL: THE END OF AN ERA

The 1980s and 1990s saw the selling of the contents of the great Manhattan apartments owned by socialites and philanthropists and decorated by Jansen and his contemporaries such as Sister Parish in a predominantly French idiom, with their American flourishes such as bar and card rooms. Jayne Wrightsman's Palm Beach home was one of the first to be sold, in 1984. The Windsor sale was 1986. The late Comtesse Diane de Castellane's collection (incorporating some of the possessions of her grandfather, the profligate Boni) was sold in Monaco in 1995. There followed the sale of the effects of Alice Tully, the Steuben glass heiress, in 1994, and of Mrs Charles Allen, Jr, a great beauty with an exquisite Jansen apartment dominated by *blanc-de-chine* white figures, in 1997. Mrs Antenor Patiño also sold the contents of her grand and much upholstered New York apartment in 1997, and Mrs John Hay Whitney (Betsey Cushing Whitney) was sold up in 1999. She had been one of the great society figures of the 1950s, with multiple residences decorated in the English country-house manner. Other important sales included: Greta Garbo in 1990; William S. Paley (Babe Paley's husband) in 1991; Jackie Kennedy in 1996; Pamela Harriman (American Ambassador to France) in 1997; and Dorothy Hirshon (formerly Mrs Jack Hearst) in 1998. Marella Agnelli's New York apartment was sold up in 2004; Her Royal Highness The Princess Margaret's private collections were sold by her heirs in 2006; the rest of Mrs Antenor Patino's collection was sold in 2010; Mrs Paul 'Bunny' Mellon died in 2014. The contents of the residence of society decorator Alberto Pinto (of Paris) were also dispersed in this period of transition. He lived like a contemporary Roman emperor, with unusually shaped green velvet rooms and dozens of dinner services in vast spaces.

These were all very different women (and a few men), but the sales of their goods do reveal a number of interesting common features. By the early twentieth century the outfitting of a home had become the domain of women. This had not been the case in the nineteenth century, when men had been intimately connected with the choice of design and decoration of houses. As a result, there is a strong 'feminine' basis to these twentieth-century designs, based on a great deal of upholstery, coordinating colours, and distinct private spaces for men and women—for example, in their dressing rooms and studies. The second point is that these people all relied on the services of very skilled decorators. Some could even re-create the effects of a room at the Palace of Pavlosk or a Proustian fantasy. People brought Europe home in miniature. They also all had in common a taste for very rare antiques. They ate from French, English, or Russian eighteenth- or nineteenth-century plates, they sat on French Louis or Germanic Biedermeier chairs, their flowers were arranged in eighteenth-century *tôle* (tin) ware, and eighteenth-century buckets served as champagne vessels. They had the best paintings and prints that they could afford. All had large libraries with many antique books. Many relied on painted effects on walls and floors, museum-quality carpets, and also custom-made furniture to complete the look. Many of the pieces they owned had a provenance to important figures of the past: Marella Agnelli, for instance, owned two impressive Louis XVI ormolu-mounted ebony and Japanese and European lacquer cabinets-on-stands that had belonged to the eighteenth-century English novelist and eccentric William Beckford and a great deal of porcelain from the last Tsar's yachts. Most had American, but the very rich had English or French, decorators. All of them had French, and many also had Russian, furniture. French furniture was Greta Garbo's private passion, along with the Renoir and other paintings that she kept concealed behind a rose damask curtain in her Manhattan apartment.

Recent years have seen the demise of the very last of the great hostesses, most notably perhaps the Americans Brooke Astor (who died in 2007), Bunny Mellon (who died in 2014 aged 103), and the Southern beauty and socialite Carol Petrie, who died in January 2015 at the age of 90. Her retailer husband Milton Petrie, believed to be worth $1 billion, owned 'Toys R Us' among many other businesses, and she lived in a beautiful Manhattan apartment full of good antiques designed by David Easton. Mrs Astor was the third wife married into one of the great American plutocrat families. She was well known for her Park Avenue apartment, with its famous brass library by Albert Hadley, her luxurious lifestyle and gala dinners, dazzling gowns by Oscar de la Renta, conjoined with serious philanthropy. Bunny Mellon, second wife of one of the United States' richest financiers, was also the Listerine and Schick razor heiress. She was a more private person, preferring to take her private jet (with its own runway) when travelling between her beloved garden in Middleburg, Virginia, and her numerous other residences around the world. Although enormously wealthy, Bunny preferred furniture made by her estate craftsmen after her own designs. Her gardening clothes might have been by Hubert de Givenchy, but she shunned publicity and could never be called vulgar.

Fig. 6.12. Jean Schlumberger (French, 1907–87), flower pot (pot de fleurs), 1960, amethyst, emeralds, diamonds, black garnet ore, terracotta, 18, 20 and 22 carat gold, 7¼ inches H x 4 inches W x 4 inches D (18.4 cm x 10.2 cm x 10.2 cm). Schlumerger began his career designing buttons for Elsa Schiaparelli in Paris. He then moved to work for Tiffany, New York. Mrs Rachel 'Bunny' Mellon owned numerous jewelled pot plants by Schlumberger, which she dotted around her various houses, possibly as little jokes, as she loved growing her own fresh flowers in very expensive hothouses. They were a modern take on the Fabergé artificial vases that she might have afforded herself, but her commissions are of their time and place, and look very 1950s, with their spikey air. That the central jewelled head detaches to become a brooch is a part of the whimsy.

The sale of Bunny Mellon's effects took place during the writing of this book, at Sotheby's in New York. Her furnishings, which included some eighteenth-century furniture in poor condition mixed in with much wicker, wood, and metalwork, netted $218 million. Her table linens embroidered in blue with a simple tree fetched more than $20,000 per set. One of her most extraordinary objects, given to the Virginia Museum of Fine Arts, was a jewelled flowerpot by the society jeweller Jean Schlumberger. Made in 1960, it includes a giant amethyst, emeralds, diamonds, black garnet, and, at the heart of the piece, a terracotta pot from her garden covered in 22-carat gold strap-work (Figure 6.12). The flower head can be detached and worn as a brooch. It is an astonishing bravura of high and low, of the exclusive and the demotic, with a design that does not teeter into the kitsch. Mellon owned many such bibelots, which must have amused her sense of the chic of poverty.

CHANGING TIMES

The interwar period brought forth new and bold ideas about luxury and the luxurious. It was an era that faced forward optimistically with a phalanx of new science, medicine, and technology that improved daily life, but was always marked by anxiety and paranoia connected with geopolitics, the cold war, and massive and divisive social change, particularly regarding the place of women and minorities. The excesses of the previous generation were seen as both decadent and old-fashioned. Luxury for the new era had to be provided with a new veneer of respectability and acceptance. Yet the tension between restraint and opulence always remained beneath the surface. By the 1950s, this could be seen in the diverging notions of luxury emerging from America: one democratic and participatory, as proposed by Hollywood films and the printed media; the other still staunchly elitist and connected to wealth and power, as in the case of continental and English luxury and the Manhattan society that could afford to access it. New technologies now became almost more important than the envelope of the house, indicating perhaps something of a return to Victorian priorities. Private planes, music, television, and elaborate security systems cost a great deal of money. For American cereal-heiress Marjorie

Merriweather Post, running an impressive household in the 1950s was as much about a private movie theatre, piped music to all parts of the house, and a private propeller plane decked out in modern chintz, as it was about her fine collection of eighteenth-century antiques, paintings of deceased Russian nobility, and Sèvres porcelain. It was also very much about staff—in her case, ones who measured each place setting at dinner. This is a continuation of a particular British caricature of luxury. It also included true eccentricities, such as an individual rainwater filtration system in the roof to deliver pure water to her private dressing room, where she had her very long hair washed and permanently waved several times a year in a nine-hour process. The public knew about Mrs Post's interests, such as square dancing, as they could study her in the magazines, and she regularly invited college students to take dinner with her, all of which was covered in the media. Where luxury existed, it was now expected that more people should be allowed to see it.

The post-war period was also one of less analysis and preoccupation with definitions of luxury. In a society in which welfare and economic achievement for the masses was more than a dream, luxury came to be perceived as something of marginal importance, a little irritating or even embarrassing, a niche hobby for the rich or—worse still—the pretentious. The counterculture of the 1960s suggested that cheap wine, good drugs, and lots of sexual relations were much more exciting and desirable than sitting at a fancy restaurant eating foreign food. When Coco Chanel returned to work in 1954 (after her 1939 'retirement' to Switzerland), her controlled and modernist 'chromatisme Chanel' was a striking foil to this counterculture and the deliberate vulgarity, especially in the 1960s. Chanel herself once said that she would not be surprised if women might start showing their 'ass' in the future; the sight of belly buttons and midriffs was enough to horrify her in the 1960s and 1970s. The middle classes grew in education, spending power, and influence around the First World, and luxury had never defined their existence.

When luxury returned with a vengeance in the deregulated environment of the 1980s, it was at first reported on rather ironically and often with great humour, as in magazines such as *Tatler* in Britain and the American *Vanity Fair*—and people sat up and noticed. Extreme luxury almost had to be explained again, often by resorting to running explanatory stories on the great 'clothes horses', couturiers, hostesses, and patrons of the past. Indeed, such stories provided most of the content of these magazines. The cost of antiques, old jewellery, and antique or 'vintage' costume began to soar. A new generation, particularly of young women and gay men, began to rediscover a legacy that had gone out of fashion in the 1970s. They rediscovered the joys of interwar Hollywood films, afternoon tea, and evening cocktails, and enjoyed watching the hugely successful television adaptation of Evelyn Waugh's *Brideshead Revisited* (1981). Rather further up the price scale, billionaires such as Malcolm Forbes (owner of *Forbes Magazine* among other things) staged parties in which guests where flown in from all around the world, events that evoked the glamour and profligacy of the Edwardian period or the 1930s. Forbes famously spent $2.5 million on his birthday in Morocco in 1989. And the great stars of the 1950s such as Elizabeth Taylor were still on hand to underline the references to luxuries past.

Everything that Money Can Buy?

Understanding Contemporary Luxury

FROM RUSSIA WITH MONEY

In late 2013, two Russian multimillionaires in their thirties competed at a London Mayfair club as to who could spend the more on drinks. In just two and a half hours they spent over £131,000 ($200,000) on fifty-five Magnums of Cristal, ninety-six bottles of Dom Pérignon (at £325 each), twenty champagne cocktails, six expresso martinis, seven mojitos, six Bellinis, ten bottles of Peroni, ten measures of 18-year-old Glenmorangie whisky, eleven bottles of vintage Krug champagne, eight bottles of Belle Époque Rosé and sixteen of Armand de Brignac, two magnums of Belvedere vodka, and two bottles of Chivas Regal whisky and, to digest it all, twelve bottles of mineral water.[1] Luckily they were not hospitalized. The news was widely reported in newspapers in the following days with comments about how the Russian *nouveaux riches* were behaving in London as if it were Monte Carlo in the Belle Époque.

Inebriation might be the appropriate expression to capture the Russian multimillionaire story, one of alcoholic profligacy and wealth that had literally gone to their heads and livers. But they are hardly exceptional: their compatriot Yevgeny Alexandrovich Chichvarkin, mobile-phone tycoon turned wine merchant in London after leaving Russia, has explained that to drink a bottle of 55-year-old Glenfiddich whisky (cost around £123,000) on a night in with friends is not excessive if you are part of a group of people who can afford yachts worth millions of dollars.[2] The reality is that the public rejoices in such insane excess: it is the stuff of dreams, a fairy tale for the twenty-first century. Tales abound of six-star hotels, of gold-plated cars, and of watches worth £33 million.[3] There are many resonances here of the hedonism of the 1980s and the television series *Lifestyles of the Rich and Famous*. The difference is that today this hyper-consumption might be photographed with an iPhone and placed immediately on the Web via Instagram; and one does not have to sit up until late to watch the American TV series. The fact that such excesses are all around us in the media and on the Web renders them somehow more 'normalized'. Such luxury is therefore not completely unreachable, as we can see it, often immediately—and this makes it both appealing and an easy target for dismissal in the moralizing presses of countries as different as England, the United States, France, and Sweden.

Luxury in the twenty-first century is on everyone's lips because it is perceived to embody the increasing disparity of wealth between a restricted global elite and the majority of us: 'the rich' versus 'the rest'. This opposition used to be a topic of concern in the differential between the developed West and the rest of the world, but after a generation of growth for the emerging economies, wealth disparity has become a home debate for countries such as the United States, the United Kingdom, and Australia, bringing a new set of concepts and concerns regarding luxury. With a chief executive earning 202 times more than the person at the bottom of the company, English journalist Zoe Williams argues that 'the tolerance band of human ability simply isn't wide enough for any one person to be 202 times better than anyone else'.[4] The perceived immorality of income disparity is mirrored in the accompanying contemporary consumption: while most of us have to do with a reasonably cheap bottle of wine, a small number of people can afford a bottle that costs not just several times as much but thousands of times as much. It seems that the multiplication of such consumption has increased since the mid-twentieth century. If one studies the liquor bills for a society party from the 1950s or even a luxury hotel menu from the 1910s, the prices are not thousands of times those of the everyday person's tipple.

Yet some might argue that the plutocrats of this world have not had it so easy since the global economic crisis of 2007–8. The crisis hit some parts of the luxury market hard. In mid-2013 the only Ferrari dealer in Greece had closed, having sold its last car more than a year earlier. The problem was not the fact that the rich of Greece could no longer afford to buy Ferraris, but that it was no longer advisable to be seen spending enormous amounts of money on cars when the country faced financial ruin. The rich—bankers, stockbrokers, and CEOs in particular—were in the firing line of a blame game and had to keep their profile low. In some cases, the reputation of entire areas had to be sanitized. At the beginning of the crisis in 2009, it was rumoured that in Larissa, in rural Thessaly, there were more Porsche Caynennes per capita than anywhere else in Europe.[5] To make things worse, governments started to pursue their wealthy citizens by asking how their declared income matched the high values of their cars, jewellery, and villas. In Italy, several owners of yachts were arrested, as on their tax returns they had declared they were on the verge of indigence. Luxury and fashion producers were not unaffected by all this: in 2012, two major Italian houses were accused of not paying tax on their revenue.[6] Luxury and luxury producers were linked to the disappearance of money to tax havens and off-shore funds. They had literally 'run off' with the profits.

The point here is not to accuse such figures of wasteful consumption, but the realization—by the taxman—that certain forms of luxury—those for the very rich—are both an enjoyment and also an asset. Yet, in some cases, the investments are not worth the money, as people can overpay. Take, for example, the fantastic villa at 116 Ocean Drive, Miami, which sold for $41.5 million (£25 million) in September 2013. It included a swimming pool with inlaid 24-carat gold tiles and gold-plated bathroom fixtures. In the 1990s it had welcomed guests such as Madonna, Cher, and Elton John. In 1997 it made the front page of all newspapers in the world when its then owner, Gianni Versace, was shot on its doorstep. Versace had spent more than $20 million on renovations to the building when he purchased it in 1992, and the family sold it in 2000. With the crash of the property market, the villa failed to find a buyer for the asking price of $125 million in 2012, and it was then reduced in early 2013 to a mere $75 million, to be sold for just over half that sum in late 2013.[7]

Luxury is therefore for the super-rich an investment, something that can be owned for a period of time, later to be sold—hopefully for a profit. This often happens with the advent of divorce, court cases, bankruptcy, or estate planning (divorce, we are told, is one of the main drivers of the auction market for decorative arts). This is the case for mansions, villas, works of art, and even the bottle of wine discussed above—such bottles are drunk much less frequently than one can imagine. This is because the rich like to enjoy life but like to part from their money somewhat less. Some research suggests that they are actually often quite parsimonious and like to maximize the financial value of their luxury. For instance, instead of buying an expensive jet, why not opt for a timeshare? There are schemes and clubs for all pockets, ranging from exclusive groups that allow access to a variety of planes whenever and wherever, to cheaper providers like Lux Jet, a company that promises its customers can 'Fly like a VIP this summer' at a price under £1,000 from London (alas Luton) to Ibiza, Palma, or Cannes. All of this with 'no gate queues; no security queues'.[8] Less than $350,000 can buy a membership of a residence club with properties all over Europe. An article published in 2009 in the UK newspaper the *Independent* reported that share ownership of yachts was on the up after the economic crises, as, in the words of Martin Gray, founder of Fractional Sailing, 'for gilded millionaires struggling to manage declining fortunes and bruised egos, it is the prudent way to keep up appearances'.[9]

LUXURY FOR THE REAL HOUSEWIFE

It would be a mistake to understand the power of luxury by blaming it on the rich and seeing it as a divisive force. In reality, luxury has become something to aspire to for vast strata of society. We might not be among those who can afford a bottle of whisky with a price tag similar to a small flat, but we are told that we can purchase instead 'luxury chocolate', or foods that are part of the 'taste the difference' range. Advertising tells us that we are unique, that we all need to be distinctive, and that luxury is the capacity to reward ourselves with something a bit pricey but not unreachable. It might be a perfume from a well-known fashion brand, designer kitchen equipment, a rare olive oil, or wine from one of France's classic wine-growing regions. Although consumers today tend to think that people have always loved French and Italian products, this is not the case. In the case of French regional wines, the allure of such products was created only between the end of the nineteenth century and the Vichy years of the Second World War, a period in which the consumption of regional products was linked to a new vision of tourism made possible via the improved roads of the Routes Nationales 6 and 7. This led to a renewed emphasis on 'regional styles' and 'folkloric traditions' adapted to a completely new luxury market that stressed the importance of *terroir* and region, rather than just urban gastronomy. The Appelation d'Origine Côntrolée (AOC), which protects consumers concerning the true identity of French wine, dates from only 1919 and gave new power to growers, rather than to wine merchants.[10]

The true achievement of luxury in the twenty-first century has been its ability to beguile as many people as possible in much the same way as mass consumption did in the post-war Western world. It plays on our inner feeling of wanting 'something better', and nurtures the rampant individualism of self-fashioning (inauthenticity, or narcissism perhaps?) that has come so much to shape our societies since the 1980s.[11] Perhaps we all secretly dream of being little Russian oligarchs who can shop for antiques at Steinitz and take over whole floors of hotels.

Figures confirm the assumption that luxury is not just the hobby of a small rich elite. Since 1982 the cost of luxury (measured by an index with the scandalous name of 'Cost of Living Extremely Well') has gone up 2.5 per cent more quickly than inflation in the United States. This means that to live the life of luxury has become very expensive. Yet the net worth of America's richest (another index named 'Forbes 400') has increased twice as fast as the cost of luxury. For those of us unfamiliar with indexes, this means that in the Unites Sates there are now many more people who can afford 'to live extremely well', even if such a life is quite costly compared to that of just a generation ago.[12]

Yet, the pervasiveness of luxury goes beyond being merely wealthy. A simple trip to a shopping street or to a mall reveals that luxury is not just about the group of people 'living extremely well'. In the Unites States alone, there are more than twenty million citizens who have assets of at least $1 million. Half of them belong to the group of the so-called baby boomers. Born between the end of the Second World War and the late 1950s, baby boomers were the children of the economic expansion of the 1950s and 1960s, the young professionals (yuppies) of the 1980s who later profited by the rise of the value in their properties in the 1990s and early 2000s. They are keen to indulge in fine up-to-date fashions, luxury cosmetics, and fine wines, and consume at levels that would have been unimaginable for the generation that preceded them (fittingly called 'the silent generation') and that perhaps will be out of the reach of the generation that has followed them, which is more acquainted with economic crises, joblessness, up- and re-cycling, and casual or precarious work.[13]

New York Times reporter Guy Trebay puts it well when he observes that today 'the client most crucial to luxury goods purveyors is no longer a Rockefeller but a Real Housewife'.[14] Yet, there is luxury and there is luxury. Social scientists have been creative in their categorizations: they put forward the idea that contemporary luxury is segmented according to both income and social/cultural capital. One such categorization uses the value of the object (and related income necessary to purchase it) and distinguishes between 'exceptional luxury' (rare and precious objects, of the highest quality, made on commission), 'intermediate luxury' (objects of great quality, produced in small batches), and 'accessible luxury' (sometimes known as 'masstige', the realm of the luxury brands).[15] Another typology is slightly more refined as it identifies four categories of luxury: 'true luxury' includes those items for which money is not a constraint, such as top-range cars, jets, and yachts; 'traditional luxury' includes instead fashion, jewellery, fragrances, premium wines and spirits; 'modern luxury living' relates instead to the search for status and identity through travel, technology, services such as hotels and spas, and online luxury; and, finally, 'life's little luxuries' is composed of the truly mass-market luxury range of affordable fashion, shoes, imported or locally produced 'organic' foods, and body-care products.[16]

Typologies are attempts at distilling a more complex reality. However, they are useful, as they point to the fact that there is a vast pool of luxury goods that are not necessarily beyond the reach of many people but are accessible and considered almost necessary for mere mortals. This, however, has created two problems. The first is how top luxury (that of the super-rich) differs from the rest of the luxury market. Sometimes referred to as 'metaluxury' or 'über luxury', the top end of the luxury market now needs to be extravagant (or elitist) beyond belief, because basic luxury is within the reach of too many today.[17] It is no longer sufficient to go to the best restaurants; one has to have a top chef employed privately at home; it is not enough to take holidays in some of the best resorts; one needs to buy or rent an entire island. Metaluxury aspires to be 'out of the market' (to own something that is extremely rare, sometimes unique, such as Bunny Mellon's unique vivid blue diamond, which sold in late 2014 for the record price of $32.6 million), precisely because most luxury is today increasingly standardized and comes with a pegged price tag attached to it.

The second problem of the enlargement of the conceptual space and market potential of luxury has been a change in the nature of production and the image of some of the best-known brands in the world. In the late 2000s journalist Dana Thomas accused the luxury industry of 'selling off' the key asset of luxury: its lustre. In a provocative book entitled *Deluxe: How Luxury Lost its Lustre*, she investigated the shallow world of the luxury brands through its producers and its customers.[18] What some had seen as the triumph of the 'democraticization of luxury', she saw instead as a strategy on the part of luxury brands to maximize their profits by trying to address all sorts of clients.[19] A case in point might be Yves Saint Laurent, a well-known producer of expensive haute couture and prêt-à-porter in the 1960s and 1970s, whose business expanded dramatically in the 1980s thanks to accessible luxury such as perfumes. Between 1979 and 1989 the sales of Saint Laurent perfumes increased sixteen times.[20] Accessible luxury used to be positioned at a much higher level, with higher entry points in terms of price. Since the 1980s, there has been a true 'luxury inflation', and now almost everything can be presented as a luxury product. Sometimes producers combine meanings that are conceptual opposites, such as that of 'affordable luxury': cinemas now often have 'classes', like an ocean-liner of the past, with better chairs, lap blankets, and even a drinks waiter. We are told, as another example, that Korean carmaker Hyundai developed a strategy to produce 'affordable luxury' sedan cars, and by 2015 this had become the fastest-growing segment of the Canadian automobile industry.[21] This is a semantic shift that would have been incomprehensible to an Edwardian gentlemen or even to a 1950s white-collar worker.

How did it happen that luxury became so omnipresent? The last thirty years have seen a transformation of mere commodities into luxuries. While in the eighteenth century a number of luxuries available only to the few became more widely obtainable commodities (populuxuries) through processes of imitation, substitution, and replacement (for example, of silver with silver plate) and production on a large scale (thus reducing costs of production per unit), the last generation has experienced the opposite trend. What once were thought of as simple, undifferentiated commodities are today perceived as luxuries. A good example of this phenomenon is something that might not immediately come across as a luxury: coffee. In 1950s America, a cup of coffee cost a dime. It was an undifferentiated commodity that was part of the consuming habits of the entire North American population. Today, coffee is both a commodity and a 'luxury'. Anyone entering one of the thousands of outlets belonging to well-known chains such as Starbucks or Costa is presented with a large variety of sizes and types. These might not be luxuries per se, but the segmentation of the market has allowed for niche coffee to find customers. Those who want a genuinely more select experience might wish to sip their coffee at the Pedrocchi Café in Padua (the nineteenth-century French author Stendhal was one of its customers) or the Café Florian in Venice, the first coffee shop in Europe. Here coffee costs a multiple of what it might cost at Starbucks and is most certainly not served in paper cups with your name on it. Yet, even if you do not care for such a refined atmosphere, you might still decide to purchase an Italian coffee machine and opt for a rare type of coffee. For instance, kopi luwak is a coffee produced by wild Asian civets eating and defecating coffee berries. By passing through the civets' bowels, the berries acquire a special aroma. For those who think this is unpleasant, prices suggest otherwise. Only 1,000 lb (454 kg) of this special coffee are produced every year, and it is sold at more than $300 a lb.[22]

One could cite a whole host of similar examples, with products ranging from beer to wallets and pens: an affluent society will always find new ways of spending its money. If economists with a social conscience warned us against the peril of overconsumption, they did not foresee that one of the strategies used by corporations would be *not* to try to sell us twenty jumpers a year when we need only two. They prefer to sell us two sweaters that cost as much as twenty. The sweater or jumper is no longer an undifferentiated piece of knitwear, but is a finely woven, ethically sourced, environmentally friendly garment produced by a famous brand, often backed by a great deal of advertising. This is what fashion studies expert Patrizia Calefato calls 'the luxurification of consumption' through advertising, shopping, fashion, and the media.[23]

We are clearly simplifying the importance both of marketing and of consumer psychology, as our aim is to show that twentieth-century luxury was born out of perfectly ordinary products, because these were, and still are, what people want and indeed *need*. The potential to sell large diamonds or eighteenth-century furniture is rather limited compared to clothing, bags, and indeed pens and coffee, things that people tend to use on a daily basis. And this explains why commodities are presented to us as luxuries and we are asked to pay prices that confirm that they are indeed luxuries. The process of mere commodities being turned into luxuries is well exemplified in the sphere of 'technoluxuries'. In the early 2000s, the author and academic James B. Twitchell proposed the idea that personal technologies ranging from microwaves to Walkmans become omnipresent (and more recently this would apply to cellphones and smartphones), yet they still retain an 'air' of exclusivity that differentiates them from mere mass-market consumer goods.[24] Apple is a case in point: a brand considered by some to belong to the luxury sphere and by others to cult or mass culture. Although producing iPhones, iPads, and iPods in their millions, Apple projects an air of dramatic design, presenting goods in a beautiful white cubic sliding box rather like perfume packaging, and adopts marketing strategies similar to those used for luxury goods. For instance, its shops are minimalist boutiques, with the most famous among them in Manhattan dominant amid the luxury shops of Fifth Avenue (Figure 7.1). Little merchandise is on display, and well-trained hipster attendants glide over to advise the clients that the new product has generally already sold out. This is even more the case with brands such as Vertu and Prada, which have made real luxury products out of mass technologies such as mobile phones, which they sell in the gigantic luxury shopping malls of Hong Kong, Bangkok, and Singapore.[25]

Fig. 7.1. The glass cube for the Apple Store, Fifth Avenue, New York, designed by Bohlin Cywinski Jackson.

THE EXPERIENCE OF LUXURY

In a world in which extravagance has become a mass phenomenon, how does luxury retain its appeal? Notwithstanding the fact that luxury is often accused of being about material overindulgence, since the early 2000s the nature—but also the value—of luxury has increasingly become *immaterial*, paradoxical as this might sound. In the words of one contemporary commentator, 'luxury is today more a condition than an object'.[26] In other words, luxury is not just about acquiring an object, but is rather a way of living, of thinking, and of aspiring. Luxury aims to recover its uniqueness not by offering expensive and exclusive goods, but by providing an experience that is unique in the acquisition and enjoyment of such goods (and increasingly services) that might not necessarily be exceptional per se. The philosopher Yves Michaud talks about the need of individuals to experience the intensity of emotions via luxury. He argues that luxury is presented as the key to 'authenticity' against a world that is increasingly dull.[27] One could, on the contrary, suggest that the world increasingly values the '*in*authentic': postmodernism encouraged all sorts of slippery characters to conjure up identities and professions in which everything was 'contingent', 'relative', and about 'appearances'. This is not the sensual economy we described as characterizing the late Victorians and the Edwardians; a good French wine today might be explained on the menu as smelling of 'smoky violets' (as at the Wine Library in Woollahra in 2015), because consumers lack the aesthetic and sensory training of wealthy, well-educated Edwardian diners, who really knew what they were smelling and tasting.

All of this is somewhat problematic for the luxury brands. Those customers who really want something *beyond* the object are less likely to be lured simply by the straightforward use of anything as crude as a mere logo. It is perhaps for this reason that Prada in 2014 began to reduce the emphasis on the emblematic triangle that appears even on the back of its T-shirts. Customers now explain that they want something beyond labels. For such consumers, 'true' luxury means the rejection of established associations like that between luxury goods and brands. Therefore, in the second decade of the twenty-first century, we have seen the emergence of 'no branding': upmarket products that conspicuously display the lack of any visible logo.[28] This phenomenon can be explained in two ways. On the one hand, customers wish to distinguish themselves from what is increasingly perceived as a mass market for luxury brands and choose a product that is not the average choice of most people. Some also fear that the conspicuous display of brands connotes a negative image of overindulgence and decadence. The 'no logo' therefore makes the product more about the experience, often intimate or shared only by those who can actually see the difference between an everyday bag and the luxury bag with no brand logo. A different interpretation of 'no logo luxury' comes instead from retailers who have realized that in order to keep sales high they need to have a more discreet approach to branding. Therefore, they are investing more in highly visible retail spaces rather than on the placement of their logo. For the customer, this means that the 'luxury element' comes not from the logo but from the experience of having purchased the good from a luxury shop, sometimes in a prominent location, an experience that is worth as much if not more than the product itself.

Marketing gurus have understood that the consumer needs to feel unique rather than to be sold a unique product. A simple, but effective, example might be perfume. Rather than selling well-known branded fragrances, a handful of London perfumers are now offering clients the chance to create their own scent. They follow the example of Parfumerie Fragonard, where, in its workshop in Eze, not far from Nice in the south of France, the company provides professional help to customers to create their own distinctive essences, which they can then purchase.[29] Here luxury is not just about purchasing a perfume that is unique, but is also about the opportunity to create it yourself, so that you become an artisan in your own right. It is as much about acquiring skills and understanding processes as it is about the total customization of the product.

The importance of customization is particularly present in luxury services. The Gateway Canyons Resort & Spa, a luxury 'discovery resort' on the border between Colorado and Utah, offers the option of custom-made cowboy boots and hats as well as a complete documentary of a client's stay produced by a professional photographer. Built by John Hendricks, the founder of the Discovery Channel, Gateway Canyons has only fifty-eight exclusive rooms and fourteen 'casitas' and provides among its many customized services 'Native American artists who offer beading classes where the spouses have taken home the jewelry that they made'.[30] The Peninsula chain of hotels, a luxury brand that originated in Hong Kong but is now branching into Europe, offers cooking classes for children, flower-arranging for ladies, and golf for men (players are helicoptered to the golf course).

Clearly this is a form of innovative marketing, but one that is still predicated on traditional gender roles, made explicit by the images on the website: attractive women, not men, arrange the bouquets.

A different kind of customized service is that of the 'genie on call': the concierge. An omnipresent figure in all high-society films, the concierge used to be the man in the lobby of a posh hotel, often accommodating impossible requests from his wealthy customers. Today, the concierge is a large part of the 'lifestyle management services' industry, catering to the needs of the super-rich. Companies such as Quintessentially Lifestyle, Les Concierges, T'Rouge, Concierge India, Concierge Alliance Global, and AmEx offer different levels of membership, costing anything between $1,000 and $15,000 a year. Les Concierges, based in India, had 250 corporate and 700 individual members in 2013. They can access services ranging from the booking of theatre seats, to legal and medical help anywhere in the world.[31]

The idea of providing service and enhancing the purchasing experience is fast becoming essential for high-end market products. This has long existed in different forms for the very rich, and has often revolved around travel. In the 1920s, an all-woman chauffeur company called the 'X Garage', led by the cross-dressing Marion Barbara 'Joe' Carstairs (a Standard oil heiress), offered to drive customers from Kensington, London, as far as Morocco.[32] And the Australian-born country girl Lady Sheila Millbanke (1895–1969, née Chisholme), who married an earl, a baronet, and a Russian prince, operated an exclusive travel agency through Harrods when she had run out of her money late in life.[33] Some of the brands working in the 'exclusive luxury' sector are well aware of the importance of service in supporting the reputation of their products, even if this comes at a cost. While most watchmakers will not service models produced before the 1960s, the world-leading horological firm Patek is able to offer a service by which each of its watches (going back to 1839) can be maintained through an archive of five million components and the use of original tools going back 175 years.[34] The acquisition of a Patek product is only the start of a relationship between customer and firm that will continue over the years and across generations. The Patek business lineage acts as an insurance that this is going to continue over the next 175 years, and this is precisely how all their advertising campaigns are structured.

In this new vision of luxury, more than simple money is required from its consumers. Time and knowledge are key concepts in the very notion of twenty-first-century luxury. The idea is not new. The sociologist Thorstein Veblen, author of the famous *Theory of the Leisure Class*, published in 1899, believed that 'distinction', the need to appear different from others, was not just achieved through the purchase and use of luxurious and expensive objects. It was also *performed* through the conspicuous expenditure of time in what we might call useless activities. Instead of working and earning money, those who can afford it simply spend money in activities that are financially unrewarding, such as playing golf, going to parties, driving around in luxury cars, and enjoying long holidays in exotic locations. One might object that these activities are linked to pleasure, but it turns out that not all of them are: the interminable high-society balls of the nineteenth and early twentieth centuries were certainly not a simple pleasure but served to signal social position and belonging, marked allegiances, and sometimes also social charity.[35] Today, spending time in 'useless' activities gives employment to an entire range of services, from hairdressers to golf caddies.

Leisure and service activities also require knowledge, sometimes very specialized. When such activities wish to signal distinction, they must be as exclusive as possible. The example of golf is fitting: it is not simply a matter of paying enormous sums to join a private club; one has also to be able to play the game. The same applies to other leisure sports such as tennis or polo. A dinner in a fancy restaurant requires good knowledge of etiquette, of ingredients and wines, plus a bit of French, the lingua franca of luxury food. Going to an auction similarly requires the need to know something about art as well as the process of bidding. One has to spend an inordinate amount of time to be able to engage in a proper way in useless activities. Luxury requires culture. Those who do not know how to behave might be as rich as Midas but will not go very far in society. And this explains why the new rich of China are fast becoming the most committed golfers in the world and fly to Old England to rent an estate and play the part of gentry squires shooting animals for the weekend. Discreet services exist in cities such as London to show the wives of the newly arrived rich Chinese how to behave, and their children might be schooled at home in how to eat food and sit at the table by a new, more private version of a nanny combined with a butler. Many of the service providers are the divorced wives of extremely wealthy men, especially from Asia, who can now sell back their expertise in the marketplace.

One of the 'experiential' areas that in recent years has been subject to intense 'luxurification' is that of food. A meal, or the use of ingredients to produce food, is part of an experience that is both extremely material (involving all the senses) but also fleeting (as nothing remains after a meal). We have already seen the importance of banquets and feasts in the Roman, medieval, and early modern courts. Food remains one of life's necessities and the source of great pleasure. We are all well aware of the kudos and cost of a Michelin-star restaurant. Started in 1900 by the Michelin Brothers (the tyre manufacturers) as a guide to visit France by car, over the course of the twentieth century the Michelin Guide came to embody the best of food internationally. Yet the criteria for receiving one, two, or three Michelin stars have little to do with either price or luxury per se. Food, but also wine, spirits, and confectionary, are appreciated not just because of their price or intrinsic taste but because of their lifestyle association. So, no one can claim to have visited Paris without paying a visit to Ladurée, the famous patisserie where one can supposedly savour the best macaroons in town. It is surely the experience of the patisserie with its faux-*ancien régime* interior that helps make these macaroons taste so much better than any others.

Yet, Ladurée (just like its neighbour, *artisan boulanger* Eric Kayser) is in fact to be found in several countries. In 2014 it even took over a small antiques shop in a far-flung Sydney suburb, becoming a favoured locale for purchasing gifts for university farewells and 'hen nights'. While emphasizing the unique experience of artisan-made pastries, its business has become multinational, even if few can pronounce it properly. Even more than material goods, experience is replicable anywhere in the world. It might not be the same as sitting in Saint-Germain-des-Prés, but it is a good approximation. The same can be said of music, one of the greatest luxuries of rich and poor alike until the twentieth century. In this case, technology (the invention of recording and the gramophone) has allowed it to become a mass product.[36] Yet quality remains a distinctive feature, and so, if one wants to hear the best of Bach performed by great musicians with perfect acoustics, one must first spend considerable amounts of money travelling to attend a concert in one of the major metropolitan concert halls. Indeed, fine music, five-star hotels, and luxury travel are the basis of the most important luxury experience tour companies.

THE SPACE AND TIME OF LUXURY

This analysis of how in the rich West luxury has become something more complex than the simple consumption of material goods can be pushed a little further to show how the concept of luxury has come to shape our views of both time and space. Sophia Coppola in her film *Bling Ring* (2013) narrates the story of a group of Californian middle-class youngsters who enter the houses of Hollywood celebrities to steal their luxury belongings. The film plays on two important themes: the boredom and alienation of middle-class life and the magnificent spaces inhabited by the super-rich.

The appeal of luxury houses and palaces has been evident since at least the Renaissance. The quest for space is perhaps a basic human need and materializes itself in the power shown by the tall medieval towers erected by rich families of the Italian city states. In fact they were often built—remember Versailles—to impress both the populace and foreign noblemen. In the twentieth century any American billionaire worthy of the name had to have a Manhattan tower, from Marjorie Merriweather Post in the 1920s to the Rockefellers to Donald Trump.[37] The ability to reproduce images in print, as we have already noted, allowed us to peep into the townhouses, luxurious apartments, chateaux, and country houses of the rich and famous. This was the great innovation of Diana Vreeland at American *Vogue* in the early 1960s; she opened up the houses of Café Society via the lush full-colour photography of Horst P. Horst and the journalism of his partner Valentine Lawford.

Yet in the last generation this fascination has intensified to the point where we think of houses and apartments not just as somewhere to live but as an asset, as something that can be 'traded up' or 'made up'. This is because—of all commodities that have become luxuries—space is perhaps the clearest example. Space (to have a roof over one's head) is a necessity, but, for most people in the West and many parts of the developing world, physical space has become a luxury. Anyone trying to buy even the smallest of apartments in London, New York, or Sydney is well aware of this. Space has become expensive also outside the West. Exclusionary housing markets now also exist in parts of cities such as Prague.[38] The average cost of a house in Beijing in 2010 was around twenty-five times the average income, and it was calculated that the cost of a 100 square metre apartment in central Beijing (*c.*$450,000) was equivalent to a salary of 1,000 years for a Chinese peasant.[39]

The proof that space has become the ultimate luxury is also to be found at the top end of the market. In London, an apartment at 1 Hyde Park will cost you the best part of $200 million.[40] In New York, 432 Park Avenue in Manhattan between 56th and 57th Street, the site of the former Drake Hotel, is the tallest residential building in the Western hemisphere. Luxury living here comes in a gradient from two-bedroom apartments (1,789 square feet) costing $9.7 million to full-floor six-bedroom penthouses (8,255 square feet) at $95 million. Three- and four-bedroom apartments are also available at $31.8 and $44.8 million respectively. There are also studio flats for sale at prices ranging from $1.5 to $3.9 million on the 28th and 29th floors, but these can only be purchased as maid's quarters for residents already owning an apartment. For those who enjoy their wine, personal wine cellars are to be purchased for as little as $158,000.[41]

The examples of London and New York might not be indicative of general trends, but they tell us that the entire property market has been moving upwards. As more and more people are excluded from buying their own homes, property is seen as a luxury. This means that the rich will go the extra mile to ensure that they have access to top-end luxury property. In an increasingly populated and connected world, it seems to be difficult to find space where calm and quiet reign. This is why luxury companies offer deserted islands, apartments the size of football pitches with views where no human being is to be seen, and holidays to the most remote parts of the globe. The crowding of our cities is instantly deleted, in an act that summons a very traditional view of luxury as extreme elitism—the ivory tower one might say—oblivious of others, of social concerns, and of collective awareness. Yet this is hardly surprising: when space is bought at over $2,000 a square foot in many world metropolises, privacy and spaciousness become luxuries that many cannot even dream of.

Time is also becoming a new luxury. Another film tells us why time itself might be a rare commodity. Justin Timberlake and Amanda Seyfield are the main characters in the film *In Time*, in which a dystopic world of the future is represented where time can be quite literally purchased. There is no longer any need for plastic surgery. Instead, there is the chance to live for ever simply by buying up time, the only luxury that is not transactional. Quite apart from the question of how long we live, time is perceived as a rare good in our everyday lives. With time, however, there is a paradox between the search for free time and leisure and the fact that those who have time to spare are either the unemployable (the traditional poor and marginalized in society), the unemployed (the new poor, increasingly middle class), or pensioners (a large part of whom are relatively poor). And this is why time too has been 'luxurified' in the form of 'quality time', intensity of experience, and short injections of pampering (spas, luxury retreats for weekends, and so on) as an antidote to the 'bad' time (stressful, busy, and unsatisfactory) spent indoors in offices, with annoying bosses, noisy shop floors, and other workplaces. This allows us to distinguish between people who simply have free time and those instead whose free time is rendered 'meaningful' by being packed with activities considered 'positive'. It is one of the key differences between the consumption of the early twenty-first century and the last decades of the twentieth. Even remote country towns in Australia with no decent shopping facilities have a foot spa now, generally run by entrepreneurial immigrants—another sign of the globalization of luxury. Once they might have opened a simple Indian or Chinese restaurant, but, following the global food revolution and the rise of gastronomy, the locals are now more likely to request sheep's milk cheese with local herbs followed by organic free-range lamb and truffled potatoes.

THE NEW CHINESE LUXURY CONSUMER

For a long time, the luxury consumer had been European and more recently North American. This is no longer the case. Already in 2004 *The Economist* predicted that the Chinese would replace the Japanese as 'the world's most fanatical luxury shoppers'.[42] The massive expansion of the luxury market since 2000 has resulted not from higher levels of consumption in Europe, the United States, and Japan, the classic luxury markets. Luxury has globalized: the new luxury consumer is as likely to be Asian as European, American, or Japanese. The numbers are impressive. The luxury goods market was estimated to be worth $86 billion worldwide in 1990. By 2008 it had doubled in size to reach $170 billion.[43] In 2013 the luxury market was worth $75 billion in the United States, $25 billion in Japan, $30 billion in China and Hong Kong (the latter being a third of the entire Chinese market), and $4 billion in Brazil.[44] Forecasts are equally optimistic: it has been estimated that in the five years up to 2020, 440 million consumers (5 per cent of the world's population) will spend $1.2 trillion on luxury goods, meaning an expansion of over 20 per cent of the sector's turnover in the six years after 2014.[45]

These impressive results have been achieved notwithstanding the fact that since 2008 the world has been enveloped by the worst economic crisis in living memory. Incomes in several Western countries have in fact gone down. Luxury firms might well have been expected to face the challenge of having no customers. At the same time, luxury brands overstretched themselves and effectively saturated their own market. This was the case, for instance, in Japan. In 2005 more than 90 per cent of Tokyo women in their twenties owned both an item by Louis Vuitton and one by Gucci, and more than half of them owned an item produced by Prada and Chanel.[46] With a staggering 80 per cent of the Japanese population already owning luxury items, an increase in sales was unlikely.[47] With the economic downturn of 2007–8, the future of the luxury market did not appear all that rosy.

Even in the early 2000s, Asia was not yet the promised land of luxury. Bangkok resembled a scene from the film *Blade Runner*. Its skytrain and overhead highways were under construction, and the very few luxury malls that existed were often approached across rubble. Hotel precincts were still the main source of interesting shopping. In India the only imported luxury goods to be seen were available in the lobbies of the few luxury hotels in large cities such as New Delhi and Mumbai. The only country that had a substantial number of outlets selling European luxury brands was Japan. Gucci had opened its first shop in 1972 in Tokyo, followed four years later by Louis Vuitton.[48] China was literally virgin land for luxury. Yves St Laurent had flirted with China in the 1980s; yet it appealed to him more as a land of inspiration than as one in which to sell luxury products. In 1991 the Italian firm Zegna opened its first store in China, a move that was regarded with bemused curiosity by the European luxury industry at the time.[49] A quarter of a century later, the picture could not be more different. China's 250 million-strong middle class can afford to buy a variety of products that could be defined as 'life's little luxuries' or 'affordable luxuries'.

But what is luxury in today's China? The *China Statistical Yearbook* for 2010 shows that ownership of durable goods varies markedly by level of income between the richest and the poorest in Chinese society. The ownership of traditional technologies such as washing machines, colour televisions, refrigerators, landline telephones, and motorcycles does not vary dramatically between the rich and the poor. Indeed, in the case of motorcycles, the richest in society are less likely to have one than the poorest. However, the richest are seventeen times more likely to own a car than the poorest in China. Some less expensive new technologies such as mobile phones are now widely used by all strata of Chinese society, and the ownership of mobile phones by the richest is just double that of the poorest. Other goods, however, such as video cameras, pianos, and exercise equipment are still 'luxuries' affordable only to the richest.

What emerges is a picture of China with at least three competing notions of luxury. First, there are consumer goods that are now common among all consumers. For this category of goods, luxury consists of owning upgraded versions (larger flat TVs, smart phones, and so on). Second, there are goods whose ownership is not yet widespread among the Chinese 'affluent society'. This is the case with cars, and therefore they retain a luxury appeal—at least until they come to fall into the previous category. Finally, marketing is creating new luxuries by generating new needs. This is the case with dishwashers, still practically unheard of by both rich and poor in China in the 2010s, but whose market potential is enormous if a need for them is created.[50]

One of the distinctive features of luxury in China is that consumer goods such as technologies and everyday appliances are more important than luxury fashion. Those who purchase LV bags and Hermès scarves are a small but important minority. According to Goldman Sachs, out of those 250 million Chinese who can afford luxury, about one million of them are active buyers of luxury goods—and fashion in particular—spending $7 billion a year. Luxury brands are of great appeal in particular to young middle-class Chinese consumers, who have no personal recollection of China under the duress of strict communism. Bruno Lannes, partner of the global management consultancy Bain & Company, says that this category of Chinese consumers 'don't need to wait until [they are] 40 or 50 years old to discovery luxury brands. There's no reason for that. You can do that at 25, even with your first salary. Why not. That gives you the taste of what it is and what you can hope for in the future.'[51]

Luxury, at least in China, has created its own 'luxury generation'.[52] These are the consumers who have made the fortune of those European luxury brands that today account for the lion's share of the market. The growth of luxury consumption has been so great in China that the government is now attempting to control it. Mainland tourists are now restricted in what they can bring back from Hong Kong and elsewhere, and the government is using the fashionable agenda of 'sustainability' in an attempt to convince consumers that they should buy less. This is a brilliant strategy. A good sustainable consumer who does not buy too much can feel very up to date and not like his or her old-fashioned parents who accumulated things; he or she might also buy fewer but more expensive things, with different meanings within the consumer matrix. China is a very interesting case, as consumption can perhaps still be effectively controlled there. We will see.

While the West imports endless quantities of cheap Chinese manufactures, China has become a buyer of European luxury. Louis Vuitton, for instance, as of 2013 had forty stores in China and was in the process of building a shopping mall.[53] Other European luxury brands have followed the trend and capitalized on the fact that China is considered the best at everything, apart from producing its own luxury goods and luxury brands.

As the political scientist Shaun Breslin perceptively observes: 'It is difficult to compete with China, but it is possible to supply China.'[54] Rolls-Royce seem to have followed such advice and now counts China as its most important market (as India had been at the time of the Maharajas). The last few years have seen a growth of nearly 50 per cent in the number of 'rollers' sold worldwide, with the best sales performance in just over 100 years of the company's existence, surpassing the high levels of the late 1970s. And all of this, *The Times* observes, notwithstanding the fact that the world is passing though one of the worst economic crises in living memory.[55]

Everyone is well aware that the dominance of European brands is not necessarily here to stay and that in the not-so-distant future Chinese firms will probably be able to out-compete European and North American luxury producers. Some firms have realized, therefore, that the potential of China is not just about selling as much as one can. Italian luxury firms, for instance, have been at the forefront in developing strategic partnerships with Chinese businesses. This is the case of Italian clothing designer Giada, founded in 2001 by Rosanna Daolio after a long experience at Max Mara. In 2005 it developed a partnership with the Chinese group RedStone. By 2011 the partnership had moved into financial investment, thus providing the capital and know-how for a relatively small luxury firm to enter the Chinese market. By 2013 RedStone's owner and CEO Yihzeng Zhao had become a well-known name in Via Montenapoleone, Milan's most fashionable shopping street.[56]

Partnerships, joint ventures, and associations allow for the improvement of production, marketing, and selling techniques in China and for a new injection of capital into smaller brands in Europe. The ultimate dream is that of convincing Chinese customers to purchase a luxury product and brand that is produced in China and perceived as Chinese.[57] This is the dream of Yang Lan, a renowned Chinese TV presenter, philanthropist, and entrepreneur. Her latest project is the creation of her namesake jewellery line that combines traditional Chinese design elements with precious gemstones and metals sourced from all over the world. South African diamonds and jade from Burma sit alongside exquisite Chinese pearls. The range is priced between a few hundred and several million US dollars.[58]

THE NEW GLOBAL LUXURY CONSUMER

In India too, luxury has become big business. It is estimated that in 2013 the luxury market in the subcontinent was worth $6 billion. Although India is still a relatively small market for luxury brands, growth over the previous decade was impressive. The sale of luxury cars grew up to 40 per cent a year and that of personal luxury goods between 15 and 20 per cent a year and by 2013 was worth $2 billion. Personal luxury goods were valued at $1.5 billion, with the remaining $2.5 billion spent on hotels, fine dining, and wines and spirits. This might be partly explained by the fact that between 2006 and 2013 the number of dollar millionaires (individuals whose onshore liquid assets were at least that figure) almost trebled from 46,000 to 132,000.[59] In 2013 more than 1.1 million households in India had an annual disposable income of $100,000.[60]

Figures alone cannot capture the fact that in India luxury is something very different from in China or other parts of Asia. The subcontinent has a very long tradition of luxury production and consumption. For centuries India produced the best of cotton cloth, fine muslin, and beautiful jewellery. The riches of the Mughal court were second to none. In the colonial period, the rich Maharajas embraced European luxury, building magnificent palaces furnished with all the European comforts and luxury novelties, and purchasing one-fifth of all Rolls-Royce cars produced in the world.

In India this historical legacy is as much a burden as it is an asset. For the new Indian middle classes, one of the barriers to engaging with luxury is its perceived exclusivity. The shopping malls of Mumbai had a hard job at convincing potential customers that they did not have to be dressed in the same high-spec brands that were for sale in order to enter a mall selling Zegna or Emporio Armani. This is because the luxury consumers of India are neither super-rich nor members of a traditional wealthy middle class. The key group consuming 'affordable luxury' is composed of HENRY (High-Earning, Not Rich Yet) consumers, who are mostly relatively young and earning between $60,000 and $80,000.[61] This explains why luxury consumers in India are very price conscious, sometimes preferring Indian brands to the more expensive European ones.[62]

India is, indeed, a country of great potential for European luxury brands, but much of it remains unrealized. At the beginning of the twenty-first century, luxury goods were a rarity in India. Louis Vuitton opened its first shop at the Oberoi Hotel in New Delhi in 2002, followed by one in Mumbai in 2004.[63] Over the next decade the French luxury brand opened another five shops. They were followed by Armani, Gucci, and Ferragamo.[64] Yet the luxury sector in India is still small, roughly a fifth of that of China. China may have had over 1,000 luxury stores in 2013, but India had only 70.[65] Part of the slow growth of luxury retailing in India is due to lack of infrastructure, complex bureaucracy, customs duties, and the exorbitant cost of rents. This means that luxury goods cost on average 30–40 per cent more in India than in other Asian markets.

The example of India suggests that the world is not yet a completely homogenized consumer space, although there is hardly a place in the world where luxury is not becoming omnipresent. Take Russia, for example, where luxury has become the symbol of wealth, especially for those 88,000 millionaires who by 2010 had accumulated enormous fortunes since the fall of communism in the early 1990s.[66] Punk dissident group Pussy Riot is now world famous for its protests against President Putin and the Orthodox Church, but its main target has been the smart luxury brand shops of St Petersburg and Moscow. On the other side of the world, in Brazil, luxury is less about social inequality than economic growth. In the two years between 2012 and 2014, more than $3 billion were spent in Brazil in the construction of 100 new malls. A new level of wealth among the rising middle classes has allowed for the expansion not just of luxury brands but also of luxury services. In 2011 Brazil was the second largest market for cosmetic surgery, for gyms, and for beauty treatments.[67]

The folly of Russian oligarchs or the pampering of Brazilian middle-class consumers are better known than the shape and size of the luxury market in places like Africa. It is estimated that Africa currently has 280,000 million-aires (18 per cent of the world total), though they are to be found mostly con-centrated in cities like Johannesburg (23,400 of them), Cape Town (9,000), and Lagos (10,000). Nigeria—and its capital city Lagos in particular—is a per-haps surprising market for luxury. The country is, for instance, the fastest-growing champagne market in the world, second only to France.[68] In April 2013, Ermenegildo Zegna opened a store in Lagos, while Porsche opened its first dealership in the exclusive area of Victoria Island, hoping to sell 300 cars a year. Similarly Mercedes-Benz has seen a steady growth in sales over the past few years.[69] As for China, the long-term aim is not just to be a consumer of European luxury goods. In March 2013, Maki Oh, a Nigerian womenswear label, was presented at New York Fashion Week and featured in *Vogue*.[70]

BRIC BY BRIC

Luxury in the twenty-first century remains a complex phenomenon. Far from having lost its lustre, luxury has achieved a global reach thanks to increasing wealth in the BRIC (Brazil, Russia, India, and China) countries and parts of the developing world. A small group of super-rich enjoy unprec-edented access to super-expensive goods and services; and yet still struggle to differentiate themselves from a much larger group of wealthy consumers for whom luxury is something to aspire to. The luxury brand has played a key role in the story of luxury since the mid-1980s, something that will be considered in more detail in the next chapter. Yet, as we have seen, branded products are not the totality of the 'luxury phenomenon'. A great deal of importance is increasingly attributed to the *experience* of luxury, either through the acts of purchasing and consuming goods or through the enjoyment of services.

8

Luxury Capitalism:

The Magic World of the Luxury Brands

D o we live in the greatest age of luxury? Recent commentators talk about the 'massification' or 'democratization' of luxury and the loss of the 'lustre' of its glow.[1] The remit of luxury seems to have changed to include the 'boutique', the 'posh', the 'stylish', and the simply overpriced. Luxury has spread to every object, from ice buckets to suitcases, from soap to chocolate. This is not a new phenomenon. In the 1950s, gift lines were retailed in sumptuous settings at boutiques such as Christian Dior that appeared like little palaces; their features continue today in the moulded plastics and faux-fixtures of the concession stores from Bangkok to New York. Yet the luxury industry today presents the acquisition of products and the *act* of shopping in themselves as almost elevated forms of cultural activity. The more cynical would see this as simply a new strategy to get people through the doors, in a pacified postmodern delirium. Or are people simply seeking new products and experiences that their grandparents could not have dreamed of? Luxury becomes a buzzword to make a brand recognized around the world but also to make any product appear as if it is a one-off, with 'signature shops' now as popular as the great museums for tourists on package holidays to Paris, London, or Milan.

This tension between the economic potential and the supposedly innate exclusivity of luxury is evident in the so-called luxury brands that today produce and retail commodities that are often also to be found in super-markets and discount outlets (which themselves use new forms of well-lit and innovative portable display cabinets to make the products appear like something from a luxurious department store). The magic world of the luxury brand is one of the most important myths of the early twenty-first century, one that is of recent creation and that has changed for ever the meaning of luxury.

THE WOLVES OF BOND STREET

In the three years between 2010 and 2013 the high-end luxury global market grew by 23 per cent, reaching an astonishing turnover of €250 billion in 2013.[2] Europe still accounts for three-quarters of this market. The sector employs an estimated 1.7 million workers worldwide. The World Luxury Brand Directory (WLBD), initiated in 2011, included as many as 672 luxury brands in 2013.[3] Luxury is big business. Just a handful of conglomerates own most of the brands that we recognize as belonging to the luxury sector. They structure their business not as small craft workshops but as multinationals, continuously seeking expansion into new markets and engaging in hostile takeovers and in the politics of exchange rates, finance, lobbying, and worldwide marketing.[4] The big luxury brands—or to be more precise the large holdings that own them—embody what could be called the 'luxury capitalism' of the twenty-first century, one based not on heavy industry, as was the case with steel, chemicals, and railways in the nineteenth century, nor on oil and electronics as happened in the twentieth century. They are the 'wolves of Bond Street', and, in contrast to the 1980s 'wolves of Wall Street', they make their money not by selling at high prices shares and futures that were bought cheaply, but by selling as expensive new luxuries things that previously were cheap commodities.

The media have been kind to the luxury brands, repeating the trope that luxury in the last generation has been 'democratized': many more people compared with just a generation ago are able to afford more than that which is merely necessary. The superfluous has become the new indispensable and an essential part of a comfortable life. As fashion became democratized after the Second World War, so luxury has undergone a similar process since around the end of the twentieth century. The luxury brands are the providers of a variety of goods, ranging from clothing to electronics, from food to hotel rooms, that consumers aspire to possess or enjoy. They surely tap into an existing demand. We prefer, however, to talk about a process of 'industrialization' of luxury, which puts the emphasis not on demand and consumers, but on supply and producers. Yet it should be clear that the industrialization of luxury 'is not only that of production. It is also that of advertising campaigns, of launches, of types of distribution, of shop chains,' and so on.[5] The capitalism of luxury has created its own world—linked to finance and global enterprise—and is fast reshaping our spatial world, that of our districts, our streets, our desires, our ambitions, and our material culture. This has been described by the novelist and academic Sarah Schulman as being a 'gentrification of the mind', going well beyond the economic transformation of physical space in large metropolises.[6]

Luxury capitalism was not created overnight. Two developments made it possible to reshape the sector into a world of multinationals and high finance: first, the fact that from the 1950s licences were used to sell luxury fashion. Dior was the first to create a modern company. Unlike previous French couturiers, the maison Dior was established in 1946 with the capital of Monsieur Boussac, the great cotton magnate of France, and only in name was it owned by chief designer Christian Dior. By contrast, some of the best-known luxury producers (including Louis Vuitton, Gucci, and Cartier) at this time retained their traditional small scale—often as a family business—positioning themselves as bastions of tradition in both their production and their business models. By the 1970s, several of them were in financial trouble. Notwithstanding the fact that they produced excellent products of undisputed quality, they were unable to market them effectively and to seize the opportunities presented by expanding international markets. Demand from non-European markets in particular required new capital and organizational forms, as was the case with the push of Western luxury producers into Japan in the 1970s. This led to the first phase of the restructuring of the luxury sector, which, however, was more about keeping up with the times than having an active role in shaping Western capitalism.

The real qualitative change for the luxury sector happened in the mid-1980s, when the young and well-connected French financier Bernand Arnault, with the help of the old guard of the French banking system, acquired the holding that owned the Boussac group, which still retained a substantial share in Christian Dior. He then acquired Lacroix in 1986 and Céline a year later. In 1988 the LVMH group (Moët Hennessy Louis Vuitton) was established.[7] Fast forward twenty-five years, and in December 2012 the LVMH group had more than 106,000 employees and a revenue of $36 billion. As of 2015, the company has sixty brands, many of which are leaders in their market sectors. Among them are Moët & Chandon champagne (ranked 77th in the top 100 global brands in 2011), TAG Heuer and Hublot watches (ranked 29th and 40th respectively in the top 50 Swiss brands), and Christian Dior (ranked 14th in the top 50 most valuable cosmetic brands).[8]

LVMH is truly a global conglomerate: its operations are based on a worldwide network of stores: there were 3,200 as of December 2012: 1,300 shops in Europe (400 in France), 650 in the USA, 1,100 in Asia (of which 370 in Japan), and another 200 in other countries. In 2013 a third of its revenue came from fashion and leather goods, 15 per cent from spirits and wines, 13 per cent from perfumes and cosmetics, 10 per cent from watches and jewellery, and a further 28 per cent from other sources.[9] LVMH is also in continuous expansion through acquisitions and alliances. In 2003, LVMH signed a joint venture with De Beers, the market leader in diamond production, controlling 40 per cent of world production.[10] In 2013 it acquired 80 per cent of the cashmere clothing firm Loro Piana and the

Hotel Saint-Barth Isle de France on the Island of St Barthélemy in the French West Indies.[11] In 2012 alone, LVMH's revenues grew by 19 per cent to €28.1 billion.[12] In that year Louis Vuitton, worth $23.5 billion, was one of the most important 'meta-brands' in the world, classified seventeenth by brand management company Interbrand.[13]

The alter ego of Monsieur Arnault is François-Henri Pinault, chairman of Artemis, the family holding that controls PPR (Pinault–Printemps–Redouté). As with Arnault, Pinault did not fall in love with luxury at first sight. Until the late 1990s, the holding owned businesses as different as retail stores and mail-order businesses operating in Western Europe, and France in particular. In 1999, PPR acquired 42 per cent of Gucci, the entirety of Yves St Laurent, and 70 per cent of the smaller Italian shoemaking company Sergio Rossi. In the following two years it acquired Boucheron, Alexander McQueen, Bottega Veneta, and Balenciaga, and formed a partnership with Stella McCartney. Today PPR owns the entirety of Gucci and Sergio Rossi, as well as Italian menswear couturier Brioni, majority stakes in jewellery brand Qeelin, Christopher Kane (fashion), Sowind (watches), and a minority stake in Altuzarra (which makes luxury, ready-to-wear women's wear). In other words, if you take a walk through a luxury mall anywhere from Bangkok to Los Angeles, the whole sweep in front of you is likely to be owned by one company. The strategy has been to acquire brands that have the potential further to diversify and innovate. An example is Bottega Veneta: when in 2001 PPR acquired the Italian leather goods manufacturer, the company's turnover was just €56 million. By 2012 its 196 shops around the world had a turnover of €300 million.[14] Now, it seems, everyone wants a woven leather wallet or pair of its expensive shoes.

Among the best-known luxury brands in 2009, four were French (Louis Vuitton, Chanel, Hermès, and Cartier), four were Italian (Gucci, Prada, Ferrari, and Bulgari), one Swiss (Rolex), and one American (Tiffany & Co.).[15] Of these, only Tiffany & Co. and Rolex remain independent luxury brands. The others belong to major holdings—those of Messieurs Arnault and Pinault but also the Richemond Group, which owns Cartier, Mont Blanc, Van Cleef & Arpels, Dunhill, Chloé, Piaget, Old England, and Baume & Mercier.[16] This group in 2010 had a turnover of €6.9 billion.[17] There are also smaller but well-known and significant players, such as the group headed by the Prada Group, which includes Prada as well as footwear brands such as Miu Miu, Church's, and Car Shoe.[18]

Business size is not the only distinctive feature of luxury capitalism. An interview with François-Henri Pinault in the prestigious *Harvard Business Review* in 2014 reveals two more hidden aspects in the life of the large luxury conglomerates. The first is that the gigantic financial size is needed not just to acquire more brands, expand into new global markets, and secure continuous R&D. According to Pinault: 'People tend to associate luxury brands with Fashion Week, which showcases design, but the reality is that to succeed, a company needs a logistics system that can deliver finished products to stores in the world very quickly.'[19] Responsiveness is key to the long-term wellbeing of the luxury brands and can be secured only by large and complex organizations. Large stocks of goods are rarely held in one store any more; thanks to modern-day computerized stock management, they can be shipped in daily according to demand. Yet all this is very different, for instance, from any of the global supermarket chains. A Chanel handbag clearly is not the same as a bottle of shampoo; the bag still has to be made, with various stages of finishing. The financial model of luxury is one of low turnovers and high profits. The Pinault group's revenue in 2013 was half what it was a decade earlier, when it included many non-luxury productions. Yet the move towards luxury has allowed the group to increase its profits by over 40 per cent.[20]

LUXURY BRANDS AND THEIR CLUBS

At this point, we need to pause to ask a rather banal question: what is a luxury brand? Luxury brands are like any other consumer brand, but their aim is to convey exclusivity and excellence by the quality and the look of their products.[21] This is achieved by drawing the attention of consumers to the high quality or novelty of materials used, or the detailed workmanship (sometimes hand-made products) employed. We are told, to cite just one example, that each of the watch parts of the Damiani Masterpiece series is produced from beginning to end by one worker, who spends up to six months on a single timepiece.[22] This comes at a cost in terms of product development and the sourcing of materials. Above all, it is something that needs to be hammered home to consumers, who might otherwise entirely miss such facts and have only a very superficial appreciation of the time, care, and sheer quality of the materials that have gone into making such a product. Here marketing campaigns and advertising play a key role in educating consumers, for better or for worse.

Exclusivity is even more difficult to achieve. It also requires the very clearest communication with the potential consumer. And other subtle strategies are here at play. Luxury brands might, for instance, create a sense of exclusivity by limiting production. Most of us might think that the more a firm sells the better, but in reality firms seek to maximize profits, and these are a combination of the quantities sold and the price that each commodity commands. Luxury brands understand that it is better to create a sense of absence, to convince their customers to pay more to obtain one of the rare goods that they sell. Failure to do so might lead to disaster and 'brand inflation' (Figure 8.1). This was the case with Pierre Cardin, a highly innovative and well-known brand in the 1960s, whose image suffered from becoming too common and accessible. A similar fate seemed to loom for Gucci, whose product line reached 22,000 items, but they were eventually able to refocus the brand.[23] Gucci, but also Prada, Vuitton, and any other respectable luxury brands, achieve exclusivity by limiting distribution. In a world in which the fake and counterfeit are often as good as the real and original, it is the difficulty of getting hold of the latter—versus the omnipresence of the former—that makes it genuine. And so we take it for granted

Fig. 8.1. 'Money Lent', Pawn Shop, Corner George and Barlow St, Sydney, 2013. Despite Australia's good reputation among the Chinese for selling only genuine luxury goods in its branded boutiques, the wares on sale here might be more dubious. The image also reveals the 'banalization' to which luxury goods are easily subjected when they are taken out of the context that their 'houses' hope to maintain.

that the more exclusive a consumer good is, the more difficult it will become to acquire. This explains why consumers do not hesitate to be on waiting lists to purchase the latest limited edition of a Prada bag or queue for hours and sometimes even days to be the first to own a new iPhone.

A third and at first apparently rather circular way to define a luxury brand is to say that it is one of the brands that are recognized as being 'luxurious'. Of course, consumers have a say in what they perceive as luxury, but a more clear direction comes from the many national organizations created to promote, protect, and first of all act as 'luxury brands clubs'. The most famous such club in the world is the Comité Colbert, founded in 1954 by Jean-Jacques Guerlain, owner of the luxury perfume and cosmetic company that is today part of LVMH. The Comité owes its name to Colbert, the controller-general of finances under Louis XIV, who worked so hard to promote key luxury sectors of the French economy such as the production of tapestries and porcelain. The connection with 'old luxury' is, therefore, explicit. In 2015 the association included seventy-eight luxury producers, ranging from Baccarat crystal to Givenchy and Hermès fashions, the Ritz hotel to Pullman Orient Express, to cite just a few. Among its members are some of the world's main producers of couture, crystal, porcelain, hotels, gastronomy, leather goods, gold, silver, and precious objects, perfumes and wine.[24]

The mission statement of the Comité is the promotion of French luxury, though since 2011 it has also represented selected non-French firms such as Montblanc (German pens and accessories) and Herend (Hungarian porcelain). Alongside promotion, a main task of the organization is the protection of luxury—for instance, against fakes and counterfeiting, or by lobbying for protective European Union legislation.[25] In practice, the Comité is the gatekeeper of luxury, a way to limit the supply not of luxury per se but, more to the point, of luxury brands. It is the equivalent of the College of Heraldry for those who wish to show a noble descent. More than half the members of the Comité Colbert are companies founded before 1914, the remainder being founded in the interwar period (18 per cent), and the period between 1946 and 1970 (17 per cent). Only 10 per cent (eight companies) were founded after 1970, although these include well-known brands such as La Maison du Chocolat (1977), the jeweller Laurenz Bäumer (1992), and the perfumier Frédéric Malle (2000).[26] The exclusivity of belonging to the Comité Colbert is further highlighted by the fact that some of France's major cultural institutions such as the Musée du Louvre, the Opéra de Paris, and the manufacturers of Sèvres, Gobelins, and Beauvais tapestries and la Savonnerie carpets are *membres associés* of this luxury club.[27]

Similar associations exist for luxury in Italy (Fondazione Altagamma), Britain (Walpole British Luxury), and Spain (Circulo Furtuny), and Germany is currently constituting its own national luxury association. The Fondazione Altagamma in Italy was established in 1992 by brands such as Alessi, Les Copains, Ferragamo, Ferré, Zegna, and Versace.[28] Altagamma is particularly active in commissioning research, and, together with the Comité Colbert and other national associations and international bodies, is keen to protect the luxury brands' reputation. They are at the forefront in the fight to preserve what could be described as the 'aura of luxury'.

THE AURA OF LUXURY

A great deal of the power of luxury brands is based on their reputation. Such reputation is not built just by producing high-quality goods or created through advertising and skilful image-building. It has to be protected. The protection of luxury today is first and foremost a protection of the 'allure and prestigious image' of the luxury brands. That sentence might sound as if it comes straight out of a promotional brochure. In fact it is a quotation from the European Union's Court of Justice in 2009 as an explanation of the First Trade Mark Directive.[29] In the same document, the Court of Justice defines such 'allure and prestigious image' as a way of bestowing 'an aura of luxury'.

It might appear unusual that a legal body should use such a 'poetic' turn of phrase. But in reality it can be interpreted as the result of a watershed change in the legislators' attitudes to the protection of trademarks. Brands— and luxury brands in particular—are first and foremost trademarks, a series of letters and symbols that come to represent either specific products or specific companies. Trademarks have been in existence since the eighteenth century, but only in the twentieth century did they become widely recognized by consumers and the public at large. They are an important tool for our shopping, ensuring that we do not need to check the quality of each item that we purchase in a supermarket. When we buy a bar of a well-known chocolate, we distinguish it from other chocolates because of its characteristic wrapping and logo. We already know the quality of the product and we trust that the product will be exactly the same as the one we bought a week or a year ago. This is a by-product of the retailing and manufacturing innovations of the nineteenth century, when increasing populations in countries such as the United States had to be satisfied with products whose processes of production and intrinsic qualities could not be easily tested.

In the case of the luxury brands, their trademarks have come to signify not just trust but also a cluster of ideas in the minds of consumers about the prestige and appeal of the product. The double 'Cs' of Coco Chanel are not just another trademark; they make us think of Paris, wonderfully dressed ladies, beautifully tailored *tailleurs*, quilted bags, and red carpets. All these ideas create an 'aura of luxury', something that is as difficult to define as it is difficult to protect. And yet it is this 'aura' that the luxury brands are determined to defend even more than their logos. They do so through a variety of means that include image-building through PR and advertising, endorsement by testimonials, and protection via laws that give brands exclusive rights of use.

European legislation on the protection of trademarks has changed substantially since the beginning of the twenty-first century. This has happened under pressure from the luxury brands, whose range of activities and products has noticeably increased to include not just clothing and accessories but also restaurants, cafés, and a variety of other consumer goods. In the 1990s, a producer of cocoa pops could legitimately have used the double 'Cs' of Chanel: this was possible as long as the product was sufficiently different from the leather bags and clothing produced and sold by Coco Chanel. Legislators thought that there would be no risk of confusion on the part of consumers between the famous luxury brand Coco Chanel and an (invented) cereal brand, Cocoa Chanel.

More recent legislation, however, has made this illegal. From the realm of fantasy, we move to a real court case of 2007 between Louis Vuitton (LV) and the company Haute Diggity Dog, which was using the name Chewy Vuiton (CV) for dogs' toys. LV objected to the use of a mark that closely resembled its own, claiming that Diggity Dog contributed to a trademark dilution by blurring and tarnishing the image of LV. Legislators were initially unconvinced that LV would suffer from the incursion: any trademark can be used for the purpose of parody (and the comic effect was clearly apparent), and LV and Diggity Dog were not operating in sectors with a strong enough level of proximity for LV customers to be under the impression that LV produced dogs' wares.[30] The existing law establishes that no one else can use the logo LV or the Vuitton name, even if there is no risk of confusion between a leather bag and dogs' toys. This happened because the luxury brands successfully convinced legislators that their 'aura' is potentially limitless and indeed might one day include products as different as fashionable accessories and cereals. While trademarks connect to specific products, the aura of luxury extends to the entire realm of notions and ideas.

A further important change in how the law deals with the 'aura' of luxury relates to distribution. Would you buy a Prada bag from a market stall? We know that such a bag sold in a market has a high probability of being fake. But let us suppose, instead, that it is a 'real' product, legitimately bought by a market-stall owner from a luxury wholesaler. Existing legislation says that this sale of 'real' products is illegal, as the owner of the trademark (Prada in this case) has the right to allow only certain retailers (its own concessions and stores, most likely) to sell Prada goods. This goes against common sense, as most traders would want as many sellers for their products as possible. Yet luxury is traditionally at least partly about *limiting* supply, and this is why the luxury brands have fought (and won) a battle for legislation that allows them to control not just the production but also the distribution of their products. This is seen as key to preserving an 'aura of luxury', as the allure and prestige of Prada or other luxury brands might conceivably be significantly tarnished if their products were made readily available on all market stalls.[31]

This restrictive legislation has two important consequences. The first is that the luxury brands have the power of stopping Internet retailers. As digital shopping is expanding year by year, the luxury brands are worried that large retailers such as Amazon or Ebay could profit from trading their branded products. Legally—at least in Europe—the luxury brands can control retailing. The second consequence relates to consumers: is it in the interest of consumers that supply is limited? Is not the principle of the free circulation of goods infringed as a consequence of the power given to the luxury brands? There is no easy answer to this question. Certainly, most consumers are probably not aware that the legitimate quest for protection by the luxury brands might be at the expense of their rights as consumers to access goods freely at the cheapest possible price.

More insidious enemies of luxury—which challenge the very reputation and aura of luxury brands—are counterfeit products. Louis Vuitton, the most copied luxury brand in the world, in 2010 had 40 in-house lawyers and 250 outside investigators and was spending $18 million a year fighting counterfeiting.[32] Counterfeiting is large and increasing by the year. In 2013 the US agencies seized goods under their Intellectual Property Rights (IPR) enforcement measures in more than 22,000 separate incidents for a value (had they been genuine) of $1.7 billion. China is the country of origin of nearly 70 per cent of the merchandise seized by US customs, valued at a staggering $1.1 billion. Clearly, counterfeiting affects not just the luxury brands, although in the United States, for instance, luxury handbags, wallets, watches, and jewellery make up 70 per cent of all seized counterfeit merchandise.[33] A similar picture emerges in Europe. In 2013, €768 million worth of goods were seized by EU customs for infringing IPR. In Europe, however, the scale of counterfeiting is four times larger than in the United States. With 87,000 incidents in 2013, a total of 36 million articles were seized. Watches accounted for 21 per cent of all value, followed by sunglasses (12 per cent), clothing (11 per cent), bags and wallets (10 per cent), perfumes and cosmetics (7 per cent), sportswear (5 per cent), and other items (34 per cent). The countries most active at prosecuting infringements of IPR are Germany, the UK, and Italy.[34]

One of the challenges of the fight against counterfeiting is to understand consumers' psychology. The luxury brands and their associations rely heavily on the law and seek the protection of the authorities. Anyone passing through a French airport will have noticed posters with a crocodile (the logo of Lacoste, a well-known French sportswear brand), informing passengers that the introduction of counterfeits into France is an offence. Needless to say, such posters are greeted with a wry smile, because fakes and counterfeits have become socially acceptable. At the end of the twentieth century counterfeit goods were purchased by those consumers who could not afford the original. There were also always tourists who bought such things home for fun; they were often cheap imitations, substandard even to the naked or inexperienced eye. Today counterfeits are not just to be found everywhere from Shanghai to San Francisco, but are often sold to people who could well afford the original.[35] Youtube videos tell you how to distinguish a counterfeit from a real product, as the quality of copies and fakes is sometimes as high as that of the original product. Indeed, as we shall see, slowly but surely the focus of regulation seems to be shifting away from the protection of the luxury brands and their profits towards the notion of protection of consumers, who are the ultimate judge of what they consume.

ETHICS AND SOCIAL FUNCTION OF A LUXURY BRAND

The economic strength of the luxury sector and the public position that the luxury brands have in today's society naturally raise the question of their social role. The luxury economy is founded upon a specific model of consumption. It constructs a series of dreams through advertising and, for example, rarefied shop interiors, and communicates to us all via television, glossy magazines, and, increasingly, the Internet. By the very action of creating desire, luxury becomes a maker of social identities. The teenage girl who dreams of having a $1,000 bag from a famous luxury brand is a potential individual customer for the luxury sector. Yet when a thousand or a million similar teenagers hold the same dream, the object of their desire becomes part of the *politics* of consumption. Luxury brands are therefore increasingly asked what they do for their consumers and for the national and global communities with which they interact.

Luxury has an undesirable nature that pushes states, groups, and individuals to argue for more regulation. This is not the regulation to protect the brand, but rather a regulation to protect consumers, perhaps from themselves. Regulation remains relatively light in this area, although the issue of consumer credit and a rise in bankruptcies should be a topic of concern both for government and the big brands (luxury included). We are not advocating a return to state interference in personal consumption along the lines of the medieval sumptuary laws. However, consumers' preferences can be managed via taxation, in particular through the imposition of consumption taxes, such as VAT. Some European states already apply a 'luxury tax' in the form of higher VAT rates on expensive goods or specific categories of commodities classified as 'luxurious', such as sports cars, yachts, second houses, or jewellery; Sweden is one example.

The luxury brands might shy away from regulation, though they have taken the notion of (voluntary) social responsibility somewhat more seriously. 'Social responsibility' relates both to the products that they sell and their role as companies in the wider society. An area that in recent years has been at the centre of attention is their responsibility towards the environment, and the respect shown in the use of natural resources and towards human beings. 'Sustainability' has become a new keyword in luxury, with many luxury brands claiming that their products are long-lasting and can be used over several generations, thus limiting waste and harm to the environment. Examples here include Savile Row suits and the advertising campaigns for Chopard watches.

A further area of socially responsible action has been charity. Several of the large brands are now engaged in charitable causes, mostly in Third World countries. Their detractors comment upon the fact that such charitable causes are selected to create maximum visibility and are turned into powerful marketing tools for the promotion of the brand itself. The ethical limits are perhaps sometimes tested, as in the case of Angelina Jolie's 2011 LV campaign, where she is shown on top of a traditional Cambodian boat in Cambodia's Siem Reap Province, holding a large LV bag. In this case, LV has no particular charitable link to Cambodia. Yet the advertisement reads 'A single journey can change the course of a life', possibly referring to the well-known fact that Jolie and her husband, Brad Pitt, adopted a Cambodian child. The endorsement by Angelina gives apparent deepness of meaning to the product and an 'ethical' context that the product by itself does not have.[36] It is perhaps hard not to feel a little cynical as one looks at such an image.

The luxury brands have also become major sponsors of the arts. The French businessman and luxury retail billionaire François-Henri Pinault, for instance, opened his art collection in Venice at the eighteenth-century Palazzo Grassi on the Grand Canal, and then, following a renovation coordinated by the famous Japanese architect Tadao Ando, moved it to the Punta della Dogana, the city's historic former customs' house in 2009. The Louis Vuitton Foundation opened its $143 million museum in the Bois de Boulogne in Paris in 2014, a magnificent building specifically designed for the purpose by Frank Gehry (Figure 8.2). Prada, which also has a foundation in Milan supporting contemporary art, started a new literary prize in 2013, in association with the Italian publisher Feltrinelli. Literary talent, however, was not allowed to roam entirely free. The 1,300 short stories received from international authors had to respond to the questions: 'Which are the realities seen by our eyes? And how do lenses filter such realities?' Needless to say, Prada's interest at the time was promoting a new line of eye frames called 'Prada Journal'.[37] More recently, Rem Koolhas, the innovative architect, has designed an art space for Miuccia Prada (the designer and entrepreneur behind Prada's current success) in Venice.[38] Luxury brand–art collaborations, as they are known in the jargon, are a fairly recent invention, whose popularity goes back only to about 2006–7. A detailed study shows that, in just a few years, luxury brand–art collaborations have become common for all brands and often have an international nature. Yet nearly three-quarters of them are limited to the visual arts; only rarely do they include the performing arts (4 per cent) and music (3 per cent). In three-quarters of cases such collaborations are based on Western art and just over a fifth (21 per cent) on the arts of Asia. Art that originates from Latin America, Australasia, and Africa is clearly underrepresented.[39]

Since 1996, the Hugo Boss Prize, worth $100,000, has been awarded annually to an artist who has made a substantial contribution to the contemporary art scene. The winner is also given the opportunity to showcase his or her work at the Guggenheim Museum in New York.[40] Luxury leather goods manufacturer Bottega Veneta started 'The Art of Collaboration' in 2002, a scheme through which every year the Italian brand selects an artist to shoot avant-garde creative commercials. More recently, in 2012 the champagne-producer Dom Pérignon launched 'The Power of Creation' collaboration, in which contemporary artists were asked to design limited-edition bottles of the famous French champagne.[41] Hermès, too, has its special prizes for avant-garde craft practitioners, such as the Swedish contemporary knitter Sandra Backlund, at the well-known festival of Hyères in Provence. Versace, a fashion brand that has made a virtue out of luxurious vulgarity, commissioned the emerging designer Anthony Vaccarello in 2013 to create a 'capsule collection'—that is to say, a small non-seasonal collection, made available online for the 'digital generation'.[42]

These are just a few examples of the extensive engagement of luxury brands with the arts, an association that was also strong in the specific case of fashion throughout the twentieth century. It is an engagement that luxury brands have used to promote both their image and good causes. Yet some might see the increasing remit of luxury as a threat to traditional

Fig. 8.2. Fondation Louis Vuitton, architect Frank Gehry, Paris, 2014. Gehry, one of the generation of 'starchitechts' (architecture stars), is himself a brand, and has even designed handbags of late for Louis Vuitton. The Louis Vuitton Foundation embeds the luxury brand into a role as contemporary Maecenas of the Arts. The building is located in the Bois de Boulogne, a park that in the nineteenth century was one of the main spaces in which women and men of leisure showed off their carriages and fashions on fine afternoons.

boundaries between business and charity, between artistic and commercial forms, or indeed, as we shall see, between private space and the marketplace. Brands have transformed themselves into 'brand worlds'—for instance, Burberry now supports its own emerging singers, with the idea being that new talent will in turn support the brand. Rather than sponsor young people's voices, the well-known Italian footwear brand Della Valle chose instead to sponsor the restoration of major Italian monuments, such as the Colosseum.

THE SPACES OF LUXURY

The American author and critic Edmund White, writing in the early years of the new millennium, observed a process of what he termed the 'boutiquification' of entire Parisian neighbourhoods. He complained that, in fashionable Saint-Germain-des-Près,

> one of the best bookstores, Le Divan, has been replaced by Dior, that one of the few record stores in the area has been cannibalized by Cartier, and Le Drugstore—a late-night complex of tobacco stand, restaurant and chemist—has been supplanted by Armani. Louis Vuitton has installed a chic shop right next to Les Deux Magots [a famous café in the area].[43]

Luxury is colonizing the spaces of our cities. In the 1960s, chain stores, especially those selling clothing, became important parts of Western Europe's urban landscape. Chains such as Gap and Next in Britain, the Italian Benetton, and (since 2000) a variety of other retail outlets that include Dorothy Perkins, Zara, Nike, or Maxmara, have become ubiquitous features of urban and metropolitan life. Together with supermarket chains (now increasingly present in city centres with smaller 'metro' retail units) and the equally pervasive chain coffee shops, clothing and accessory chains have been accused of imposing homogeneity not just in the visual appearance of what have been described as 'clone towns', but also in the experience of shopping.[44] This is a phenomenon particularly marked in

Northern Europe and North America, but its effects are now visible from Lisbon to Istanbul, from Riga to Rome.

Yet since the early years of the new millennium a new process has been at play: a new wave of specifically *luxury* outlets has come to dominate our cities. The luxury brands have claimed their own space within the very centre of the city. With the expansion of demand for luxury, both established and new luxury brands, from Chanel and Dior to Bottega Veneta and Marc Jacobs, could no longer find sufficient retail space and visibility within department stores or in their old and cramped venues in exclusive back alleys. Their new clientele is quantitatively and qualitatively different from the customers that they had in the 1980s and even 1990s. By pursuing larger sales and in the attempt to attract even wider numbers of customers, luxury brands have had to move to prime locations, especially in large cities, sometimes fighting for space against supermarkets and mass retailing.

The example of the famous Galleria in Milan might help explain this change and the consequent paradox that it has created. Just off the beautiful Piazza Duomo in the centre of Milan, the Galleria Vittorio Emanuele II was built in the 1870s to rival the grand Parisian arcades, adding a bit of class to the city of Milan that in the nineteenth century was better known for its factories than its fashion. For over a century, the Galleria retained its architectural uniqueness and shopping exclusivity: it was the mecca of elite shopping, with high-class artisanal names, including Samini and Prada, the latter then known for small luxuries, bags, and travel goods. Today the experience of the Galleria is different. The two most prominent outlets are the famous fast-food chain McDonalds and (one might say) the even more well-known luxury chain Louis Vuitton. Hordes of tourists pass through the Galleria, dropping into Louis Vuitton before indulging in a Big Mac, unless they have a very expensive glass of champagne at Biffi, in order to amuse themselves watching the tourists jostling about.

The physical closeness of 'mass' and 'luxury' in the Milanese galleria might appear exceptional, but a similar trend can be seen in many shopping streets in London, Paris, and New York, and also in smaller centres such as Bologna in Italy or Nice in France. In the attempt to amplify desire, the luxury brands have consciously chosen both the strategies and the locations formerly used by mass retailing. The historic city of Bologna, for instance, with its medieval towers and Renaissance square, is a mecca of luxury shopping. We were once asked by a colleague where 'the real people' of Bologna shop, as in the city centre nothing can be found but luxury brand shops. Within the space of just a few hundred yards there is LV, Armani, Frette (purveyors of luxury bed and bath linens), and two Gucci outlets. These luxury retailers have now colonized both the spaces where mass retailers once did business as well as those of independent shops, who can no longer afford the high rents. The 'new luxury' of the luxury brands has replaced the 'old luxury' of specialized bookshops, antiques shops, tobacconists, haberdashers, glove and millinery vendors, and traditional bars and cafés.

The effect is disorienting: in some cases the homogeneity of mass distribution has mutated into an homogeneity of luxury: from city to city we find again and again the same luxury brands, the same products, and the same shop-window dressings. In other cases, luxury has taken over the historic parts of town. Take Ferragamo's headquarters in Florence, for instance: occupying the Renaissance Palazzo Spini Feroni in the centre of Florence, Ferragamo has an impressive number of spacious shop windows overlooking the Arno River, just a few steps from the Ponte Vecchio. While Ferragamo has been there since the 1930s, other famous brands have moved in, creating a 'citadel of luxury' in which elegant shops, ornate churches, and world-famous museums seem to form a seamless cityscape. Ferragamo itself is not just a shop but also a museum, thus transporting the cultural tourism that surrounds the shop into its own premises. This idea was taken by Prada to a new extreme with its recent 'Pradasphere' pop-up shops in spaces such as London's Harrods or Hong Kong's Ferry Pier, which simulate very accurately the appearance of an extra-glamorous museum, once you enter their portals. Charming attendants whisper gently about the genesis of the brand, as they display examples of Prada's early travelling cases and art deco handbags in beautifully lit vitrines.

The visibility of luxury retailing is integral to the creation of desire and to securing big sales. Yet it is also a curse, if it leads to a tarnishing of the image of the brand. This is the reason why access and exclusivity have to be negotiated spatially as well as via advertising and marketing. Despite what has been said about the rise of online shopping, space still matters. This means, in practical terms, that one must secure the use of areas of a city that have cultural cachet and historical fame. In Paris, luxury concentrates itself in well-known areas of the city, in the rue Saint-Honoré (already the centre of the luxury trades in the eighteenth century) and especially in the Champs Elysées, perhaps the best-known boulevard in France, with large pavements, cafés, and panoramic views of the city. Today a stroll in the Champs is like reading the Yellow Pages of luxury. The queues that snake around Louis Vuitton probably leave the people who consider themselves to be 'real' fashionistas disdainful and jaded. Yet the crowds must presumably be queuing for something. And, indeed, the materials and textures on sale inside are still as luxurious, high quality, and high price as they have ever been.

But what to do when there is no cultural cachet or history to rely upon? This is very much the case in Dubai. A city of malls that rises from the desert, Dubai is fast becoming a world shopping mecca.[45] A visit to the famous Mall of the Emirates, however, shows that luxury is both an opportunity and a challenge. Located next to the Bhur Dubai, the tallest building in the world, the mall has more than 560 international brands and 700 stores. The many luxury brands and designer outlets have been assembled around a court, at the centre of which is not an ordinary café but the Armani Caffé Dubai. A cascade of diamond-shaped glass strings, two large escalators, and high-pile carpet provide an element of drama and distinguish this part of the mall from the rest, where the non-luxury stores are located. Another of the city's well-known malls, the Dubai Mall, went a step further. Here, one can walk through a charming European luxury alley (see Figure 8.3).

Fig. 8.3. A Dubai mall imitating a street in Paris or London, 2013. It is unclear which city this architecture is meant to suggest. It resembles the luxury shopping pedestrian mall adjacent to Rodeo Drive, Beverly Hills, Los Angeles, made famous in many American films, which is itself a simulation of various European locations or a cobbled street in either Paris or London.

It is unclear if this is supposed to be Paris or London, but the mock eighteenth-century architecture provides a sense of differentiation from the rest of the mall and combines a classic Parisian arcade and an idyllic shopping street. All this is within a synthetically cooled shopping mall on the edge of a desert, with the heat outside standing at 45 degrees centigrade. Then again, if Dubai does not have the architecture of Paris or London, why not simply build it?

There is a popular argument that the spread of luxury brands brings homogeneity and eliminates the diversity of different types of retail business that are able to flourish throughout the world. However, this is actually rather difficult to support if one looks at the global picture. Luxury goods are, in fact, perhaps sold through a wider variety of types of outlet than is the case in any other sector. The spaces of luxury are multiple. As an example, let us contrast two emerging Asian economies, China and South Korea. In 2014, while in China two-thirds of all luxury products were sold in shops located in shopping malls, in Korea 75 per cent of luxury goods were sold in department stores. Both in South Korea and Japan—but the same can be said for France, Italy, the United Kingdom, and Germany—few luxury goods are sold in shopping malls. Yet among European countries there are substantial differences as well. In the United Kingdom, 40 per cent of luxury goods were sold in well-known department stores, compared to 35 per cent in France, 28 per cent in Germany, and only 8 per cent in Italy. In Italy, 81 per cent of luxury goods were sold by independent shops (so called 'street-level' shops), which now constitute a substantial share of the shopping streets of the *Bel Paese*.[46] By contrast, in none of the major Asian luxury consumer economies (India, China, Japan, South Korea, Hong Kong, and Singapore) did the street-level retailing of luxury goods account for more than 6 per cent of sales. In the case of Hong Kong this is remarkable, as the metropolis has more big brands than any capital city in the West: eight Gucci stores compared to six in London and Paris, seven Hermès stores compared to just five in London, three in Paris, and two in New York.[47] India stands out for the high percentage (47 per cent) of luxury goods sold in duty free and especially within hotel corridors off the lobby, a nice older take on luxury shopping and one that guarantees security and peace. Brazil and the Middle East have in common the fact that 91 and 85 per cent respectively of luxury goods were sold in shopping malls. In the United States, 21 per cent of luxury goods were sold in outlets, a form of luxury retailing that seems to have similar success only in Japan.[48]

Retailing is key to the success of the luxury brands. Luca Solca, managing director of global luxury goods at BNP Paribas, reports that luxury brands are effectively becoming retailers and that in the next few years direct distribution will increase at the expense of franchising and sale via department stores.[49] Essentially, therefore, we are likely to see luxury-brand shops mushrooming in our city centres, shopping malls, and airports. The strategy of focusing on mono-brand shops, however, comes at a cost. Louis Vuitton sells its products through its own boutiques, ensuring a total control of its image and a cull on fakes. Yet it is one of the few luxury brands that has not launched a perfume, as this would necessitate its distribution via perfume concessions in department stores and elsewhere.[50] The brand prefers instead to invest in its own distinctive shop outlets in some of the world's most prominent streets, squares, and boulevards.

While the brand is the same and the goods are more or less standardized across the globe, this is not the case for the experience offered to customers. LV, for instance, has an architecture department that was founded in 1998 and manages the architecture, layout, and furnishing of all its 460 stores. It cooperates with architects of the calibre of Peter Marino and Jun Aoki.[51] 'Signature shops' are becoming landmarks in the best-known shopping streets in the major global cities. Architect Peter Marino has made a name for himself by working for luxury brands such as Chanel (five shops between 2001 and 2005), Fendi (two shops), Vuitton (four), and Dior (three), as well as Armani, and Barney's Stores in New York and Beverly Hills.[52] Giorgio Armani in 2001 commissioned Tadao Ando to restructure the old Nestlé building in Milan. The new 3,400 square metre space accommodated a theatre and the Armani showroom and commercial offices. The Prada boutiques, designed by significant contemporary architects such as Herzog & de Meuron and Rem Koolhaas, present themselves as akin to a gallery crossed with a skatepark. Dior Homme, meanwhile, employed contemporary artists such as Ugo Rondinone to design a changing room of black rubber that vibrates like a heartbeat. Much money is spent in order to create a unique experience.

THE LIMINAL SPACES OF LUXURY

The expansion and industrialization of luxury have created a kind of 'luxury invasion' of our everyday lives.[53] But at the same time one of the dangers for luxury brands is that of overexposure. In targeting expanding and increasingly amorphous markets, they have had to resort to increasingly generic media channels: television, newspapers, magazines, and now increasingly the Internet. They do so both by targeting precise customer segments in terms of age and income, but also by communicating in the most generic way possible. An example of the broad generic approach is the prodigiously successful Dior campaign 'J'adore Dior', in which famous actresses from the past and supermodels from the present participate in a catwalk at the centre of which is not fashionable clothing but a bottle of the 'J'adore' perfume. Waiting in a London airport, one of the authors was subjected to 'J'adore Dior' for a couple of hours. Beaming screens invaded the boredom of the quotidian toil of early twenty-first-century airport alienation. It is unknown quite what percentage of the other passengers that day resisted the impulse of purchasing 'J'adore' for their loved ones.

Airports represent the 'liminal' spaces of the twenty-first century par excellence, threshold spaces of ambiguity and sometimes disorientation, where the traveller is caught between cultures and traditions. It is therefore perhaps no surprise that they have been relentlessly colonized by luxury brands. The main creators of the modern duty-free system were the American Chuck Feeney and Robert W. Miller, who set up the Duty Free Shoppers Group corporation in 1960.[54] For a long time, duty free was synonymous with cheap alcohol and cigarettes, but since the terrorist attacks of 9/11 airports have become places where people are trapped for increasingly long periods. And among these crowds of potential consumers there are, typically, large numbers of businessmen and holidaymakers with sufficient disposable income to travel over long distances. Luxury has here found its captive audience. Heathrow Terminal 5 is a case in point: designed by Richard Rogers and inaugurated in 2008, the building is 400 metres long and 170 metres wide and cost in excess of £4 billion. It also includes more than 100 shops and restaurants. The giants of British retail distribution such as W. H. Smith and Boots are present, but the terminal also has shops by Gucci (which also has shops in three of the other four terminals), Mulberry (with shops in all five terminals), Montblanc, Prada, Tiffany, Dior, and Harrods, to name but a few. Meanwhile, in Terminal 4 the keen brand-spotter will spy luxury names such as Zegna, Etro, McQueen, Hugo Boss, Bally, Burberry, Bulgari, Paul Smith, and Ferragamo.[55] More than 30 per cent of all perfumes and 20 per cent of all cognac worldwide are bought at duty free.

Travellers do not just purchase luxury goods at airports when they happen to be travelling; increasingly, they actually travel around the world *in order* to purchase luxury goods. This is especially the case with Chinese consumers. A 2014 report reveals that, of Chinese travellers abroad, 100 per cent admitted to going shopping, compared to 90 per cent who said they had been sightseeing, 85 per cent who had sampled the local cuisine, and just over 20 per cent who had been to bars, nightclubs, or pubs while on holiday.[56] In 2014 the most popular destinations for the rising Chinese middle classes were Hong Kong, Macao, South Korea, Thailand, Japan, Taiwan, and Singapore, all relatively local destinations and with excellent European and North American branded goods shopping. The United States, Britain, and France were only the eighth, ninth, and tenth most popular destinations. Yet the *dream* destinations for Chinese travellers are all European, including France, Italy, the United Kingdom, Switzerland, Germany, Spain, Greece, and Sweden.[57]

What is important here—and should be carefully evaluated by the dream countries for Chinese travellers—is that shopping constitutes 43 per cent of total spending by travellers (equivalent to nearly $2,000).[58] Those going to Europe in 2013 splashed out on luxuries including bags, clothes, and shoes, jewellery, and watches, spending in France just over 7,000 Rmb (Chinese Yuan) on bags alone (this is about $1,100, which is double what is spent on luxury goods by Chinese tourists in other countries). Australia, too, is an increasingly attractive destination for Chinese tourists in terms of luxury goods, as they escape the high taxes and duties that they face at home.[59] The same can be said of the European destinations, though more subtle reasons than money push Chinese consumers to buy abroad. These reasons are mostly to do with perception: the Chinese think that the luxury goods that they purchase in Paris or Milan are of better quality than what they can get in Beijing or Shanghai. They trust that, away from the world centre of counterfeiting, the probability of buying a fake is lower, and, above all, they like buying the product in or near to its place of origin. There is nothing more rewarding than buying Dior in Paris, Armani in Milan, or Burberry in London (whether or not their products are manufactured in these places is, of course, another question).

The mismatch between reality and perception or between the 'dream space' of luxury and its actual retail manifestation is nowhere more evident than on the Internet. The luxury brands have long resisted cyberspace, finding it difficult to protect and control their image. This is why even today some luxury brands use the Web as nothing more than a shop window, although others such as Prada cleverly use the Web to show customers parts of their collections and to generate interest in the product, rather than selling it there per se.[60] Attitudes vary considerably. A study completed in 2011 showed that the high-end jewellery- and watch-maker

Cartier was very Web savvy, with more than 100 pages on its website, whereas similarly traditional companies with similar pedigrees, such as the silverware firm Christofle (founded 1830), had just forty pages, and the luxury bed-linen company Yves Delorme (founded 1845) had no website at all.[61] Hotel brands such as the exclusive Peninsula had only partial websites until about 2012; they now have very detailed magazine-style sites with histories and images of the brand, shots with models using the spaces of the hotel, and vignettes of Peninsula 'experiences'.

If the online message proposed by the luxury brands remains partial at best, the same can be said of their engagement with the Web as a tool to sell their products and interact with their clients and the public at large. In 2006, Guy Salter, then deputy chairman of Walpole, the association representing British luxury brands, warned the sector that the development of an online retailing strategy was a priority. Nearly a decade on, e-commerce is growing but struggles to re-create the experience, attention to detail, and customization offered in shops. The luxury brands fear for the worst. The Internet has made the difference between original and counterfeit difficult to detect. A considerable proportion of the stock for sale on the Web is blatantly infringing copyright and is sold at one-tenth of the original's price (a Louis Vuitton counterfeit purse can be acquired online for, say, $115 instead of $1,100).[62] Yet Tim Philips, in his book *Knock Off* (2005), claims that the luxury brands' lack of an online presence actually encourages the purchase of counterfeits, with consumers trusting dubious online retailers in the absence of legitimate online retailers.[63] Online retailers of counterfeits also undermine the integrity of traditional distributive channels: a few years ago a Birkin handbag sold on Ebay became the subject of an intense bidding war that ultimately led to the bag being sold for more than double its original price tag of $6,000.[64] In this case, the artefact was genuine, and what bidders wanted was to avoid a long waiting list.

But the Web consists of much more than just advertising and marketing. A great part of what people think about a brand comes from cyberspace.

Fashion blogs, for instance, are as recent as 2003. Yet already by 2006 bloggers had achieved enormous prestige in the hierarchy of the fashion industry and within fashion communication. That year, forty bloggers were for the first time given press passes to attend New York Fashion Week. Four years later, Dolce & Gabbana took the decision to sit the bloggers in the front row, elbow to elbow, one might say, with the aristocracy of fashion such as Anna Wintour of American *Vogue* and Suzy Menkes of the *International Herald Tribune*.[65] Bloggers replicate traditional formats to be found in the fashion press, but the Web also increasingly has the potential to be a tool of *interaction*. The mid-market luxury handbag brand Coach, for instance, in 2012 used the Web to launch a campaign to 'Design a Coach Tote[bag]' that led to 3,000 design submissions, the best of which were eventually put into production. This is crowd-sourcing, a form of participation that is not about buying but about interacting with the brand at a more creative level. Apart from the thousands of submissions, the campaign produced six million page views and more than 100,000 people rated the designs submitted.[66]

LUXURY AND NATIONAL IDENTITIES

Luxury is today a phenomenon that goes beyond the confines of national markets and local denominations. Yet simply to equate luxury brands with a handful of globally known labels is overly reductive. 'Internationally recognizable' brands are well advertised and supported by the power of capital. However, the world of the luxury brands also includes important 'niche brands' and products that are unique and more exclusive than the big brands, even though they might not be as well recognized by consumers. Many of the tailors in Savile Row in London, for instance, do not advertise in luxury and fashion magazines, but their products and the prestige of their logo are well above those of any high-street luxury brand. They might have one or two shops only, but their clientele is truly global.[67]

The idea that 'niche' necessarily means restricted geographical reach is incorrect. Take a relatively small firm like the Italian company Furla, for example; an independent brand that produces 'affordable luxury' hand-bags, wallets, and shoes, and that exports 76 per cent of all its production.[68]

A third type of brand that is key to understanding the luxury market is the 'collective brand'. The most recognized among them is 'Made in Italy', a concept that was invented in the 1950s to promote Italian fashion and design. The idea of a collective trademark goes back to the nineteenth century and extends to regional products that excel in quality, such as the cutlery of Sheffield, the wines of Champagne, and the glass of Bohemia or Murano. National and regional denominations rely on formal and informal mechanisms such as the use of collective trademarks of systems of certification. The best known among them is that of the Champagne region. A proposal for the granting of a special 'appellation' goes back to 1908, but it was only in 1927 that the French government intervened to delineate the borders of the Champagne region, and nine years later it created an 'Appellation d'Origine Contrôlée' for Champagne.[69]

There is an apparent contradiction in the fact that, in an age of globalization, brands are deeply national, indeed often regional and subnational. A French product is sold across the world simply because it is French. Yet the definition of what 'French' might mean for producers and consumers alike is less than clear. The global recomposition of the luxury market has in recent years presented a unique opportunity to reshape the geographies of luxury provenance. Since the eighteenth century, specific nations—with France at the top of the pyramid, followed by England and in the twentieth century Italy—became synonymous with fashion, style, and luxury. France remained the home of both fashion (haute couture) and luxury in the twentieth century, though the rise of luxury has shown the importance of Italy as well. Britain, by contrast, suffered from a perceived stuffiness of elite culture and the success instead of demotic pop culture (Carnaby, rather than Bond, Street), to the detriment of Britain's traditional luxury industry (high-quality men's shoes, trench coats, impeccable tailoring Savile Row-style, or the magnificence of Edwardian outfitters). Only since the mid-2000s has the British luxury goods industry made a comeback, though not necessarily in its traditional forms.

The case of British luxury is indicative of the complexity of the relationship between the national identity of luxury and its global ambitions. While English men's tailoring enjoys the patronage of a select international clientele and steady business, British luxury brands have also made inroads in global markets. Burberry is perhaps the best known among them. Under the able stewardship of head designer and later CEO Chris Bailey, what used to be a rather decayed niche brand has become the embodiment of modern luxury. The 2014 Burberry campaign visually conveyed the secret of the brand's success: it shows English fashion model Cara Delevingne transformed into a modern Mary Poppins dressed in Burberry and holding a Burberry-patterned umbrella while flying over the stormy skyline not of London but of Shanghai.[70] The transposition of Mary Poppins to China is far from a coincidence: with China accounting for 20 per cent of Burberry's sales, this is part of a reshaping of a classic British children's character (admittedly written by an expatriate Australian author) into a hybrid that blends the essence of Britain and the skyline of the rising oriental economies. Britishness needs to be marketed to Chinese consumers.

A great deal of the national appeal of brands is created by cultural associations cemented through the clever use of advertising at a global level. Globalization, however, creates at the same time a sense of brand displacement. The 'country of production' of a product is often different from the 'country of origin' of the brand: the brand might be French or Italian, whereas the product might have been produced in China or South Korea. When Burberry moved production to China in 2007, the loss of 300 jobs in the Rhondda Valley of Wales made world news: Kate Moss, Prince Charles, and the Archbishop of Canterbury were all dismayed. Burberry was accused of 'corporate greed', public opinion felt betrayed, and people wondered whether a search for cost reduction was necessary when a Burberry shirt cost £60.[71] At the same time, exposés by the likes of Dana Thomas and Naomi Klein put forward a new ethical dimension, revealing that the working conditions and workers' wages of luxury production in China, South-East Asia, and other developing countries were little or no better than in the sweatshops churning out cheap commodities. The situation becomes even more complex if one considers an example such as the city of Prato in Tuscany, where many Chinese workers are employed in sometime clandestine workshops to produce handbags for leading Italian fashion brands. It was rumoured in 2007 that these workshops produced a bag for €20 that was later sold for €400.[72]

The luxury sector is playing with fire, as globalization of production and distribution threatens to blur the identity of brands. Are consumers negatively affected by the fact that Jaguar or Louis Vuitton might be produced in China rather than England and France respectively? Marketing researchers such as Qing Wang at the Warwick Business School think that they are, at least in those cases when the symbolic value of the luxury brand is intangible and emotional. The preservation of a close relationship between manufacturing and origin is important when brands rely on an identity that associates them with key values of their country of origin.[73] By contrast, no one cares or even is surprised that Nike, iPhones, and even Land Rover cars are produced in Asia, because it is their technological features and attributes that bestow upon them the 'luxury' label. In 2013, Bentley, the British luxury car producer, announced the move of part of its production to Bratislava, Slovakia. Unlike the Burberry story, this particular story hardly made the headlines anywhere, notwithstanding the core importance of 'Britishness' to the Bentley brand. The Queen's car-maker is, of course, actually owned by the very German company Volkswagen, which in this case saw an opportunity to reduce costs by offshoring production to Slovakia, where the Porsche Cayenne is also produced.[74] The entry level VW Polo is made in South Africa, but one has to ask the sales representatives to find this out, and the more expensive models are still made in Europe. How is a consumer to know?

THE TIME OF LUXURY

The luxury brands have not just invaded the *spaces* of streets and department stores. They also play with the concepts of Time and History. As discussed in the Introduction, luxury finds its *raison d'être* in quality (real or perceived), aesthetics, expense, and the *past*.[75] The past is often invoked in luxury brands' marketing campaigns as a quest for 'authenticity'. It is claimed that products 'embody' skills, quality, and traditions that have been passed down from generation to generation of craftsmen and skilled producers. 'Authenticity' means appropriating the 'thickness' of the past, its tradition and patina, all of which are key to an 'aura of luxury'.[76]

Two periods that continue to attract the collective imagination of consumers are the Italian Renaissance and the French eighteenth century. They have been used by the luxury sector as the backdrop to convey a sense of exclusivity, a world of excess, taste, and fun. Italian brands use the Renaissance architecture of Rome, Florence, and Venice, not just in a quest for national identity, but in the association between the magnificence and splendour of the Italian Renaissance courts and present-day luxury products. French luxury uses the eighteenth century, with references to the architectural splendour of Louis XIV, Louis XV's fashion-mad mistress Madame de Pompadour, and Louis XVI's queen, Marie Antoinette. Countless advertising campaigns have been set at Versailles, still the most coveted imaginary centre of French luxury, over two centuries after the Revolution.

The luxury sector wishes to give lustre to its brands by invoking their pedigree. A bit like a noble family, it uses the past to provide a sense of continuity and success. For some brands, this is no invention. The oldest among them belong to the watch and jewellery market and include brands such as Breguet (est. 1775), Tiffany (1837), Cartier (1847), Bulgari (1884), and the more recent Rolex (1908). The leather and accessories market includes well-known luxury brands established in the nineteenth century such as Hermès (1837), Louis Vuitton (1854), and the early twentieth-century Prada (1913), Ferragamo (1920), and Gucci (1922). By contrast, and with the exception of Burberry (est. 1856) and Chanel (1910), all the best-known luxury brands in clothing and fashion were established after the Second War World: Dior (1946), Givenchy (1952), YSL (1962), Armani (1974), and Versace (1978).[77] To get around this perceived lack of long-term pedigree, some of the most illustrious brands from the history of fashion have in recent years been resurrected by the big luxury conglomerates. For instance, Balenciaga (*maison* closed in 1968) and, more recently still, Schiaparelli (*maison* closed in 1954). The 2013 relaunch of Schiaparelli coincided with the auction sale of Schiaparelli's 1938–9 Zodiac jacket, which achieved a staggering £110,000 and a great deal of publicity.[78] (It is rumoured that this outfit was in the personal wardrobe of Marlene Dietrich.) Similar smart clothes were also seen in the 2011 movie *W.E.* about the Duchess of Windsor filmed by Madonna.

The age of a brand is, of course, not the only indicator of its pedigree. Continuity is just as valuable.[79] We mentioned earlier that two important brands such as Chanel and St Laurent did not even mention their founders on their websites. This is because in both cases they failed to produce an heir and therefore their life stories cannot be told as the foundation of a dynasty.[80] Quite different is the case with Hermès, a company whose CEO, Axel Dumas, is part of the sixth generation of the Hermès family.[81] The same can be said of Bulgari (fourth generation), Esteé Lauder (third generation), Prada (third generation), and Riedel (eleventh generation).[82] The search for a long-term pedigree often also encourages luxury brands to bask in the illustrious reflected glory of previous (famous) owners of their products. Watchmaker Patek, for instance, is proud to have had among its customers Leo Tolstoy, Albert Einstein, Marie Curie, Andy Warhol, Eric Clapton (who collected them), Joe DiMaggio (who celebrated his signing of the first six-figure sum in Major League Baseball with a Patek), Pope Pius IX, and Queen Victoria, who apparently owned the first keyless winding stem Patek.[83] The New York Cartier show in 2009 showed Mary Pickford's vanity case, the tutti-frutti dress clips that belonged to Cole Porter's wife, Grace Kelly's poodle pin, and jewellery belonging to wealthy customers such as Mrs J. P. Morgan and Gertrude Vanderbilt. The show could not do without Elizabeth Taylor's many jewels, including 'La Peregrina', a pear-shaped pearl that had been owned by (among others) Queen Mary I of England and the Spanish queens Margarita and Isabel, before Richard Burton purchased it at auction for Taylor in 1972 (it was then remounted in a necklace of diamonds and rubies by Cartier).[84]

The past is deeply ingrained in many of the products sold by luxury brands. One of the best-known logos in the world, the LV monogram, has been used since it was patented by Georges Vuitton in 1905 and is said to have been inspired by the quatrefoil in stone of the Palazzo Ducale in Venice and other medieval decorative motifs.[85] Tiffany's Blue Box and Hermès' Orange Box have been in use since 1837 and 1945 respectively. Cartier's logo has been in use in a nearly unaltered form since the early twentieth century, and Bulgari's distinctive logo in Roman letters since 1933. Prada still uses the Savoy royal family's coat of arms as the 'official supplier of the Royal Family of Italy' (conferred in 1919), even though Italy has been a republic since 1946.[86]

Prada's attachment to royal symbols is indicative of how luxury capitalism wishes to hide carefully its modern organization behind the veneer of history. Unlike high fashion in clothing, which is now often future oriented, luxury often sees value in the past, even if that is simply understood as 'timelessness'. Frédéric de Narp, president and chief executive of Cartier North America, says that 'there is no fashion at Cartier, there are no seasonal products. There is just the timelessness of something valuable cherished for generation after generation.'[87] Ironically, of course, it was often society women and figures of style, with their fingers very much on the pulse of the times, such as Cartier's jewellery director Jeanne Toussaint, who came up with many of the ideas for those famous Cartier jewels of the 1930s, 1940s, and 1950s, such as the iconic 'big cat', which are now so central to the 'timeless' Cartier image. Such women can hardly be said to have been *beyond* fashion in any sense, although some may well have been *in advance* of it.

The luxury brands today play a major role in the market for elite goods and in reshaping the notion of luxury embraced by most Western and also now many Asian people. The creation of large conglomerates and the emergence of luxury as big business is recent, yet it has had profound implications for our everyday lives. Luxury brands have created new desires, have reshaped communication, have colonized our shopping streets, and have even used history and time itself to create a sense of lineage and pedigree in real or sometimes mythical past.

Conclusion

Luxury: Towards a Richer History

The author J. B. Priestley wrote of England in the 1930s:

> Modern England is rapidly Blackpooling itself. Notice how the very mod-
> ern things, like the film and wireless and sixpenny stores, are absolutely
> democratic, making no distinction whatever between their patrons: if you
> are in a position to accept what they give—and very few people are not in
> that position—then you get neither more nor less than what anybody else
> gets, just as in the popular restaurants there are no special helpings for
> favoured patrons but mathematical portions for everybody. There is almost
> every luxury in this world except the luxury of power or the luxury of pri-
> vacy. (With the result that these are the only luxuries that modern auto-
> crats insist upon claiming for themselves. They are far more austere than
> most of the old tyrants ever were, but they are all greedy for power and
> sticklers for privacy.)[1]

Priestley was not the only one to complain about the debasement of luxury, what he called 'Blackpooling' after the well-known working-class
seaside resort in the north-west of England. He blamed a democracy or
levelling of consumption that provided 'no special helpings for favoured
patrons'. Rising levels of consumption were eroding the traditional luxury
of the upper and the more privileged sections of the middle classes. Power
and privacy remained as the only real surviving luxuries, according to
Priestley.

Fast forward eighty years, and we can hear echoes of Priestley's complaints in many popular and academic treatments of luxury today, though couched in more politically correct tones. One of the leading scholars of fashion, the philosopher Gilles Lipovetsky, observed in the early 2000s that 'Luxury has multiplied and "exploded": there is no longer *one* luxury, but several luxuries, of *various* levels and for different consumers'.[2] Lipovetsky proposed the argument that one can see a 'democraticization' of luxury in which luxury—or better to say access to luxury goods—has come to be perceived as a contemporary 'right'. The other side of the coin is that such a 'right of access to the superfluous' must be supported by a large-scale system of distribution. The luxury market increasingly resembles the contents of a supermarket because it is aimed at satisfying the needs of the masses. The fashion journalist Dana Thomas has written in a similar vein of how luxury has 'lost its lustre' (indeed, this was the subtitle of her book).[3] Lipovetsky, on the other hand, takes a lesson from history and argues instead that new forms of luxury continually emerge aimed at providing something more than 'luxury for everyone'. In this view, luxury is a dynamic entity, continually evolving over time.

Indeed, as we have seen in our journey through the history of luxury in this book, the concept of luxury and the material forms that it assumes have never been fixed in time. The notion of luxury is always historically contingent. The world of Renaissance luxury, for instance, has to be understood in relation to the rise of court culture. A prince's splendid buildings, fine clothing, and fabulous jewellery did not simply express expenditure or consumption—as they might do in the present—but functioned as badges of dignity and honour. The pursuit of luxury at this time was the *duty* of a ruler, as it embodied the riches and power of the state. By the eighteenth century, the notion of luxury had been reconfigured under the pressure of new ideas about its civic and economic value and the influence of new commodities from Asia and other parts of the world. New luxury goods satisfied the aspirations of richer and poorer consumers alike and helped to shape modern consumption patterns and at the same time to drive innovation in manufacturing, at least in Europe. The eighteenth century bears many resemblances to the present, albeit the history of luxury is far from linear. The nineteenth century might be seen as the golden age of luxury, but this was the luxury of the rich entrepreneurial bourgeoisie, of robber-barons and of impecunious noblemen. Luxury became elitist, high class, and whimsical. It was a tool to distinguish a new international class of rich, well-connected, and mundane elites ranging from the 'million dollar princesses', to the interwar jet set and café society. The period from the Second World War to the late twentieth century was, by contrast, one of decreasing wealth inequality.[4] Luxury remained, but its forms were more discreet and its appeal more limited. It was only in the 1980s that luxury reappeared in the media as a leitmotif; yet since then its rise has been meteoric. By the early 2000s it had entered the popular consciousness to such a degree that—as Lipovetsky argues—it came to be perceived as a 'right'.

The latest incarnations of luxury should be read not as some 'absolute', but in the light of the long historical evolution of the concept and the changing material and social practices that it has assumed over time, although this is not to deny that some of the features of contemporary luxury are indeed new. The period since the 1980s has seen a new form of capitalism based on the global production and distribution of 'luxury goods'—bags, clothing, cars, fragrances, and other consumer goods—whose production and distribution rely on ubiquitous and powerful conglomerates. This new form of luxury has found new consumers as well. Its success is based on satisfying what we might call the 'aspirational society', an ever more global society in which consumers increasingly feel they have the 'right' to luxury.

One of the problems of narrating a history of luxury derives from the fact that in each era there was no singular idea of luxury. Luxury—both as a concept and as a material practice—has been the subject of vehement debate and disagreement since antiquity. Both vituperated against and welcomed in almost equal measure, luxury is today both the embodiment of deep inequality and at the same time—some argue—a form of participation in democracy. It is a force of economic growth (a large-scale and expanding industry) as well as the cause of massive consumer debt. It is a source of exploitation of labour (especially in the developing economies), while also providing a vital underpinning for highly skilled craftsmanship and manufacturing ingenuity. These brief contrasting examples help remind us that luxury thrives on its own internal ambiguity.

In our history, we have given space not just to the desires and ambitions of consumers. Production remains an important part of the story of luxury. Throughout its long history, luxury has been linked to skilful craftsmanship and innovation. Often sitting somewhere between the realm of the artist and that of the artisanal craftsman, the producer of luxury goods has pushed the technical, technological, and aesthetic boundaries of the material world since antiquity. Today the idea is prevalent that luxury captures the essence of dying skills: the hand-crafted and labouriously produced object that requires a set of traditional skills, often acquired through years of training. We like the rarity value that such craft production confers, which often of course results in high prices for the finished object. We like to emphasize the local, the unique, and the peculiar, setting these comforting qualities against more alienating narratives of global homogeneity and industrial mass production. The global brands that today dominate the 'luxury industry' understandably struggle to reconcile this aspiration to authenticity, to quality, and to craftsmanship, with the 'industrial' model of their production.

A final, related contradiction that characterizes luxury particularly acutely in the present is a tension between its universalizing ambitions and its innate local nature. Luxury goods are often seen as the 'genuine' fruit of the *genius loci*—a quality captured by the French word *terroir* (as for instance in the case of champagne). Luxury thrives on the knowledge of the particular, of local contexts, and it relies on clearly defined communi-ties of producers and consumers alike. Yet at the same time, luxury—like fashion—aspires to be *global*, to be enjoyed by transnational elites whose only real connection might well be their shared enjoyment of the same luxuries. An international group of rich businessmen meeting in Hawaii might, for instance, have very little in common other than that they are expected to be conversant with the quality of a specific type of champagne from a specific cellar.

As we were finishing the writing of this book, we visited a new type of luxury exhibition entitled 'What is Luxury?', held at the Victoria and Albert Museum in the spring and summer of 2015. This exhibition took a brave stand, and banished shopping bags with large logos or dresses by famous couturiers. There were no 'J'adore Dior' and no LV monograph wallpaper. There was no whisky, cognac, or champagne, or diamond rings, even though such objects understandably represent the essence of luxury for many contemporary consumers. But the very absence of the expected panoply of luxury items from the exhibition posed interesting questions. Might not luxury be moving in exciting directions in the not-too-distant future? For instance, what if currently omnipresent chemical materials deriving from hydrocarbons become scarce? Could plastic then become as rare as gold? Could privacy—as Priestley once suggested—become the ulti-mate new luxury, especially in an age when the vast majority of us will probably have to be 'connected up' online? Can we envisage a future in which luxury and commercial capitalism once again separate from each other? Is it an idle luxury to indulge in such speculation?

NOTES

Introduction. Luxury: A Rich History and a History of Riches

1. Andrew Wallace-Hadrill, *Rome's Cultural Revolution* (Cambridge: Cambridge University Press, 2008), 348.
2. See, e.g., John Sekora, *Luxury: The Concept in Western Thought: Eden to Smollett* (Baltimore: Johns Hopkins University Press, 1977); Christopher Berry, *The Idea of Luxury: A Conceptual and Historical Investigation* (Cambridge: Cambridge University Press, 1994); William Howard Adams, *On Luxury: A Cautionary Tale: A Short History of the Perils of Excess from Ancient Times to the Beginning of the Modern Era* (Washington: Potomac Books, 2012).
3. See, e.g., Maxine Berg, *Luxury and Pleasure in Eighteenth-Century Britain* (Oxford: Oxford University Press, 2005); Berry, *Idea of Luxury*; Richard Goldthwaite, 'The Economy of Renaissance Italy: The Preconditions for Luxury Consumption', *I Tatti Studies in the Italian Renaissance*, 2 (1987), 15–39; Guido Guerzoni, and Gabriele Troilo, 'Silk Purses out of Sows' Ears: Mass Rarefaction of Consumption and the Emerging Consumer-Collector', in Marina Bianchi (ed.), *The Active Consumer* (London: Routledge, 1998), 174–98; Linda Levy Peck, *Consuming Splendor: Society and Culture in Seventeenth-Century England* (Cambridge: Cambridge University Press, 2005). And in French: Jean Castarède, *Le Luxe* (Paris: Puf, 1992); Philippe Perrot, *Le Luxe: Une richesse entre faste et confort, XIIIe–XIXe siècle* (Paris: Seuil, 1995); Jacques Marseille (ed.), *Le Luxe en France du siècle des 'lumières' à nos jours* (Paris: ADHE, 1999); Olivier Assouly and Pierre Bergé (eds), *Le Luxe: Essais sur la fabrique de l'ostentation* (Paris: Institut français de la mode, 2004); Yves Michaud, *Le Nouveau Luxe: Experiences, arrogance, authenticité* (Paris: Éditions Stock, 2013).
4. See, e.g., Robert H. Frank, *Luxury Fever: Money and Happiness in an Era of Excess* (Princeton: Princeton University Press 2000); Dana Thomas, *Deluxe: How Luxury Lost its Lustre* (London: Penguin, 2008).
5. Michaud, *Le Nouveau Luxe*, 56.
6. Olivier Assouly, 'Le Luxe, un art de la dépense', in *Universalia 2011* (Paris: Encyclopaedia Universalis, 2011), 154.
7. Sekora, *Luxury*, 24.
8. Thorstein Veblen, *The Theory of the Leisure Class: An Economic Study of Institutions* (New York: MacMillan, 1899); Georg Simmel, *Philosophie der Mode* (Berlin:

Pan-Verlag, 1905); Werner Sombart, *Luxus und Kapitalismus* (Munich: Duncker & Humblot, 1913; English trans. *Luxury and Capitalism,* Ann Arbor: University of Michigan Press, 1967).

9. Personal communication with Dr Glenn Adamson, Museum of Art and Design, New York.

10. Olivier Assouly and Pierre Bergé (eds), *Le Luxe: Essais sur la fabrique de l'ostentation* (Paris Éditions de l'Institut français de la mode et Éditions du regard, 2005); Berg, *Luxury and Pleasure in Eighteenth-Century Britain*; Berry, *Idea of Luxury*; Jean Castarède, *Histoire du luxe en France* (Paris: Eyrolles, 2007); Goldthwaite, 'The Economy of Renaissance Italy'; Richard Goldthwaite, 'The Empire of Things: Consumer Demand in Renaissance Italy', in Francis William Kent, Patricia Simons, and John Christopher Eade (eds), *Patronage, Art, and Society in Renaissance Italy* (Canberra: Canberra Humanities Research Centre; Oxford: Oxford University Press, 1987), 153–75; Perrot, *Le Luxe*; Thomas, *Deluxe*; Jan de Vries, 'Luxury in the Dutch Golden Age in Theory & Practice', in Maxine Berg and Elizabeth Eger (eds), *Luxury in the Eighteenth Century: Debates, Desires and Delectable Goods* (Basingstoke: Palgrave, 2003), 41–56; Evelyn Welch, *Shopping in the Renaissance: Consumer Cultures in Italy, 1400–1600* (New Haven and London: Yale University Press, 2005).

Chapter 1. Luxury, Antiquity, and the Allure of the Antique

1. Allison Karmel Thomason, *Luxury and Legitimation: Royal Collecting in Ancient Mesopotamia* (Aldershot: Ashgate, 2005).

2. Kelly Olson, 'Matrona and Whore: The Clothing of Women in Roman Antiquity', *Fashion Theory*, 6/4 (2002), 413.

3. John Baines, 'On the Status and Purposes of Ancient Egyptian Art', *Cambridge Archaeological Journal*, 4/1 (1994), 69.

4. Cit. in David Braund, 'The Luxuries of Athenian Democracy', *Greece & Rome*, 41/1 (1994), 44.

5. Braund, 'Luxuries', 46.

6. Cit. in John Sekora, *Luxury: The Concept in Western Thought: Eden to Smollett* (Baltimore: Johns Hopkins University Press, 1977), 35.

7. Krishan Kumar, 'Greece and Rome in the British Empire: Contrasting Role Models', *Journal of British Studies*, 51/1 (2012), 79.

8. Quintillian, *Institutes* 8, pref. 19–20.

9. Cit. in Andrew Dalby, *Empire of Pleasures: Luxury and Indulgence in the Roman World* (London: Routledge, 2000), 267.

10. Cit. in Sekora, *Luxury*, 30.

11. Cit. in Grant Parker, '*Ex Oriente Luxuria*: Indian Commodities and Roman Experience', *Journal of the Economic and Social History of the Orient*, 45/1 (2002), 57.

12. Cit. in Andrew Wallace-Hadrill, *Rome's Cultural Revolution* (Cambridge: Cambridge University Press, 2008), 315.
13. Dalby, *Empire of Pleasures*, 10–11.
14. Francesca C. Tronchin, 'Roman Collecting, Decorating, and Eclectic Practice in the Textual Sources', *Arethusa*, 45 (2012), 338–9.
15. Cit. in Dalby, *Empire of Pleasures*, 271.
16. Lowell Bowdith, 'Propertius and the Gendered Rhetoric of Luxury and Empire: A Reading of 2.16', *Comparative Literature Studies* 43/3 (2006), 315.
17. Giuseppe Dari-Mattiacci and Anna E. Plisecka, 'Luxury in Ancient Rome: An Economic Analysis of the Scope, Timing and Enforcement of Sumptuary Laws', *International Journal of Roman Law, Legal History and Comparative Law*, 1 (2012), 216.
18. Barbara Levick, 'Morals, Politics, and the Fall of the Roman Empire', *Greece & Rome*, 29/1 (1982), 56.
19. John H. D'Arms, 'The Culinary Reality of Roman Upper-Class Convivia: Integrating Texts and Images', *Comparative Studies in Society and History*, 46/3 (2004), 431.
20. Wallace-Hadrill, *Rome's Cultural Revolution*, 329–30.
21. Anton Ervynck, Wim Van Neer, Heide Hüster-Plogmann, and Jörg Schibler, 'Beyond Affluence: The Zooarchaeology of Luxury', *World Archaeology*, 34/3 (2003), 428–41.
22. Corrie Bakels and Stefanie Jacomet, 'Access to Luxury Foods in Central Europe during the Roman Period: The Archaeobotanical Evidence', *World Archaeology*, 34/3 (2003), 542.
23. Ervynck et al., 'Beyond Affluence', 437.
24. Alexandra Livarda, 'Date, Rituals and Socio-Cultural Identity in the North-Western Roman Provinces', *Oxford Journal of Archaeology*, 32/1 (2013), 107, 108.
25. Lucia Amalia Scatozza Höricht, 'Le Orificerie romane', in Rosanna Cappelli (ed.), *Bellezza e lusso: Immagini e documenti di piaceri della vita* (Rome: Leonardo Arte, 1992), 63.
26. A. Heron de Villefosse, 'Le Trésor de Boscoreale', *Monuments et mémoires*, 5 (1899), 39–43.
27. Katherine M. D. Dunbabin, 'The Waiting Servant in Roman Art', *American Journal of Philology*, 124/3 (2003), 444.
28. Dunbabin, 'Waiting Servant', 454.
29. Dunbabin, 'Waiting Servant', 463.
30. Olson, 'Matrona and Whore', 399.
31. Cit. in Scatozza Höricht, 'Le Orificerie romane', 63.
32. Phyllis Culham, 'The "Lex Oppia"', *Latomus*, 41/4 (1982), 788.
33. Culham, '"Lex Oppia"', 793.
34. Courtesy Kelly Olson, communication with the authors.
35. Scatozza Höricht, 'Le Orificerie romane', 65.
36. Olson, 'Matrona and Whore', 387–420. We thank Dr Olson for sharing her work on men's dress currently in progress.

37. Cit. in Neil W. Bernstein, 'Adoptees and Exposed Children in Roman Declamation: Commodification, Luxury and the Threat of Violence', *Classical Philology*, 104 (2009), 339–40.

38. Bernstein, 'Adoptees', 342.

39. Karen Rose Matthews, 'Expressing Political Legitimacy and Cultural Identity through the Use of Spolia on the Ambo of Henry II', *Medieval Encounters*, 5/2 (1999), 156–83.

40. Jonathan Scott, *The Pleasures of Antiquity: British Collectors of Greece and Rome* (New Haven: Yale University Press, 2003), 1.

41. Cit. in Evelyn Welch, *Shopping in the Renaissance: Consumer Cultures in Italy, 1400–1600* (New Haven and London: Yale University Press, 2005), 292.

42. Isobel dos Guimarães Sá, 'The Uses of Luxury: Some Examples from the Portuguese Courts from 1480 to 1580', *Análise social*, 44/192 (2009), 595.

43. Scott, *Pleasures of Antiquity*, 4–5.

44. Scott, *Pleasures of Antiquity*, 13.

45. Scott, *Pleasures of Antiquity*, 14–21.

46. Cit. in Manfred Pfister (ed.), *The Fatal Gift of Beauty: The Italies of British Travellers* (Amsterdam: Rodopi, 1996), 145.

47. Cit. in Christopher Hibbert, *The Grand Tour* (New York: Putnam, 1969), 159.

48. Cit. in S. Sprague Allen, *Tides in English Taste (1619–1800)* (New York: Rowman and Littlefield, 1969), 234–7.

49. Cit. in Scott, *Pleasures of Antiquity*, 221.

50. H. Roux Ainé, *Herculaneum et Pompéi: Recueil général des peintures, bronzes, mosaïques, etc.* (Paris: Librarie de Firmin Didot Frères, 1840), pp. xvi–xvii.

51. Cit. in Diego Saglia, 'Consuming Egypt: Appropriation and the Cultural Modalities of Romantic Luxury', *Nineteenth-Century Contexts*, 24/3 (2002), 324.

52. Cit. in Saglia, 'Consuming Egypt', 320.

53. Saglia, 'Consuming Egypt', 321. The service remained with the Dukes of Wellington until 1979, when it was acquired by the Victoria and Albert Museum. Today all but one plate is on loan to English Heritage and displayed at Apsley House, London.

54. See, e.g., Timothy Mowl, *Horace Walpole: The Great Outsider* (London: John Murray Publishers, 1996).

55. Charles Saumarez Smith, *Eighteenth-Century Decoration: Design and the Domestic Interior in England* (New York: H. N. Abrams, 1993), 237.

56. Cit. in J. Mordaunt Crook, 'Strawberry Hill Revisited – II', *Country Life*, 14 June (1973), 1730.

57. [Horace Walpole], *A Description of the Villa of Mr Horace Walpole, Youngest Son of Sir Robert Walpole Earl of Orford at Strawberry-Hill near Twickenham, Middlesex. With an Inventory of the Furniture, Pictures, Curiosities, &c.* (Strawberry-Hill: Thomas Kirgate, 1784), p. iii.

58. Jeffrey Cass, 'Homoeroticism and Orientalism in William Beckford's *Vathek*: Liberalism and the Problem of Pederasty', in Diane Long Hoeveler and Jeffrey Cass (eds), *Interrogating Orientalism: Contextual Approaches and Pedagogical Practices* (Columbus: Ohio State University Press, 2006), 107–20.

59. Aaron Betsky, *Queer Space: Architecture and Same-sex Desire* (New York: William Morrow & Company, 1997), 70.

60. Anita McConnell, 'William Beckford', in Matthew and Brian Harrison (eds), *Oxford Dictionary of National Biography. From the Earliest Times to the Year 2000* (Oxford: Oxford University Press, 2004), 731–7.

61. William Hazlitt, 'Fonthill Abbey', in *The Complete Works of William Hazlitt*, ed. P. P. Howe, 21 vols (London: J. M. Dent, 1933), xviii. 173.

62. Hazlitt, 'Fonthill Abbey', xviii. 174.

63. Saglia, 'Consuming Egypt', 325.

64. Horace Walpole's letter to his cousin, Henry Conway, 5 August 1761, In J. Mordaunt Crook, 'Strawberry Hill Revisited – I', *Country Life*, 7 June (1973), part I, no pagination in W. S. Lewis's proof copy, Lewis Walpole Library, Yale University.

Chapter 2. Luxury, the Church, and the Court in the
Late Middle Ages and Renaissance

1. Ronald Recht, *Believing and Seeing. The Art of Gothic Cathedrals*, trans. Mary Whittall (Chicago and London: University of Chicago Press, 2008), 114. French edn, 1999.

2. Recht, *Believing and Seeing*, 84.

3. Recht, *Believing and Seeing*, 99.

4. Maureen C. Miller, *Clothing the Clergy: Virtue and Power in Medieval Europe, c.800–1200* (Ithaca, NY: Cornell University Press, 2014), 41.

5. Miller, *Clothing the Clergy*, 45.

6. Miller, *Clothing the Clergy*, 145, 153–6.

7. See, e.g., Susan Mosher Stuard, *Gilding the Market: Luxury and Fashion in Fourteenth-Century Italy* (Philadelphia: University of Pennsylvania Press, 2006).

8. Odile Blanc, 'From Battlefields to Court: The Invention of Fashion in the Fourteenth Century', in Désirée G. Koslin and Janet E. Snyder (eds), *Encountering Medieval Textiles and Dress: Objects, Texts, Images* (New York: Macmillan Palgrave, 2002), 157–72; Sarah-Grace Heller, 'Fashion in French Crusade Literature: Desiring Infidel Textiles', in Koslin and Snyder (eds), *Encountering Medieval Textiles*, 103–19; Françoise Pipponier and Perrine Manne, *Dress in the Middle Ages* (New Haven: Yale University Press, 2000), esp. 99–113.

9. Georges Duby, *Art and Society in the Middle Ages* (Cambridge: Polity Press, 2000), 46. French edn, 1995.

10. Johan Huizinga, *The Waning of the Middle Ages* (1999; Mineola, NY: Dover Publications, 1999), 228.

11. Edwin Hall, *The Arnolfini Betrothal: Medieval Marriage and Enigma of Van Eyck's Double Portrait* (Berkeley and Los Angeles, and London: University of California Press 1994), 115.

12. Daniel Roche, *The Culture of Clothing: Dress and Fashion in the 'Ancien Régime'*, trans. J. Birrell (Cambridge: Cambridge University Press, 1994).

13. See Chapter 3.

14. Luca Molà, *The Silk Industry of Renaissance Venice* (Baltimore: Johns Hopkins University Press, 2000).

15. Lisa Monnas, 'Silk Cloths Purchased for the Great Wardrobe of the Kings of England, 1325–1462', *Textile History*, 20/2 (1989), 283–307; Lisa Monnas, *Merchants, Princes, and Painters: Silk Fabrics in Italian and Northern Paintings, 1300–1500* (New Haven and London: Yale University Press, 2008).

16. Cit. in Jeffrey S. Widmayer, 'The Sumptuary Laws of Manuscript Montpellier H119', *Romance Notes*, 46/2 (2006), 132.

17. Negley B. Harte, 'State Control of Dress and Social Change in Pre-Industrial England', in D. C. Coleman and A. H. John (eds), *Trade, Government and Economy in Pre-Industrial England* (London: Weidenfeld and Nicolson, 1976), 134.

18. Sarah-Grace Heller, 'Anxiety, Hierarchy, and Appearance in Thirteenth-Century Sumptuary Laws and the *roman de la rose*', *French Historical Studies*, 27/2 (2004), 312–13.

19. Heller, 'Anxiety, Hierarchy, and Appearance', 329, 335.

20. Heller, 'Anxiety, Hierarchy, and Appearance', 318.

21. Heller, 'Anxiety, Hierarchy, and Appearance', 319.

22. Law of 1294, cit. in Heller, 'Anxiety, Hierarchy, and Appearance', 345.

23. A. Liva, 'Note sulla legislazione suntuaria nell'Italia centro-settentrionale', in A. G. Cavagna and Graziella Butazzi (eds), *Le trame della moda* (Rome: Bulzoni, 1995), 34.

24. Maria Giuseppina Muzzarelli, 'Il corpo spogliato: Multe, scomuniche e stratagemmi per il rispetto delle leggi suntuarie', *Micrologus*, 15 (2007), 407.

25. Catherine Kovesi Killerby, *Sumptuary Law in Italy, 1200–1500* (Oxford: Oxford University Press, 2002).

26. Helmut Puff, 'The Sodomite's Clothes. Gift-Giving and Sexual Excess in Early Modern Germany and Switzerland', in Anne L. McClanan and Karen Rosoff Encarnacion (eds), *The Material Culture of Sex, Procreation and Marriage in Premodern Europe* (Basingstoke: Palgrave, 2002), 261.

27. Giovanni Pontano, *De splendore* (1498), cit. in Evelyn Welch, 'Public Magnificence and Private Display: Giovanni Pontano's "De Splendore" (1498) and the Domestic Arts', *Journal of Design History*, 15 (2002), 222.

28. Pipponier and Manne, *Dress in the Middle Ages*.

29. Maria Hayward, 'Luxury or Magnificence? Dress at the Court of Henry VIII', *Costume*, 30 (1996), 37. See also Maria Hayward, *Dress at the Court of King Henry VIII* (Leeds: Maney, 2007).

30. Hayward, 'Luxury or Magnificence?', 39.

31. Anne F. Sutton, 'Order and Fashion in Clothes: The King, his Household and the City of London at the End of the Fifteenth Century', *Textile History*, 22/2 (1991), 253–76.

32. Kay Staniland, 'Clothing Provision and the Great Wardrobe in the Mid-Thirteenth Century', *Textile History*, 22/2 (1991), 239–52.

33. Yassana Croizat, '"Living Dolls": François I Dresses his Women', *Renaissance Quarterly*, 60/1 (2007), 94–130.

34. For an anthropological analysis of colours in history and their meaning, see the extensive work by Pastoreau. Michel Pastoreau, *Colours of our Memories* (Cambridge: Polity, 2012); and his 'colour trilogy': Michel Pastoreau, *Blue: The History of a Color* (Princeton: Princeton University Press, 2001); *Black: The History of a Color* (Princeton: Princeton University Press, 2008); *Green: The History of a Color* (Princeton: Princeton University Press, 2014).

35. Janet Arnold, *Elizabeth's Wardrobe Unlock'd* (Leeds: Maney & Son, 1988); Susan Frye, 'Sewing Connections: Elizabeth Tudor, Mary Stuart, Elizabeth Talbot, and Seventeenth-Century Anonymous Needleworkers', in Susan Frye and Karen Robertson (eds), *Maids and Mistresses, Cousins and Queens: Women's Alliances in Early Modern England* (New York: Oxford University Press, 1999), 165–82. See also Ann Rosalind Jones and Peter Stallybrass, *Renaissance Clothing and the Materials of Memory* (Cambridge: Cambridge University Press, 2000); Roy Strong, *Portraits of Queen Elizabeth I* (Oxford: Clarendon Press, 1963); Margaret Swain, *Figures on Fabric: Embroidery Design Sources and Their Application* (London: Adam & Charles Black, 1980).

36. Cit. in Aileen Ribeiro, *Fashion and Fiction: Dress in Art and Literature in Stuart England* (New Haven and London: Yale University Press, 2005), 81.

37. Timothy Mowl, *Elizabethan and Jacobean Style* (London: Phaidon, 2001), 22.

38. Christy Anderson, 'Monstrous Babels: Language and Architectural Style in the English Renaissance', in Georgia Clarke and Paul Crossley (eds), *Architecture and Language: Constructing Identity in European Architecture, 1000–1600* (Cambridge: Cambridge University Press, 2000), 160.

39. Anderson, 'Monstrous Babels', 161.

40. 'The Sea-Dog Table', in Gervase Jackson-Stops (ed.), *Treasure Houses of England. Five Hundred Years of Private Patronage and Art Collecting* (National Gallery of Art, Washington, New Haven, and London: Yale University Press, 1985), 108–10.

41. 'Sea-Dog Table', 108–10.

42. *Chambers' Cyclopaedia* (1728, 2 vols, with the 1753 supplement): digitized by the University of Wisconsin Digital Collections Center.

43. Pamela Clabburn, *The National Trust Book of Furnishing Textiles* (London: Viking, 1988), 189–90.

44. Laurence Fontaine, *The Moral Economy: Poverty, Credit, and Trust in Early Modern Europe* (Cambridge: Cambridge University Press, 2014), 223.

45. Ribeiro, *Fashion and Fiction*, 96.

46. Johan Huizinga, *The Autumn of the Middle Ages*, trans. Rodney J. Payton and Ulrich Mammitzsch (Chicago: University of Chicago Press 1996), pp. xv–xvi.

47. Lars Kjaer and A. J. Watson, 'Feasts and Gifts: Sharing Food in the Middle Ages', *Journal of Medieval History*, 37 (2011), 3.

48. Kjaer and Watson, 'Feasts and Gifts', 2.

49. Thomas DaCosta Kaufmann, *Court, Cloister & City: The Art and Culture of Central Europe 1450–1800* (Chicago: University of Chicago Press, 1995), 25

50. Baldessare Castiglione, *The Book of the Courtier*, ed. Leonard Eckstein (New York: Scribner's, 1903), 278.

51. Maria Bogucka, 'Gesture, Ritual, and Social Order in Sixteenth- to Eighteenth-Century Poland', in Jan Bremmer and Herman Roodenburg (eds), *A Cultural History of Gesture* (Ithaca, NY, 1991), 190–209.

52. Norbert Elias, *The Civilizing Process*, trans. Edmund Jephcot, 2 vols (Oxford: Blackwell, 1982).

53. Peter Burke, *The Italian Renaissance* (2nd edn, Princeton: Princeton University Press, 1987), 9.

54. On this point, see George W. McClure, *The Culture of Profession in Late Renaissance Italy* (Toronto: University of Toronto Press, 2004), 155, 167.

55. Cit. in Umberto Eco, *Art and Beauty in the Middle Ages* (New Haven: Yale University Press, 1986), 9.

56. Welch, 'Public Magnificence', 211–21.

57. Luigi Prestinenza Puglisi, *HyperArchitecture: Spaces in the Electronic Age* (Basle: Birkhäuser, 1999).

58. Cit. in Leora Auslander, *Taste and Power: Furnishing Modern France* (Berkeley and Los Angeles, and London: University of California Press, 1996), 91.

59. Auslander, *Taste and Power*, 51.

60. Auslander, *Taste and Power*.

61. Lawrence Stone, *The Crisis of the Aristocracy, 1558–1641* (Oxford: Oxford University Press, 1965), 266.

Chapter 3. Luxury and the Exotic: The Appeal of the Orient

1. NBC News, 'Ming Bling: $36M for "Chicken Cup" in Record for China Porcelain' <http://www.bloomberg.com/news/2014-04-08/-chicken-cup-sets-china-auction-record-with-36-million.html> (accessed 2 November 2015).

2. 'Imperial Chinese Porcelain. Meiyintang Marvels: The Finest Private Collection of Chinese Porcelain in the West is about to be Sold', *The Economist*, 17 March 2011 <http://www.economist.com/node/18385704> (accessed 2 November 2015).

3. Peter Stabel, '"Le Goût pour l'Orient": Demande cosmopolite et objets de luxe à Bruges à la fin du Moyen Âge', *Histoire urbaine*, 30/1 (2011), 22.

4. Paul Freedman, 'Spices and Late-Medieval European Ideas of Scarcity and Value', *Speculum*, 80 (2005), 1209.

5. Cit. in Muriel J. Hughes, 'Marco Polo and Medieval Silk', *Textile History*, 6 (1975), 121.

6. Cit. in Hughes, 'Marco Polo', 121.

7. Cit. in Hughes, 'Marco Polo', 123.

8. François Bernier, *Travels in the Mogul Empire AD 1656–1668*, ed. Archibald George Constable (London: Oxford University Press, 1916), 268.

9. Bernier, *Travels in the Mogul Empire*, 268.

10. Bernier, *Travels in the Mogul Empire*, 269.

11. Bernier, *Travels in the Mogul Empire*, 269.

12. Mark Zebrowski, 'Glamour and Restraint', in *First under Heaven: The Art of Asia* (London: Hali Publications Limited, 1997), 171–2.

13. Zebrowski, 'Glamour and Restraint', 177.

14. Gülru Necipolu, 'Süleyman the Magnificent and the Representation of Power in the Context of Ottoman–Hapsburg-Papal Rivarly', *Art Bulletin*, 71/3 (1989), 401–27.

15. Opher Mansour, 'Picturing Global Conversion: Art and Diplomacy at the Court of Paul V', *Journal of Early Modern History*, 17/5 (2013), 532.

16. Giorgio Riello, '"With Great Pomp and Magnificence": Royal Gifts and the Embassies between Siam and France in the 1680s', in Zoltán Biedermann, Anne Gerritsen, and Giorgio Riello (eds), *Global Gifts: The Material Culture of Diplomacy in Early Modern Eurasia* (forthcoming).

17. Sanjay Subrahmanyam, *Courtly Encounters: Translating Courtliness and Violence in Early Modern Eurasia* (Cambridge, MA.: Harvard University Press, 2012), 172.

18. Cit. in Maria Ruvoldt, 'Sacred to Secular, East to West: The Renaissance Study and Strategies of Display', *Renaissance Studies*, 20/5 (2006), 652–3.

19. Isobel dos Guimarães Sá, 'The Uses of Luxury: Some Examples from the Portuguese Courts from 1480 to 1580', *Análise social*, 44/192 (2009), 592.

20. Sabine Haag, *Ambras Castle in Innsbruck* (Vienna: Ambras Casle, 2013).

21. Richard Hakluyt, *The Principal Navigations, Voyages, Traffiques, and Discoveries of the English Nation* (Glasgow: J. MacLehose and Sons, 1903–5), vii. 116–17.

22. Hakluyt, *The Principal Navigations*, vii. 117.

23. Hakluyt, *The Principal Navigations*, vii. 117.

24. Stabel, '"Le Gout pour l'Orient"', 28.

25. R. W. Lightbown, 'Oriental Art and the Orient in Late Renaissance and Baroque Italy', *Journal of the Warburg and Courtauld Institutes*, 32 (1969), 228–79. They are

extremely rare, as only sixty-two pieces are known to exist. They are distinctive by their mark bearing the symbol of the cathedral of Santa Maria Novella in Florence. Nine of the sixty-two known pieces are at the Musée de Sèvres on the outskirts of Paris.

26. This was the case not just in Europe, but also, for example, in India and Persia. See Anne Gerritsen and Giorgio Riello, 'Spaces of Global Interactions: The Material Landscapes of Global History', in Anne Gerritsen and Giorgio Riello (eds), *Writing Material Culture History* (London: Bloomsbury, 2015), 112.

27. See Gerritsen and Riello, 'Spaces of Global Interactions', 111.

28. Daniel Walker, *Flowers Underfoot: Indian Carpets of the Mughal Era* (London: Thames and Hudson, 1998).

29. Anne Goldar, *Tulipmania: Money, Honor, and Knowledge in the Dutch Golden Age* (Chicago: University of Chicago Press, 2007).

30. H. Walter Lack, *Garden Eden: Masterpieces of Botanical Illustration* (Cologne: Taschen, 2001).

31. Jenny Uglow, *A Little History of British Gardening* (London: Chatto and Windus, 2004); Ronald Blythe, 'Heavens on Earth: Writers and Gardens', *Country Life*, 1 May (1986), 1172–4; Carolyn Fry, *The Plant Hunters: The Adventures of the World's Greatest Botanical Explorers* (Chicago: University of Chicago Press, 2013).

32. Peter McNeil, 'Everlasting: The Flowers in Fashion and Textiles', in Roger Leong (ed.), *Everlasting: The Flowers in Fashion and Textiles* (Melbourne: National Gallery of Victoria, 2005), 14–23.

33. Beverly Lemire and Giorgio Riello, 'East and West: Textiles and Fashion in Eurasia in the Early Modern Period', *Journal of Social History*, 41/4 (2008), 887–916.

34. Beverly Lemire, 'Domesticating the Exotic: Floral Culture and the East India Calico Trade with England, *c.*1600–1800', *Textile: The Journal of Cloth and Culture*, 1/1 (2003), 65–85.

35. See John Styles, *The Dress of the People: Everyday Fashion in Eighteenth-Century England* (New Haven: Yale University Press, 2007); Beverly Lemire, *Fashion's Favourite: Cotton Trade and the Consumer in Britain, 1660–1800* (Oxford: Oxford University Press, 1992).

36. Giorgio Riello, *Cotton: The Fabric that Made the Modern World* (Cambridge: Cambridge University Press, 2013), esp. ch. 7.

37. Monika Bincsik, 'European Collectors and Japanese Merchants of Lacquer in "Old Japan"', *Journal of the History of Collections*, 20/2 (2008), 218.

38. Danielle O Kisluk-Grosheide, 'A Japanned Cabinet in the Metropolitan Museum of Art', *Metropolitan Museum Journal*, 19/20 (1986), 85.

39. Alexandra Curvelo, 'The Disruptive Presence of the Namban-*jin* in Early Modern Japan', *Journal of the Economic and Social History of the Orient*, 55 (2012), 584–5.

40. Rhonda K. Garelick, *Mademoiselle: Coco Chanel and the Pulse of History* (New York: Random House, 2014).

41. See Simon Schama, *The Embarrassment of Riches: An Interpretation of Dutch Culture in the Golden Age* (London: HarperCollins, 1987).

42. Bernard Mandeville, *The Fable of the Bees; or, Private Vices, Public Benefits...* (London: C. Bathurst, 1795), 42.

43. Maxine Berg and Helen Clifford, 'Introduction', in Maxine Berg and Helen Clifford (eds), *Consumers and Luxury: Consumer Culture in Europe, 1650–1850* (Manchester: Manchester University Press, 1999), 3.

44. Jan de Vries, 'Luxury in the Dutch Golden Age in Theory and Practice', in Maxine Berg and Elizabeth Eger (eds), *Luxury in the Eighteenth Century: Debates, Desires and Delectable Goods* (Basingstoke: Palgrave, 2003), 43.

45. Olivier Assouly, 'Le Luxe, un art de la dépense', in *Universalia 2011* (Paris: Encyclopaedia Universalis, 2011), 152.

46. Cissie Fairchilds, 'The Production and Marketing of Populuxe Goods in Eighteenth-Century Paris', in John Brewer and Roy Porter (eds), *Consumption and the World of Goods* (London and New York, 1993), 228–48.

47. Cit. in Brenda Collins, 'Matters Material and Luxurious: Eighteenth and Early Nineteenth-Century Irish Linen Consumption', in Jacqueline Hill and Colm Lennon (eds), *Luxury and Austerity* (Dublin: University College Dublin Press, 1999), 114.

48. Maxine Berg, 'New Commodities, Luxuries and their Consumers in Eighteenth-Century England', in Berg and Clifford (eds), *Consumers and Luxury*, 63–85. See also Maxine Berg, *Luxury and Pleasure in Eighteenth-Century Britain* (Oxford: Oxford University Press, 2005). A more cautious view is expressed for the seventeenth century by Linda Levy Peck, *Consuming Splendor: Society and Culture in Seventeenth-Century England* (Cambridge: Cambridge University Press, 2005).

49. Giorgio Riello, 'Asian Knowledge and the Development of Calico Printing in Europe in the Seventeenth and Eighteenth Centuries', *Journal of Global History*, 5/1 (2010), 1–29.

50. Christine Velut, 'Between Invention and Production: The Role of Design in the Manufacture of Wallpaper in France and England at the Turn of the Nineteenth Century', *Journal of Design History*, 17/1 (2004), 55–69.

51. John Cornforth, *Early Georgian Interiors* (New Haven and London: Yale University Press, 2004).

52. M. Cassidy-Geiger (ed.), *Fragile Diplomacy: Meissen Porcelain for European Courts, ca. 1710–63* (New Haven and London: Yale University Press, 2007).

53. Oliver Impey, 'Japanese Export Art of the Edo Period and its Influences on European Art', *Modern Asian Studies*, 18/4 (1984), 686–7.

54. Impey, 'Japanese Export Art', 688.

55. Christoph Jeggle, 'Economies of Quality as a Concept of Research on Luxury', in Rengenier C. Rittersma (ed.), *Luxury in the Low Countries: Miscellaneous Reflections on Netherlandish Material Culture, 1500 to the Present* (Brussels: Pharo Publishing, 2010), 36.

56. Paul F. Hsai, 'Chinoiserie in Eighteenth Century England', *American Journal of Chinese Studies*, 4 (1997), 239.

57. David Porter, 'Chinoiserie and the Aesthetics of Illegitimacy', *Studies in Eighteenth-Century Culture*, 28 (1999), 27–54.

58. Cit. in David M. Mitchell, 'The Influence of Tartary and the Indies on Social Attitudes and Material Culture in England and France, 1650–1730', in Anna Jolly (ed.), *A Taste for the Exotic: Foreign Influences on Early Eighteenth-Century Silk Design* (Riggisberg: Abegg-Stiftung, 2007), 31.

59. Mitchell, 'Influence of Tartary', 42.

60. Ulrike Grimm, 'Favourite, a Rare Place Exuding the Spirit of an Age when Chinoiseries Reigned Supreme', in Jolly (ed.), *A Taste for the Exotic*, 85

61. *London Chronicle*, 9–12 April 1757, vol. 1, 348.a

62. Molière's *bourgeois gentilhomme*: see full text at <http://www.gutenberg.org/files/2992/2992-h/2992-h.htm> (accessed 2 November 2015).

63. 'Turquerie', *Metropolitan Museum of Art Bulletin*, 26/5 (1968), 233.

64. Julia Anne Ladweber, 'Turkish Delight: The Eighteenth-Century Market in Turqueries and the Commercialization of Identity in France', *Proceedings of the Western Society for French History*, 30 (2002), 206–7. See also Alexander Bevilacqua and Helen Pfeifer, 'Turqueries: Culture in Motion, 1650–1750', *Past & Present*, 221 (2014), 75–118.

65. Cit. in Ladweber, 'Turkish Delight', 204.

66. Fairchilds, 'The Production and Marketing of Populuxe Goods', 230.

67. Wan-Chen Chang, 'The Goncourt Brothers' Chinese Art Collection', in *A Taste for China: Paris 1743–1930* (Paris: Musée Guimet and Hong Kong Museum of Art, 2008), 101.

68. Chang, 'The Goncourt Brothers' Chinese Art Collection', 111–12.

69. Chang, 'The Goncourt Brothers' Chinese Art Collection', 113.

70. Marie-Catherine Rey, 'A Taste for China: A Portrait of the French Lover of Chinese Art', in *A Taste for China*, 41–2.

71. Phyllis Floyd, 'Documentary Evidence for the Availability of Japanese Imagery in Europe in Nineteenth-Century Public Collections', *Art Bulletin*, 68/1 (1986), 106.

72. P.-A. Renoir, 'Grammar 1883–84' (unpublished manuscript), cit. in Robert L. Herbert, *Nature's Workshop: Renoir's Writings on the Decorative Arts* (New Haven and London: Yale University Press, 2000), 152.

73. Jean-Paul Desroches, 'Artistic Paris in the 1930s', in *A Taste for China*, 128–31.

74. Monika Bincsik, 'European Collectors and Japanese Merchants of Lacquer in "Old Japan"', *Journal of the History of Collection*, 20 (2008), 222.

75. He later authored, as a result of his 1876–7 travels in Japan, Christopher Dresser, *Japan: Its Architecture, Art and Art Manufactures* (London: Longmans, 1882).

76. Ellen E. Roberts, 'A Marriage of "The Extreme East and the Extreme West": Japanism and Aestheticism in Louis Comfort Tiffany's Rooms in the Bella Apartments', *Studies in the Decorative Arts*, 13/2 (2006), 9–11.

77. Cit. in Joe Earle, 'The Taxonomic Obsession: British Collectors and Japanese Objects, 1852–1986', *Burlington Magazine*, 128/1005 (1986), 865.

78. Bincsik, 'European Collectors', 223.

79. See, e.g., the bestseller Edmund De Waal, *The Hare with Amber Eyes: A Hidden Inheritance* (London: Vintage, 2011), whose narrative rotates around a collection of *netsukes* inherited from the author's uncle.

80. Cit. in Phyllis Floyd, 'Documentary Evidence for the Availability of Japanese Imagery in Europe in Nineteenth-Century Public Collections', *Art Bulletin*, 68/1 (1986), 115.

81. Roger Scruton, *Beauty: A Very Short Introduction* (Oxford: Oxford University Press, 2009), 168.

82. Robert Baldick, 'Introduction', in Joris-Karl Huysmans, *Against Nature (A Rebours)*, trans. Robert Baldick (Harmondsworth: Penguin, 1959), 13. (Original edn 1884.)

83. Edgar Munhall, *Whistler and Montesquiou: The Butterfly and the Bat* (New York and Paris: Frick Collection/Flammarion, 1995).

84. 'Fiat Chrysler to Spin off Ferrari into Separate Unit' <www.bbc.com/news/business-29817720> (accessed 2 November 2015).

Chapter 4. Housing Luxury: From the *Hôtel Particulier*
to the Manhattan Cooperatives

1. Mariana Valverde, 'The Love of Finery: Fashion and the Fallen Woman in Nineteenth-Century Social Discourse', *Victorian Studies*, 32/2 (1989), 168–88.

2. On the concept of comfort, see John E. Crowley, *The Invention of Comfort: Sensibilities and Design in Early Modern Britain and Early America* (Baltimore: Johns Hopkins University Press, 2001).

3. Ursula Priestley and Penelope J. Corfield, 'Rooms and Room Use in Norwich Housing, 1580–1730', *Post-Medieval Archaeology*, 16 (1982), 93–123.

4. Richard Wilson and Alan Mackley, *Creating Paradise: The Building of the English Country House 1660–1880* (London and New York: Hambledon and London, 2000).

5. Peter Thorold, *The London Rich: The Creation of a Great City from 1666 to the Present* (London: Viking, 1999).

6. M[onsieur] D'Archenholz (Johann Wilhelm von Archenholz), *A Picture of England: Containing a Description of the Laws, Customs, and Manners of England* (London: Edward Jeffery, 1789), i. 148–9.

7. D'Archenholz, *A Picture of England*, i. 148–9.

8. Daniel Roche, *The People of Paris: An Essay in Popular Culture in the 18th Century* (Leamington Spa: Berg, 1987), and Daniel Roche, *A History of Everyday Things:*

The Birth of Consumption in France, 1600–1800 (Cambridge: Cambridge University Press, 2000).

9. Katie Scott, *The Rococo Interior: Decoration and Social Spaces in Early Eighteenth-Century Paris* (New Haven and London: Yale University Press, 1995), 86.

10. R. G. Saisselin, 'Neo-Classicism: Images of Public Virtue and Realities of Private Luxury', *Art History*, 4/1 (1981), 15. See also Charissa Bremer-David (ed.), *Paris: Life & Luxury in the Eighteenth Century* (Los Angeles: Paul Getty Museum, 2011).

11. Rochelle Ziskin, *The Place Vendôme: Architecture and Social Mobility in Eighteenth-Century Paris* (Cambridge: Cambridge University Press, 1999), 2.

12. Scott, *Rococo Interior*, 104.

13. Saisselin, 'Neo-Classicism', 14.

14. Piero Camporesi, *Exotic Brew: The Art of Living in the Age of Enlightenment*, trans. Christopher Woodall (Cambridge: Polity Press, 1994).

15. Colin Jones, *Madame de Pompadour: Image of a Mistress* (London: National Gallery and Yale University Press, 2002), 51.

16. Saisselin, 'Neo-Classicism', 20.

17. Saisselin, 'Neo-Classicism', 20, 30.

18. Ziskin, *Place Vendôme*.

19. Mimi Hellman, 'Furniture, Sociability, and the Work of Leisure in Eighteenth-Century France', *Eighteenth-Century Studies*, 32/4 (1999), 415–45.

20. Ziskin, *Place Vendôme*, 24, 48–9.

21. Jean-François de Bastide, *The Little House: An Architectural Seduction*, trans. Rodolphe el-Khoury (Princeton: Princeton Architectural Press, 1996), introduction by R. el-Khoury, 'Architecture in the Bedroom', 19–54; extract, 57–110.

22. See also Chapter 3.

23. John Carr, *The Stranger in France, or, a Tour from Devonshire to Paris, Illustrated by Engravings in Aqua Tinta of Sketches Taken on the Spot* (London: J. Johnson, 1803), 184.

24. Yannick Chastang, *Paintings in Wood: French Marquetry Furniture* (London: Wallace Collection, 2001).

25. John Morley, *Furniture: The Western Tradition. History. Style. Design* (London: Thames and Hudson, 1999).

26. Reed Benhamou, 'Imitation in the Decorative Arts of the Eighteenth Century', *Journal of Design History*, 4/1 (1991), 4.

27. Carolyn Sargentson, *Merchants and Luxury Markets: The* Marchands Merciers *of Eighteenth-Century Paris* (Malibu and London: Victoria and Albert Museum and the J. Paul Getty Museum, 1996).

28. Bettina Dietz and Thomas Nutz, 'Collections Curieuses': The Aesthetics of Curiosity and Elite Lifestyle in Eighteenth-Century Paris', *Eighteenth-Century Life*, 29/3 (2006), 54.

29. Dietz and Thomas Nutz, '*Collections Curieuses*'.

30. Jones, *Madame de Pompadour*, 105–7.

31. See also Chapter 1.

32. Alan Phipps Darr et al., *The Dodge Collection of Eighteenth-Century French and English Art in the Detroit Institute of Arts* (New York: Hudson Hills Press, 1996), 55.

33. Anna Jolly (ed.), *Fürstliche Interieurs: Dekorationstextilien des 18. Jahrhunderts* (Riggisberg: Abegg-Stiftung, 2005).

34. Leora Auslander, *Taste and Power: Furnishing Modern France* (Berkeley and Los Angeles, and London: University of California Press, 1996).

35. Mark Evans (ed.), *Princes as Patrons: The Art Collections of the Princes of Wales from the Renaissance to the Present Day. An Exhibition from the Royal Collection* (London: Merrell Holberton and National Museums & Galleries of Wales and the Royal Collection, 1998), 69–120.

36. Peter Mandler, *The Fall and Rise of the Stately Home* (New Haven: Yale University Press, 1997), 63.

37. John Martin Robinson, *The Latest Country Houses, 1945–83* (London, Sydney, and Toronto: Bodley Head, 1984), 40.

38. Francis Watson, 'Mentmore and its Art Collections', in *Mentmore: Catalogue of French and Continental Furniture, Tapestries and Clocks*, sold on behalf of the Executors of the 6th Earl of Roseberry and his family. *Vol. 1. Furniture* (London: Sotheby Parke Bernet, May 1977), p. x.

39. Christoper Wilk (ed.), *Western Furniture, 1350 to the Present Day* (London: Philip Wilson and Victoria and Albert Museum, 1996), 13.

40. Yannick Chastang, *Paintings in Wood: French Marquetry Furniture* (London: Wallace Collection, 2001), 66.

41. Donald Albrecht and Jeannine Falino, 'An Aristocracy of Wealth', in Donald Albrecht and Jeannine Falino (eds), *Gilded New York: Design, Fashion, and Society* (New York: Museum of the City of New York and Monacelli Press, 2013), 22. Jeannine Falino, 'Blazed with Diamonds: New Yorkers and the Pursuit of Jeweled Ornament', in Albrecht and Falino (eds), *Gilded New York*, 75.

42. Bernard Morel, *The French Crown Jewels: The Objects of the Coronations of the Kings and Queens of France Followed by a History of the French Crown Jewels from Francois I up to the Present Time* (Antwerp: Fonds Mercator, 1988), 375.

43. Albrecht and Falino, 'An Aristocracy of Wealth', 22.

44. Michael Hall, *The Victorian Country House: From the Archives of County Life* (London: Aurum, 2009), 16.

45. Hall, *Victorian Country House*, 17–18.

46. Hall, *Victorian Country House*, 19.

47. Jane Ridley, *Bertie: A Life of Edward VII* (London: Chatto and Windus, 2012), 271.

48. Anne de Courcy, *Margot at War: Love and Betrayal in Downing Street, 1912–1916* (London: Weidenfeld and Nicolson, 2014), 37.

49. Hall, *Victorian Country House*, 158.

50. Hall, *Victorian Country House*, 158.

51. Note written by Renoir in 1883–4, cit. in Robert L. Herbert, *Nature's Workshop: Renoir's Writings on the Decorative Arts* (New Haven and London: Yale University Press), 120.

52. Consuelo Vanderbilt Balsan, *The Glitter and the Gold: The American Duchess—in her Own Words* (1953; London: Hodder & Stoughton, 2012), 22.

53. Vanderbilt Balsan, *The Glitter and the Gold*, 9; see also p. 72 in this book for the Field of the Cloth of Gold.

54. Mandler, *Fall and Rise*, 93.

55. Mandler, *Fall and Rise*, 163.

56. Oliver Garnett et al., *Standen, West Sussex* (London: National Trust, 1993), 40.

57. Oliver Garnett et al., *Standen, West Sussex*, 43.

58. *The Jewels and Objets de Vertu of The Honorable Clare Booth Luce* (New York: Sotheby's, 19 April 1988), no pagination.

59. Cit. in Charlotte Gere and Marina Vaizey, *Great Women Collectors* (London: Philip Wilson Publishers and Harry N. Abrams, 1999), 156.

60. Ruth Brandon, *The Dollar Princesses: The American Invasion of the European Aristocracy 1870–1914* (London: Weidenfeld and Nicolson, 1980).

61. Clive Aslet, *An Exuberant Catalogue of Dreams: The Americans who Revived the Country House in Britain* (London: Aurum Press, 2013), 90–7.

62. Robinson, *Latest Country Houses*, 27.

63. De Courcy, *Margot at War*, 43–50.

64. De Courcy, *Margot at War*, 93–4. The famous couturier Lucille, Lady Duff Gordon, was one of the survivors.

65. Robinson, *Latest Country Houses*, 44.

66. Greg King, *A Season of Splendour: The Court of Mrs Astor in Gilded Age New York* (Hoboken, NJ: John Wiley and Sons, 2009), 393–4.

67. For the definitive account of the decline of the British land-owning classes see David Cannadine, *Aspects of Aristocracy: Grandeur and Decline in Modern Britain* (New Haven and London: Yale University Press, 1994).

68. Michael Hall, *The Victorian Country House: From the Archives of County Life* (London: Aurum Press, 2009), 75.

69. Hall, *Victorian Country House*, 95.

70. *Christie's Magazines*, June–July–August 2000, *Collecting Issue*, 42.

71. Cit. in *Christie's Magazines*, June–July–August 2000, *Collecting Issue*, 42

72. *Christie's Magazines*, June–July–August 2000, *Collecting Issue*, 45.

73. Steven Gaines, *The Sky's the Limit: Passion and Property in Manhattan* (New York: Back Bay Books, 2006), 41–2.

74. 'List of Countries by the Number of US Dollar Billionaires' <http://en.wikipedia.org/wiki/List_of_countries_by_the_number_of_US_dollar_billionaires> (accessed 1 March 2015).

75. Gaines, *Sky's the Limit*, 77.

76. Gaines, *Sky's the Limit*, 3.
77. Gaines, *Sky's the Limit*, 7.
78. Gaines, *Sky's the Limit*, 2.
79. Gaines, *Sky's the Limit*, 174–7.
80. Molly W. Berger, *Hotel Dreams: Luxury, Technology, and Urban Ambition in America, 1829–1929* (Baltimore: Johns Hopkins University Press, 2011).
81. Huguette Clark, 'Reclusive Heiress, Dies at 104', *New York Times*, 24 May 2011. See also Bill Dedman and Paul Clark Newell, Jr, *Empty Mansions: The Mysterious Life of Huguette Clark and the Spending of a Great American Fortune* (New York: Random House, 2013).
82. *An American Dynasty: The Clark Family Treasures* (New York: Christie's, Spring 2014).

Chapter 5. Luxury and Decadence at the Turn of the Twentieth Century

1. Arjun Appadurai (ed.), *The Social Life of Things: Commodities in Cultural Perspective* (Cambridge: Cambridge University Press, 1986).
2. Jane Ridley, *Bertie: A Life of Edward VII* (London: Chatto and Windus, 2012).
3. Elsie de Wolfe, *The House in Good Taste* (1913; New York, Rizzoli, 2004), 25.
4. Sîan Evans, *Mrs Ronnie: The Society Hostess who Collected Kings* (London: National Trust Books, 2013), 55.
5. Cit. in Anne De Courcy, *Diana Mosley* (London: Vintage Books, 2004), 201.
6. Cit. in Evans, *Mrs Ronnie*, 87.
7. Evans, *Mrs Ronnie*, 150. Mrs Greville left an estate worth approximately £39 million in 2010 money. Her wines were sold at auction and included 1,000 bottles of claret. Evans, *Mrs Ronnie*, 166.
8. De Wolfe, *House in Good Taste*, 134.
9. Alistair O'Neill, *London: After a Fashion* (London: Reaktion, 2007).
10. William Shawcross, *The Queen Mother: The Official Biography* (New York: Alfred P. Knopf, 2009), 692.
11. Shawcross, *Queen Mother*, 164.
12. De Wolfe, *House in Good Taste*, 141.
13. De Courcy, *Diana Mosley*, 306.
14. Edgar Munhall, *Whistler and Montesquiou: The Butterfly and the Bat* (New York and Paris: Frick Collection/Flammarion, 1995).
15. Robert Baldick, 'Introduction', in Joris-Karl Huysmans, *Against Nature (A Rebours)*, trans. Robert Baldick (Harmondsworth: Penguin, 1959). (Original edn 1884.)
16. Munhall, *Whistler and Montesquiou*. Pierre Arizzoli-Clémentel, *The Textile Museum, Lyons* (Paris: Musées et Monuments de France, 1996).

17. John McMullin, 'We Went to India', British *Vogue* (December 1938).

18. Charles Scheips, *Elsie de Wolfe's Paris: Frivolity before the Storm* (New York: Harry N. Abrams, 2014).

19. 'Brilliant Balls in Paris', British *Vogue*, 9 August 1939.

20. Sam Staggs, *Inventing Elsa Maxwell: How an Irrepressible Nobody Conquered High Society, Hollywood, the Press and the World* (London: St Martin's Press, 2012).

21. Donald Albrecht and Jeannine Falino, 'An Aristocracy of Wealth', in Donald Albrecht and Jeannine Falino (eds), *Gilded New York: Design, Fashion, and Society* (New York: Museum of the City of New York and Monacelli Press, 2013), 45.

22. Deborah Davis, *Party of the Century: The Fabulous Story of Truman Capote and the Black and White Ball* (Hoboken, NJ: John Wiley & Sons, 2006).

23. Lee Radziwill, *Happy Times* (New York: Assouline, 2000), 58.

24. Phyllis Magidson, 'A Fashionable Equation: Maison Worth and the Clothes of the Gilded Age', in Albrecht and Falino (eds), *Gilded New York*, 111.

25. Amy de la Haye and Valerie D. Mendes, *The House of Worth: Portrait of an Archive* (London: V&A Publishing, 2014), 56.

26. Jeannine Falino, 'Blazed with Diamonds: New Yorkers and the Pursuit of Jeweled Ornament', in Albrecht and Falino (eds), *Gilded New York*, 59.

27. Robert L. Herbert, *Nature's Workshop: Renoir's Writings on the Decorative Arts* (New Haven and London: Yale University Press, 2000), 36–7.

28. Shawn Waldron, 'Horst's World in Colour', in S. Brown (ed.), *Horst: Photographer of Style* (London: V&A Publishing, 2014), 153–62.

29. Cit. in Christopher Rowell, *Polesden Lacey, Surrey* (London: National Trust, 1999), 69.

30. Her Majesty Queen Elizabeth the Queen Mother to D'Arcy Osborne, 28 July 1934, cit. in William Shawcross (ed.), *Counting One's Blessings: The Selected Letters of Queen Elizabeth the Queen Mother* (London: Macmillan, 2012), 202.

31. Charles Wilson, 'Economy and Society in Late Victorian Britain', *Economic History Review*, 18/1 (1965), 190.

32. Wilson, 'Economy and Society', 190.

33. Wilson, 'Economy and Society', 187.

34. Keith Thomas, 'Diary', *London Review of Books*, 5 February 2015, p. 43.

35. Andrew Godley and Bridget Williams, 'Democratizing Luxury and the Contentious "Invention of the Technological Chicken" in Britain', *Business History Review*, 83 (2009), 267.

36. Godley and Williams, 'Democratizing Luxury', 267–90.

37. Paul Johnson, 'Conspicuous Consumption and Working-Class Culture in Late-Victorian and Edwardian Britain', *Transactions of the Royal Historical Society*, 38 (December 1988), 27–42.

38. Consuelo Vanderbilt Balsan, *The Glitter and the Gold: An American Duchess—in her Own Words* (1953; New York: Hodder, 2012), 15.

39. Charlotte Gere and Marina Vaizey, *Great Women Collectors* (London: Philip Wilson Publishers and Harry N. Abrams, 1999), 113.
40. Her Majesty Queen Elizabeth the Queen Mother to the Hon. Lady Johnston, 30 December 1989, cit. in Shawcross (ed.), *Counting One's Blessings*, 508.
41. Valentin V. Skurlov, 'In Search of Fabergé Flowers in Russia', in Joyce Lasky Reed and Marilyn Pfeifer Swezey (eds), *Fabergé Flowers* (New York: Harry N. Abrams, 2004), 107.
42. Jane Brown, *The Pursuit of Paradise: A Social History of Gardens and Gardening* (London: HarperCollins, 1999), 258–9.
43. Anne de Courcy, *Margot at War: Love and Betrayal in Downing Street, 1912–1916* (London: Weidenfeld and Nicolson, 2014), 289.
44. Mary and John Gribbins, *Flower Hunters* (Oxford: Oxford University Press, 2008), 175.
45. Catherine Ziegler, *Favored Flowers: Culture and Economy in a Global System* (Durham, NC: Duke University Press, 2007), 22.
46. Ziegler, *Favored Flowers*, 23.
47. Johnson, 'Conspicuous Consumption and Working-Class Culture'.
48. Ziegler, *Favored Flowers*.
49. Her Majesty Queen Elizabeth the Queen Mother to D'Arcy Osborne, 4 December 1924, cit. in Shawcross (ed.), *Counting One's Blessings*, 131.
50. Robin W. Winks, *Cloak and Gown, Scholars in the Secret War, 1939–1961* (London: Harvill Press, 1987), 259.
51. Valentine Lawford, 'Fashions in Living: The Duke and Duchess of Windsor in Paris', American *Vogue*, 143/7 (1 April 1964), 176–87, 190–4.
52. Ryan Linkof, '"The Photographic Attack on His Royal Highness": The Prince of Wales, Wallis Simpson and the Prehistory of the Paparazzi', *Photography & Culture*, 4/3 (2011), 277–92.
53. John Cornforth, 'The Duke and Duchess of Windsor's House in Paris', *Country Life*, 25 June 1987, pp. 120–5.
54. Hugo Vickers, 'My Bathroom is my Castle', *German Architectural Digest* (September 2008), 176–81; Peter McNeil, 'The Duke of Windsor and the Creation of the "Soft Look"', in Patricia Mears (ed.), *Ivy Style: Radical Conformists* (New York, New Haven, and London: Yale University Press; Fashion Institute of Technology, 2012), 44–51.

Chapter 6. Between False Poverty and Old Opulence:
Luxury Society in the Twentieth Century

1. Stephen Gundle, *Glamour: A History* (Oxford: Oxford University Press, 2008), 164. See also other important works on glamour, a concept until recently left

unexplored and unconnected to luxury: Joseph Rosa et al., *Glamour: Fashion, Design, Architecture* (New Haven: Yale University Press, 2004); Judith Brown, *Glamour in Six Dimensions: Modernism and the Radiance of Form* (Ithaca, NY: Cornell University Press, 2009); Carol Dyhouse, *Glamour: History, Women, Feminism* (London: Zed Books, 2011); Virginia Postrel, *The Power of Glamour: Longing and the Art of Visual Persuasion* (New York: Simon & Schuster, 2013).

2. Cit. in Ulrich Lehmann, *Tigersprung: Fashion in Modernity* (Cambridge, MA: MIT Press, 2000), 14.

3. Kenneth E. Silver, 'Flacon and Fragrance: The New Math of Chanel No. 5', in Harold Koda and Andrew Bolton (eds), *Chanel* (New York: Metropolitan Museum of Art with Yale University Press, 2005), 30–3.

4. Elsie de Wolfe, *The House in Good Taste* (1913; New York: Rizzoli, 2004), 17.

5. Paul Morand, *L'Allure de Chanel* (1976); *The Allure of Chanel*, trans. Euan Cameron (London: Pushkin Collection, 2008), 43.

6. Morand, *L'Allure de Chanel*, 47.

7. Morand, *L'Allure de Chanel*, 51.

8. Paul Iribe, *Défense du luxe* (Montrouge: Draeger Frères, 1932; repr. 1933); translation by the authors.

9. Rhonda K. Garelick, *Mademoiselle: Coco Chanel and the Pulse of History* (New York: Random House 2014), 235–6.

10. *Encyclopédie des arts decoratifs et industriels modernes au xxème siecle*, 12 vols (Paris: Office Centrale d'Éditions et de Librairie, 1925), iii. 38; translation by the authors.

11. Donica Belisle, *Retail Nation, Department Stores and the Making of Modern Canada* (Vancouver: UBC Press, 2011), 130.

12. Peter McNeil, 'Myths of Modernism: Japanese Architecture, Interior Design and the West, c.1920–1940', *Journal of Design History*, 5/4 (1992), 291.

13. Stefania Ricci, 'Made in Italy: Ferragamo and Twentieth-Century Fashion', in Giorgio Riello and Peter McNeil (eds), *Shoes: A History from Sandals to Sneakers* (Oxford and New York: Berg, 2006), 306–25.

14. Mo Amelia Teitelbaum, *The Stylemakers: Minimalism and Classic-Modernism, 1915–45* (London: Philip Wilson, 2010).

15. Teitelbaum, *Stylemakers*, 134.

16. Peter McNeil, ' "Designing Women": Gender, Sexuality and the Interior Decorator, c.1890–1940', *Art History*, 17/4 (1994), 631–57.

17. Cecil Beaton, *The Glass of Fashion* (London: Cassell, 1954), 176.

18. Franz Schulze, *Philip Johnson: Life and Work* (Chicago: University of Chicago Press, 1994), 191–3.

19. Schulze, *Philip Johnson*, 204–5.

20. Schulze, *Philip Johnson*, 204.

21. See Peter Dormer, 'Mies, Modernism and the Moon...and Back Again', in Peter Dormer, *The New Furniture. Trends & Traditions* (London, Thames and Hudson, 1987), 8–22.
22. The curators of the comprehensive collection of the late Marlene Dietrich's legacy kindly read from these amusing typed records at a visit of the Costume Committee of the International Council of Museums, Berlin, 2005.
23. Clint Hill and Lisa McCubbin, *Mrs Kennedy and Me* (New York: Gallery Books, 2012).
24. The Duchess of Devonshire's brother-in-law and heir to the title married John Fitzgerald Kennedy's younger sister Kathleen. They both died in their twenties.
25. Charlotte Mosley (ed.), *In Tearing Haste: Letters between Deborah Devonshire and Patrick Leigh Fermor* (London: John Murray, 2008), 98.
26. Verena Pawlowsky, 'Luxury Item or Urgent Commercial Need? Occupational Position and Automobile Ownership in 1930s Austria', *Journal of Transport History*, 34/2 (2013), 189. The value of the Austrian case is that the printed vehicle ownership records survive intact for all cars on the road in that period, and all names and occupations can be tracked.
27. Her Majesty Queen Elizabeth the Queen Mother to Queen Elizabeth II, 7 July 1953, cit. in William Shawcross (ed.), *Counting One's Blessings: The Selected Letters of Queen Elizabeth the Queen Mother* (London: Macmillan, 2012), 471.
28. Cit. in Jeffrey L. Meikle, 'Into the Fourth Kingdom: Representations of Plastic Materials, 1920–1950', *Journal of Design History*, 5/3 (1992), 180–1.
29. Roland Barthes, *Mythologies*, trans. J. Cape (London: Grafton Books, 1972), 97–9.
30. Peter Wollen, 'Plastics: The Magical and the Prosaic', in Mark Francis and Margery King (eds), *The Warhol Look: Glamour, Style'. Fashion* (Boston: Andy Warhol Museum, Boston, and Bulfinch Press, 1997), not paginated.
31. Meikle, 'Into the Fourth Kingdom', 174.
32. Amy Schellenbaum, 'In 1955, the Fontainebleau Hotel was Irrepressibly Glamorous' <http://curbed.com/archives/2014/09/19/in-1955-the-fontainebleau-hotel-was-irrepressibly-glamorous.php > (accessed 19 March 2015).
33. Rebecca Arnold, 'Looking American: Louise Dahl-Wolfe's Fashion Photographs of the 1930s and 1940s', *Fashion Theory*, 6/1 (2002), 45–60.
34. A. M. Stuart, *Empress of Fashion: A Life of Diana Vreeland* (New York: HarperCollins, 2012), 119.
35. *Vogue's Book of Houses, Gardens, People: Photographed by Horst, Text by Valentine Lawford. Introduction by Diana Vreeland* (London: Bodley Head, 1963; repr. every year until 1968 by Condé Nast publications).
36. Cherie Burns, *Searching for Beauty: The Life of Millicent Rogers, the American Heiress who Taught the World about Style* (New York: St Martin's Press, 2011).
37. Cit in. Annette Tapert and Diana Edkins, *The Power of Style: The Women who Defined the Art of Living Well* (London: Aurum Press, 1994), 70.

38. Margaret Maynard, *Out of Line* (Sydney: UNSW Press, 2001).

39. Marco Urizzi, ' "Jusqu'au bout du rêve": Neo and Aulic Romanticism, in René Gruau's Art', in Elisa Tosi Brandi (ed.), *Gruau and Fashion-Illustrating the 20th Century* (Milan: Silvana Editoriale, 2009), 126–45.

40. Anita Loos, *'Gentlemen Prefer Blondes': The Illuminating Diary of a Professional Lady* (1925; New York: Boni & Liveright, Inc., 1926), 35.

41. Loos, *'Gentlemen Prefer Blondes'*, 41.

42. Loos, *'Gentlemen Prefer Blondes'*, 94.

43. Loos, *'Gentlemen Prefer Blondes'*, 127.

44. The expression 'Here's to the ladies who lunch —aren't they the best' was made into a famous Broadway song by Stephen Sondheim for the musical *Company* (1970). The song was belted out by the alcoholic and slightly depressive character played by the late Elaine Stritch.

45. Truman Capote, *Answered Prayers: The Unfinished Novel. III. La Côte Basque* (1986; London: Penguin, 1993), 156–7.

46. Lee Radziwill, *Happy Times* (New York: Assouline, 2000), 100.

47. James Archer Abbott, *Jansen* (New York: Acanthus Press, 2006).

48. Debora Silverman, *Selling Culture: Bloomingdale's, Diana Vreeland, & the New Aristocracy of Taste in Reagan's America* (New York: Pantheon, 1986).

49. Mario Praz, *An Illustrated History of Interior Decoration: From Pompeii to Art Nouveau*, trans. William Weaver (London: Thames and Hudson, 1964).

Chapter 7. Everything that Money Can Buy?

Understanding Contemporary Luxury

1. Alistair Foster, 'Multi-Millionaire Russians in Battle of the Bar Bills', *Evening Standard*, 13 October 2013, p. 5.

2. 'Exile in Mayfair: Millionaire Yevgeny Chichvarkin's New Life in London', *Guardian*, 27 December 2013. It is estimated that more than 150,000 Russians live in London, attracted by the favourable tax conditions offered. Maria Eugenia Girón, *Inside Luxury: The Growth and Future of the Luxury Goods Industry: A View from the Top* (London: LID Publishing, 2010), 136.

3. £33 million is the cost of a Graff Diamond Hallucination ladies watch with 110-carat gems around a small dial.

4. Zoe Williams, 'A Burberry-Style Profits Warning Is Nothing to Envy', *Guardian*, 13 September 2012, p. 34.

5. Helena Smith, 'Ferrari Sales in Greece Slow to a Standstill', *Guardian*, 20 August 2013, p. 23.

6. 'Verifiche fiscali sulla griffe del lusso: "Milioni all'Estero" ', *Corriere della sera*, 31 December 2012, p. 22.

7. 'Versace Mansion for Sale', *Guardian*, 25 July 2013; Carol Driver, 'Gianni Versace's Miami Mansion Reopens as Luxury Hotel', *Mail Online*, 17 March 2014.

8. <http://www.lux-jet.com/> (accessed 2 November 2015).

9. Cit. in Mark Tungate, *Luxury World: The Past, Present and Future of Luxury Brands* (London and Philadelphia: Kogan Page, 2009), 71.

10. Gilles Laferté, 'The Folklorization of French Framing: Marketing Luxury Wine in the Interwar Years', *French Historical Studies*, 34/4 (2011), 682, 699.

11. Mike Featherstone, 'The Rich and the Super-Rich: Mobility, Consumption and Luxury Lifestyles', in Nita Mathur (ed.), *Consumer Culture, Modernity and Identity* (New Delhi: Sage, 2014), 3–5.

12. Scott DeCarlo, 'The Price of the Good Life', *Forbes*, 192/5, 7 October 2013.

13. Melissa Hoffmann, 'Old Money, New Money', *Adweek*, 55/15, 14 April 2014.

14. Guy Trebay, 'When Cartier Was Just for the Likes of Liz', *New York Times*, 26 April 2009, p. ST8.

15. Jean-Claude Dumas and Marc de Ferrière le Vayer, 'Les Métamorphoses du luxe vues d'Europe', *Entreprises et histoires*, 46 (2007), 10–11. 'Masstige' is a combination of the words 'mass' and 'prestige' and is described as 'prestige for the masses'.

16. Anghuman Ghosh and Sanjeev Varshney, 'Luxury Goods Consumption: A Conceptual Framework Based on Literature Review', *South Asian Journal of Management*, 20/2 (2013), 147.

17. Rebecca Robins and Manfredi Ricca, *Meta-Luxury: Brands and the Culture of Excellence* (New York: Palgrave Macmillan, 2012); Alessandro Quintavalle, 'Über Luxury: For Billionaires', in Jonas Hoffmann and Ivan Coste-Manière (eds), *Global Luxury Trends: Innovative Strategies for Emerging Markets* (New York: Palgrave Macmillan, 2013), 51–76. See also Tungate, *Luxury World*.

18. Dana Thomas, *Deluxe: How Luxury Lost its Lustre* (London: Penguin, 2008).

19. Thomas, *Deluxe*. See also Yves Michaud, *Le Nouveau Luxe: Experiences, arrogance, authenticité* (Paris: Éditions Stock, 2013), 11

20. Dumas and de Ferrière le Vayer, 'Les Métamorphoses', 10–11.

21. Chris Soren, 'Living beyond our Means', *Maclean's*, 127/12, 31 March 2014.

22. 'That and $30 Gets You a Cuppa Joe', *Newsweek Global*, 162/17, 5 February 2014.

23. Patrizia Calefato, *Luxury: Fashion, Style and Excess* (London: Bloomsbury, 2014), 12.

24. James B. Twitchell, *Living it Up: Our Love Affair with Luxury* (New York: Columbia University Press, 2002), 61–5.

25. Brommer et al., 'Le Luxe aujourd'hui', 182.

26. Marcello Matté, 'Articolo di lusso', *Settimana*, 19 January 2014, p. 3.

27. Michaud, *Le Nouveau Luxe*, 16–20.

28. Jane Bainbridge, 'Discreet Luxury', *Marketing*, 1 October 2013.

29. Andrea Doyle, 'Choose your Luxury', *Incentive*, 188/3 (May–June 2014).

30. Doyle, 'Choose your Luxury'.

31. Arunima Mishra, 'Genies on Call', *Business Today*, 1 September 2013, pp. 91–4.

32. Kate Summerscale, *The Queen of Whale Cay: The Extraordinary Story of 'Joe' Carstairs, the Fastest Woman on Water* (New York: Penguin, 1999).

33. Robin Wainwright, *Sheila: The Australian Ingenue who Bewitched British Society* (Sydney: Allen and Unwin, 2014).

34. 'Africa: The New Mecca for Luxury Brands', *African Business* (October 2013).

35. Bonnie G. Smith, *Ladies of the Leisure Class: The Bourgeoisies of Northern France in the 19th Century* (Princeton: Princeton University Press, 1981).

36. Elizabeth Wilson, 'Luxury', *Luxury*, 1/1 (2014), 19–20.

37. Calefato, *Luxury*, 81.

38. Andrew Cook, 'The Expatriate Real Estate Complex: Creative Destruction and the Production of Luxury in Post-Socialist Prague', *International Journal of Urban and Regional Research*, 34/3 (2010), 611–28.

39. Carolyn Cartier, 'Class, Consumption and the Economic Restructuring of Consumer Space', in Minglu Chen and David S. G. Goodman (eds), *Middle Class China: Identity and Behaviour* (Cheltenham: Edward Elgar, 2013), 38.

40. 'One Hyde Park' website < http://www.onehydepark.com/#/index (accessed 10 November 2014).

41. 'Amenities in the Sky', *New York Times*, 18 May 2013.

42. Cit. in Pierre Xiao Lu, *Elite China: Luxury Consumer Behavior in China* (Singapore: John Wiley & Sons, 2008), 69.

43. Ghosh and Varshney, 'Luxury Goods Consumption', 147.

44. 'Luxury in India at $6 Billion and Growing', *Women's Wear Daily*, 205/69, 5 April 2013.

45. 'Luxe Spending to Grow to $1.2 Trillion', *Women's Wear Daily*, 207/19, 9 January 2014.

46. R. Chadha and P. Husband, *The Cult of the Luxury Brand: Inside Asia's Love Affair with Luxury* (London: Nicholas Brealey International, 2006), p. x.

47. Girón, *Inside Luxury*, 99.

48. Girón, *Inside Luxury*, 102.

49. 'Africa: The New Mecca for Luxury Brands', 19.

50. Cartier, 'Class, Consumption and the Economic Restructuring', 37.

51. Cit. in 'Luxury Lures China's Young Wealth', CCTV.com <http://english.cntv.cn/program/bizasia/20101008/102949.shtml> (accessed 25 August 2014).

52. See, e.g., Jacqueline Tsai, *La Chine et le luxe* (Paris: Odile Jacob, 2008), 199–221.

53. Y. Hemantha, 'Research Note: Status of Luxury Branding in India', *IUP Journal of Management*, 10/4 (2013), 67.

54. Shaun Breslin, 'Power and Production: Rethinking China's Global Economic Role', *Review of International Studies*, 31 (2005), 751.

55. 'Rolls Royce Defies Downturn', *The Times* (2011).

56. 'Giada: Così la Cina entra nel salotto del lusso', *Corriere della sera*, 9 September 2013, p. 10.

57. Jonas Hoffmann and Betina Hoffmann, 'Paths for the Emergence of Global Chinese Luxury Brands', in Hoffmann and Coste-Manière (eds), *Global Luxury Trends*, 25–36.
58. 'Chinese Brands Tap Lucrative Luxury Market', CCTV.com <http://english.cntv.cn/program/bizasia/20101008/102418.shtml> (accessed 25 August 2014).
59. 'Luxury in India at $6 Billion and Growing', *Women's Wear Daily*, 205/69, 5 April 2013.
60. Shweta Pamj and Manu Kaushik, 'Money Can Buy You Luxe', *Business Today*, 1 September 2013, p. 33.
61. Pamj and Kaushik, 'Money Can Buy You Luxe', 31–3.
62. Y. Hemantha, 'Research Note: Status of Luxury Branding in India', *IUP Journal of Management*, 10/4 (2013), 69.
63. 'Luxury Goods in India: Maharajah's in the Shopping Mall', *The Economist*, 2 June 2007, p. 76–7.
64. Manu Kaushik, 'Oui for Louis', *Business Today*, 1 September 2013, p. 40.
65. Pamj and Kaushik, 'Money Can Buy You Luxe', 38.
66. Bainbridge, 'Discreet Luxury'; Maria Eurgena Giròn, *Inside Luxury*, 133.
67. Claudio Diniz, Glyn Atwal, and Douglas Bryson, 'Understanding the Brazilian Luxury Consumer', in Glyn Atwal and Douglas Bryson (eds), *Luxury Brands in Emerging Markets* (Basingstoke: Palgrave, 2014), 9–11. See also Jonas Hoffmann, 'Luxi Brasil and Osklen's New Luxury', in Hoffmann and Coste-Manière (eds), *Global Luxury Trends*, 37–50.
68. Stephanie Findley, 'Nouveau-Riche and Loving It', *Canadian Business*, 86/11–12, 15 July 2013.
69. 'Africa: The New Mecca for Luxury Brands', 14–19.
70. Findley, 'Nouveau-Riche'.

Chapter 8. Luxury Capitalism: The Magic World of the Luxury Brands

1. Dana Thomas, *Deluxe: How Luxury Lost its Lustre* (London: Penguin, 2008).
2. Tuna N. Amobi, 'Apparel, Accessories & Luxury Goods', *Standard & Poor's Industry Investment Reviews*, 1 August 2014.
3. Olga Louisa Kastner, *When Luxury Meets Art: Forms of Collaboration between Luxury Brands and the Arts* (New York: Springer Gabler 2014), 73.
4. In 2014, for instance, the makers of Kelly bags and silk scarves warned that their operating profits were down because of negative exchange rates. 'Hermès Sounds the Alarm over Currency Concerns', *Women's Wear Daily*, 208/14, 21 July 2014.

5. Yves Michaud, *Le Nouveau Luxe: Experiences, arrogance, authenticité* (Paris: Éditions Stock, 2013), 46.

6. Sarah Schulman, *The Gentrification of the Mind: Witness to a Lost Generation* (Berkeley and Los Angeles, and London: University of California Press, 2012).

7. Maria Eugenia Giròn, *Inside Luxury: The Growth and Future of the Luxury Goods Industry: A View from the Top* (London: LID Publishing, 2010), 157–8.

8. 'Company Profile: LVMH Moët Hennessy Louis Vuitton SA', *MarketLine*, 21 November 2013, pp. 1–3.

9. 'Company Profile: LVMH Moët Hennessy Louis Vuitton SA', 3–5.

10. Giròn, *Inside Luxury*, 71.

11. 'Company Profile: LVMH Moët Hennessy Louis Vuitton SA', 6.

12. Manu Kaushik, 'Oui for Louis', *Business Today*, 1 September 2013, 42.

13. Eugénie Briot and Christel de Lassus, 'La Figure de l'entrepreneur fondateur dans le récit de marque et la construction de la personnalité de la marque de luxe', *Management International*, 17/3 (2013), 51–2.

14. François-Henri Pinault, 'How I Did It', *Harvard Business Review* (March 2014), 42–5.

15. Giròn, *Inside Luxury*, 186.

16. Giròn, *Inside Luxury*, 159.

17. Michaud, *Le Nouveau Luxe*, 71.

18. For an overview of the birth of the luxury conglomerates, see Alain Chatriot, 'La Construction récente des groups de luxe français: Mythes, discours et pratiques', *Entreprise et histoire*, 46 (2007), 143–56.

19. Pinault, 'How I Did It', 46.

20. Pinault, 'How I Did It', 46.

21. Liselot Hudders, Mario Pandelaere, and Patrick Vyncke, 'Consumer Meaning Making: The Meaning of Luxury Brands in a Democratised Luxury World', *International Journal of Market Research*, 55/3 (2013), 393.

22. 'Gli orologi de nuovi artigiani (con stampanti 3D)', *Corriere della sera*, 21 December 2013, p. 44.

23. Silvia Bellezza and Anat Keinan, 'Brand Tourists: How Non-Core Users Enhance the Brand Image by Eliciting Pride', *Journal of Consumer Research*, 41 (2014), 397.

24. James B. Twitchell, *Living it Up: Our Love Affair with Luxury* (New York: Columbia University Press, 2002), 126–8. <http://www.comitecolbert.com/les_maisons.html> (accessed 2 November 2015).

25. <https://fr.wikipedia.org/wiki/Comit%C3%A9_Colbert> (accessed 2 November 2015).

26. For a list of all companies belonging to the Comité Colbert, see Briot and de Lassus, 'La Figure de l'entrepreneur fondateur', 60–2.

27. <https://fr.wikipedia.org/wiki/Comit%C3%A9_Colbert> (accessed 2 November 2015).

28. Fondazione Altagamma, 'Studi e ricerche' <http://www.altagamma.it/sezione2.php?Id=64&Lingua=ita> (accessed 2 November 2015).

29. Court of Justice of the European Union, 23 April 2009, case C-59/08. We thank Alberto Musso of the University of Bologna for the information provided concerning the legislative framework on trademarks. See also Alberto Musso, 'Domain names e marchi in Internet nell'evoluzione giurisprudenziale', in *Diritto e nuove tecnologie* (Bologna: Gedit, 2007), 45–68, and Vito Mangini and Alberto Musso Alberto, 'L'incidenza del diritto dell'Unione europea sulla disciplina della proprietà industriale o intellettuale e della concorrenza', in *L'incidenza del diritto dell'Unione europea sullo studio delle discipline giuridiche nel cinquantesimo della firma del Trattato di Roma* (Naples: Editoriale Scientifica, 2008), 283–90.

30. 'Trademark Parody Gives Louis Vuitton Something to Chew on', *Journal of the Academy of Marketing Science*, 36 (2008), 435–6.

31. This was not the case until the 1990s, when the European Court of Justice established that trademark owners had a say about the distribution of their products only if they showed that violation 'seriously damages the trade mark reputation' (Court of Justice of European Union, 4 November 1997, case C-337/95).

32. Michel Chevalier and Pierre Lu, *Luxury China: Market Opportunities and Potential* (Singapore: John Wiley & Sons, 2010), 178.

33. US Department of Homeland Security, 'Intellectual Property Rights Seizures Statistics Fiscal Year 2013' <http://www.cbp.gov/sites/default/files/documents/2013%20.IPR%20Stats.pdf> (accessed 2 November 2015).

34. European Commission, 'Report on EU Customs Enforcement of Intellectual Property Rights: Results at the EU Border 2013' <http://ec.europa.eu/taxation_customs/resources/documents/customs/customs_controls/counterfeit_piracy/statistics/2014_ipr_statistics_en.pdf> (accessed 2 November 2015).

35. Pierre Xiao Lu, *Elite China: Luxury Consumer Behavior in China* (Singapore: John Wiley & Sons, 2008), 130.

36. Paul-Gérard Pasols, *Louis Vuitton: The Birth of Modern Luxury* (New York: Harry N. Abrams, 2012), 367.

37. Matteo Persivale, 'Il segreto degli sguardi (con stile)', *Corriere della sera*, 21 December 2014, p. 45.

38. Rachel Cooke, 'Miuccia Prada: I hate the idea of being a collector. I really hate it' <http://www.theguardian.com/fashion/2015/may/17/miuccia-prada-i-hate-the-idea-of-being-a-collector?utm_source=Subscribers&utm_campaign=71ec61aea9-&utm_medium=email&utm_term=0_d2191372b3-71ec61aea9-417371553> (accessed 2 November 2015).

39. Kastner, *When Luxury Meets Art*, 80–2.

40. Kastner, *When Luxury Meets Art*, 92.

41. Kastner, *When Luxury Meets Art*, 83.
42. 'L'"audace" Vaccarello per la digitale Versus', *Corriere della sera*, 21 December 2013, p. 45.
43. Edmund White, *The Flâneur: A Stroll through the Paradoxes of Paris* (London: Bloomsbury, 2001), 18.
44. 'Cambridge Beats Exeter for Title as UK's Ultimate "Clone Town" ', *Independent*, 15 September 2010.
45. Mike Featherstone, 'The Rich and the Super-Rich: Mobility, Consumption and Luxury Lifestyles', in Nita Mathur (ed.), *Consumer Culture, Modernity and Identity* (New Delhi: Sage, 2014), 24.
46. 'Altagamma Retail Evolution 2014', 2 <http://www.brand-news.it/wp-content/uploads/downloads/2015/01/Altagamma-Retail-Presentation-January-2015-LS.pdf> (accessed 2 November 2015).
47. Giròn, *Inside Luxury*, 125.
48. 'Altagamma Retail Evolution 2014', 2.
49. 'Luxe Spending to Grow to $1.2 Trillion', *Women's Wear Daily*, 207/19, 9 January 2014.
50. Jean Claude Brommer et al., 'Le Luxe aujourd'hui', *Entreprises et histoire*, 46 (2007), 184.
51. Pasols, *Louis Vuitton*, 308–10.
52. Giròn, *Inside Luxury*, 94.
53. Featherstone, 'The Rich and the Super-Rich', 29.
54. Giròn, *Inside Luxury*, 125–6.
55. Heathrow, 'Heathrow Airport Shops A–Z' <http://www.heathrow.com/shops-and-restaurants/shops-a-z> (accessed 2 November 2015).
56. 'Foreign Travel for the Masses', *China Confidential–FT*, 16 January 2014, point 3.6.
57. 'Foreign Travel for the Masses', *China Confidential–FT*, 16 January 2014, point 3.
58. 'Foreign Travel for the Masses', *China Confidential–FT*, 16 January 2014, point 3.6.
59. Euromonitor International, 'Luxury Goods in Australia' <http://www.euromonitor.com/luxury-goods-in-australia/report> (accessed 2 November 2015).
60. Mark Tungate, *Luxury World: The Past, Present and Future of Luxury Brands* (London and Philadelphia: Kogan Page, 2009), 135–7.
61. Briot and de Lassus, 'La Figure de l'entrepreneur', 52, 55.
62. Stephanie Geiger-Oneto, Betsy D. Gelb, Doug Walker, and James D. Hess, ' "Buying Status" by Choosing or Rejecting Luxury Brands and their Counterfeits', *Journal of the Academy of Marketing Science*, 41 (2013), 359.
63. Tungate, *Luxury World*, 136–7. See Tim Philips, *Knock Off: The True Story of the World's Fastest Growing Crime* (London: Kogan Page, 2005).
64. Geiger-Oneto et al., ' "Buying Status" ', 359.

65. Rasa Stankeviciute, 'Occupation Fashion Blogging: Relation between Blogs and Luxury Fashion Brands', in Jonas Hoffmann and Ivan Coste-Manière (eds), *Global Luxury Trends: Innovative Strategies for Emerging Markets* (New York: Palgrave Macmillan, 2013), 78.

66. Christoph Fuchs, Emanuela Prandelli, Martin Schreider, and Darren W. Dahl, 'All That is Users Might not be Gold: How Labeling Products as User Designed Backfires in the Context of Luxury Fashion Brands', *Journal of Marketing*, 77 (2013), 76.

67. We are grateful to the company Henry Poole for hosting the Luxury Network in its premises in July 2013.

68. We thank Giovanna Furlanetto of Furla for this information.

69. Tungate, *Luxury World*, 156–7.

70. Jess Cartner-Morley, 'Burberry Brings a Touch of London to Shanghai', *Guardian*, 3 May 2014, p. 9.

71. Steven Morris, 'Male Voice and a Jazz Band Play Burberry out of the Rhondda', *Guardian*, 31 March 2007, p. 9; Carole Cadwalladr, 'Squaring up to Burberry', *Observer Magazine*, 25 March 2007, pp. 35–9.

72. Tungate, *Luxury World*, 27–8.

73. Qing Wang, 'Understanding Chinese', *Core*, 1 (2013), 14–15.

74. 'New Bentley Made in Slovakia?', *Guardian*, 20 March 2013, p. 32.

75. Anghuman Ghosh and Sanjeev Varshney, 'Luxury Goods Consumption: A Conceptual Framework Based on Literature Review', *South Asian Journal of Management*, 20/2 (2013), 147.

76. For a critical overview, see Steven Poole, 'Give me the Real Thing', *New Statesman*, 1–7 March 2013, pp. 24–8.

77. Gilles Auguste and Michel Gutsatz, *Luxury Talent Management: Leading and Managing a Luxury Brand* (New York: Palgrave Macmillan, 2013), 4–5.

78. 'Schiap, la giacca zodiaco vale più di 130 mila euro', *Corriere della sera*, 21 December 2013, p. 47.

79. For the analysis of seven of the most prominent 'luxury dynasties' (Cartier, Chanel, Ferragamo, Gucci, Hermès, Louis Vuitton, and Rolls-Royce), see Yann Kerlau, *Les Dynasties du luxe* (Paris: Perrin, 2010). Notice that Kerlau includes Chanel as one of the first fashion houses that continued after the death of its founder.

80. Briot and de Lassus, 'La Figure de l'entrepreneur', 52, 55.

81. Auguste and Gutsatz, *Luxury Talent Management*, 3–4, 7. See also Jean-Pierre Blay, 'La Maison Hermès, du dernier siècle du cheval à l'ère de l'automobile', *Histoire Urbaine*, 12 (2005), 69–88.

82. Auguste and Gutsatz, *Luxury Talent Management*, 3–4, 7.

83. 'Africa: The New Mecca for Luxury Brands', *African Business* (October 2013).

84. Cit. in Trebay, 'When Cartier Was Just for the Likes of Liz', p. ST8.

85. Pasols, *Louis Vuitton*, 120–2.

86. Auguste and Gutsatz, *Luxury Talent Management*, 4–5.
87. Cit. in Guy Trebay, 'When Cartier Was Just for the Likes of Liz', p. ST8.

Conclusion. Luxury: Towards a Richer History

1. J. B. Priestly, *English Journey* (London: Heinemann/Gollancz, 1934), 402.
2. Gilles Lipovetsky, *Il tempo del lusso* (Palermo: Sellerio, 2007), 16.
3. Dana Thomas, *Deluxe: How Luxury Lost its Lustre* (London: Penguin, 2008).
4. Thomas Piketty, *Capital in the Twenty-First Century* (Cambridge, MA: Belknap Press, 2014)

SELECT BIBLIOGRAPHY

A Taste for China: Paris 1743–1930 (Paris: Musée Guimet and Hong Kong Museum of Art, 2008).

Abbott, James Archer, *Jansen* (New York: Acanthus Press, 2006).

Adams, William Howard, *On Luxury: A Cautionary Tale: A Short History of the Perils of Excess from Ancient Times to the Beginning of the Modern Era* (Washington: Potomac Books, 2012).

Albrecht, Donald, and Jeannine Falino, 'An Aristocracy of Wealth', in Donald Albrecht and Jeannine Falino (eds), *Gilded New York: Design, Fashion, and Society* (New York: Museum of the City of New York and Monacelli Press, 2013), 11–50.

Arnold, Janet, *Elizabeth's Wardrobe Unlock'd* (Leeds: W. S. Maney & Son, 1988).

Assouly, Olivier, and Pierre Bergé (eds), *Le Luxe: Essais sur la fabrique de l'ostentation* (Paris: Institut français de la mode, 2004).

Atwal, Glyn, and Douglas Bryson (eds), *Luxury Brands in Emerging Markets* (Basingstoke: Palgrave, 2014).

Auguste, Gilles, and Michel Gutsatz, *Luxury Talent Management: Leading and Managing a Luxury Brand* (New York: Palgrave Macmillan, 2013).

Auslander, Leora, *Taste and Power: Furnishing Modern France* (Berkeley and Los Angeles, and London: University of California Press, 1996).

Beaton, Cecil, *The Glass of Fashion* (London: Cassell, 1954).

Beaton, Cecil, 'Beverly Hills Hotel, January 1970', in Hugo Vickers (ed.), *The Unexpurgated Beaton: The Cecil Beaton Diaries as they Were Written* (London: Phoenix, 2002), 32–5.

Berg, Maxine, 'New Commodities, Luxuries and their Consumers in Eighteenth-Century England', in Maxine Berg and Helen Clifford (eds), *Consumers and Luxury: Consumer Culture in Europe, 1650–1850* (Manchester: Manchester University Press, 1999), 63–85.

Berg, Maxine, *Luxury and Pleasure in Eighteenth-Century Britain* (Oxford: Oxford University Press, 2005).

Berg, Maxine, and Helen Clifford (eds), *Consumers and Luxury: Consumer Culture in Europe, 1650–1850* (Manchester: Manchester University Press, 1999).

Berger, Molly W., *Hotel Dreams: Luxury, Technology, and Urban Ambition in America, 1829–1929* (Baltimore: Johns Hopkins University Press, 2011).

Berry, Christopher, *The Idea of Luxury: A Conceptual and Historical Investigation* (Cambridge: Cambridge University Press, 1994).

Blanc, Odile, 'From Battlefields to Court: The Invention of Fashion in the Fourteenth Century', in Désirée G. Koslin and Janet E. Snyder (eds), *Encountering Medieval Textiles and Dress: Objects, Texts, Images* (New York: Macmillan Palgrave, 2002), 157–72.

Brandon, Ruth, *The Dollar Princesses: The American Invasion of the European Aristocracy 1870–1914* (London: Weidenfeld and Nicolson, 1980).

Braund, David, 'The Luxuries of Athenian Democracy', *Greece & Rome*, 41/1 (1994), 41–8.

Bremer-David, Charissa (ed.), *Paris: Life & Luxury in the Eighteenth Century* (Los Angeles: Paul Getty Museum, 2011).

Brown, Jane, *The Pursuit of Paradise: A Social History of Gardens and Gardening* (London: HarperCollins, 1999).

Brown, S. (ed.), *Horst: Photographer of Style* (London: V&A Publishing, 2014).

Burke, Peter, *The Italian Renaissance* (2nd edn, Princeton: Princeton University Press, 1987).

Burns, Cherie, *Searching for Beauty: The Life of Millicent Rogers, the American Heiress who Taught the World about Style* (New York: St Martin's Press, 2011).

Calefato, Patrizia, *Luxury: Fashion, Style and Excess* (London: Bloomsbury, 2014).

Cartier, Carolyn, 'Class, Consumption and the Economic Restructuring of Consumer Space', in Minglu Chen and David S. G. Goodman (eds), *Middle Class China: Identity and Behaviour* (Cheltenham: Edward Elgar, 2013), 34–53.

Castarède, Jean, *Le Luxe* (Paris: Puf, 1992).

Castarède, Jean, *Histoire du luxe en France* (Paris: Eyrolles, 2007).

Castiglione, Baldessare, *The Book of the Courtier*, ed. Leonard Eckstein (New York: Scribner's, 1903).

Chadha, R., and P. Husband, *The Cult of the Luxury Brand: Inside Asia's Love Affair with Luxury* (London: Nicholas Brealey International, 2006).

Chevalier, Michel, and Pierre Lu, *Luxury China: Market Opportunities and Potential* (Singapore: John Wiley & Sons, 2010).

Cornforth, John, 'The Duke and Duchess of Windsor's House in Paris', *Country Life*, 25 June 1987, pp. 120–5.

Coudert, Thierry, *Café Society, Socialites, Patrons, and Artists: 1920–1960* (Paris: Flammarion, 2010).

Crowley, John E., *The Invention of Comfort: Sensibilities and Design in Early Modern Britain and Early America* (Baltimore: Johns Hopkins University Press, 2001).

D'Arms, John H., 'The Culinary Reality of Roman Upper-Class Convivia: Integrating Texts and Images', *Comparative Studies in Society and History*, 46/3 (2004), 428–50.

DaCosta Kaufmann, Thomas, *Court, Cloister & City. The Art and Culture of Central Europe 1450–1800* (Chicago: University of Chicago Press, 1995).

Dalby, Andrew, *Empire of Pleasures: Luxury and Indulgence in the Roman World* (London: Routledge, 2000).

Dari-Mattiacci, Giuseppe, and Anna E. Plisecka, 'Luxury in Ancient Rome: An Economic Analysis of the Scope, Timing and Enforcement of Sumptuary Laws', *International Journal of Roman Law, Legal History and Comparative Law*, 1 (2012), 189–216.

Davis, Deborah, *Party of the Century: The Fabulous Story of Truman Capote and the Black and White Ball* (Hoboken, NJ: John Wiley & Sons, 2006).

de la Haye, Amy, and Valerie D. Mendes, *The House of Worth: Portrait of an Archive* (London: V&A Publishing, 2014).

de Wolfe, Elsie, *The House in Good Taste* (1913; New York: Rizzoli, 2004).

Dietz, Bettina, and Thomas Nutz, '*Collections Curieuses*: The Aesthetics of Curiosity and Elite Lifestyle in Eighteenth-Century Paris', *Eighteenth-Century Life*, 29/3 (2006), 54.

dos Guimarães Sá, Isobel, 'The Uses of Luxury: Some Examples from the Portuguese Courts from 1480 to 1580', *Análise social*, 44/192 (2009), 589–604.

Duby, Georges, *Art and Society in the Middle Ages* (Cambridge: Polity Press, 2000). French edn, 1995.

Eco, Umberto, *Art and Beauty in the Middle Ages* (New Haven: Yale University Press, 1986).

Elias, Norbert, *The Civilizing Process*, trans. Edmund Jephcot, 2 vols (Oxford: Blackwell, 1982).

Evans, Mark (ed.), *Princes as Patrons: The Art Collections of the Princes of Wales from the Renaissance to the Present Day. An Exhibition from the Royal Collection* (London: Merrell Holberton and National Museums & Galleries of Wales and the Royal Collection, 1998).

Evans, Sîan, *Mrs Ronnie: The Society Hostess who Collected Kings* (London: National Trust Books, 2013).

Fairchilds, Cissie, 'The Production and Marketing of Populuxe Goods in Eighteenth-Century Paris', in John Brewer and Roy Porter (eds), *Consumption and the World of Goods* (London and New York, 1993), 228–48.

Falino, Jeannine, 'Blazed with Diamonds: New Yorkers and the Pursuit of Jeweled Ornament', in Donald Albrecht and Jeannine Falino (eds), *Gilded New York: Design, Fashion, and Society* (New York: Museum of the City of New York and Monacelli Press, 2013), 51–82.

Featherstone, Mike, 'The Rich and the Super-Rich: Mobility, Consumption and Luxury Lifestyles', in Nita Mathur (ed.), *Consumer Culture, Modernity and Identity* (New Delhi: Sage, 2014), 3–44.

Frank, Robert H., *Luxury Fever: Money and Happiness in an Era of Excess* (Princeton: Princeton University Press 2000).

Gaines, Steven, *The Sky's the Limit: Passion and Property in Manhattan* (New York: Back Bay Books, 2006).

Garelick, Rhonda K., *Mademoiselle: Coco Chanel and the Pulse of History* (New York: Random House, 2014).

Gere, Charlotte, and Marina Vaizey, *Great Women Collectors* (London: Philip Wilson Publishers and Harry N. Abrams, 1999), 113.

Ghosh, Anghuman, and Sanjeev Varshney, 'Luxury Goods Consumption: A Conceptual Framework Based on Literature Review', *South Asian Journal of Management*, 20/2 (2013), 146–59.

Giròn, Maria Eugenia, *Inside Luxury. The Growth and Future of the Luxury Goods Industry: A View from the Top* (London: LID Publishing, 2010).

Goldthwaite, Richard, 'The Empire of Things: Consumer Demand in Renaissance Italy', in Francis William Kent, Patricia Simons, and John Christopher Eade (eds), *Patronage, Art, and Society in Renaissance Italy* (Canberra: Humanities Research Centre; Oxford: Oxford University Press, 1987), 153–75.

Goldthwaite, Richard, 'The Economy of Renaissance Italy: The Preconditions for Luxury Consumption', *I Tatti Studies in the Italian Renaissance*, 2 (1987), 15–39.

Guerzoni, Guido, and Gabriele Troilo, 'Silk Purses out of Sows' Ears: Mass Rarefaction of Consumption and the Emerging Consumer-Collector', in Marina Bianchi (ed.), *The Active Consumer* (London: Routledge, 1998), 174–98.

Hall, Michael, *The Victorian Country House: From the Archives of County Life* (London: Aurum, 2009).

Harte, Negley B., 'State Control of Dress and Social Change in Pre-Industrial England', in D. C. Coleman and A. H. John (eds), *Trade, Government and Economy in Pre-Industrial England* (London: Weidenfeld and Nicolson, 1976), 132–65.

Hayward, Maria, *Dress at the Court of King Henry VIII* (Leeds: Maney, 2007).

Heller, Sarah-Grace, 'Fashion in French Crusade Literature: Desiring Infidel Textiles', in Désirée G. Koslin and Janet E. Snyder (eds), *Encountering Medieval Textiles and Dress: Objects, Texts, Images* (New York: Macmillan Palgrave, 2002), 103–19.

Hellman, Mimi, 'Furniture, Sociability, and the Work of Leisure in Eighteenth-Century France', *Eighteenth-Century Studies*, 32/4 (1999), 415–45.

Hibbert, Christopher, *The Grand Tour* (New York: Putnam, 1969).

Hill, Clint, and Lisa McCubbin, *Mrs Kennedy and Me* (New York: Gallery Books, 2012).

Hoffmann, Jonas, and Ivan Coste-Manière (eds), *Global Luxury Trends: Innovative Strategies for Emerging Markets* (New York: Palgrave Macmillan, 2013).

Hudders, Liselot, Mario Pandelaere, and Patrick Vyncke, 'Consumer Meaning Making: The Meaning of Luxury Brands in a Democratised Luxury World', *International Journal of Market Research*, 55/3 (2013), 391–412.

Huizinga, Johan, *The Waning of the Middle Ages* (1999; Mineola, NY: Dover Publications, 1999).

Impey, Oliver, 'Japanese Export Art of the Edo Period and its Influences on European Art', *Modern Asian Studies*, 18/4 (1984), 685–97.

Jeggle, Christoph, 'Economies of Quality as a Concept of Research on Luxury', in Rengenier C. Rittersma (ed.), *Luxury in the Low Countries: Miscellaneous Reflections on Netherlandish Material Culture, 1500 to the Present* (Brussels: Pharo Publishing, 2010), 27–44.

Jolly, Anna, *A Taste for the Exotic: Foreign Influences on Early Eighteenth-Century Silk Design* (Riggisberg: Abegg-Stiftung, 2007).

Jones, Ann Rosalind, and Peter Stallybrass, *Renaissance Clothing and the Materials of Memory* (Cambridge: Cambridge University Press, 2000).

Jones, Colin, *Madame de Pompadour. Image of a Mistress* (London: National Gallery and Yale University Press, 2002).

Karmel Thomason, Allison, *Luxury and Legitimation: Royal Collecting in Ancient Mesopotamia* (Aldershot: Ashgate, 2005).

Kastner, Olga Louisa, *When Luxury Meets Art: Forms of Collaboration between Luxury Brands and the Arts* (New York: Springer Gabler, 2014).

Kerlau, Yann, *Les Dynasties du luxe* (Paris: Perrin, 2010).

Kovesi Killerby, Catherine, *Sumptuary Law in Italy, 1200–1500* (Oxford: Oxford University Press, 2002).

Lemire, Beverly, 'Domesticating the Exotic: Floral Culture and the East India Calico Trade with England, c.1600–1800', *Textile: The Journal of Cloth and Culture*, 1/1 (2003), 65–85.

Lemire, Beverly, and Giorgio Riello, 'East and West: Textiles and Fashion in Eurasia in the Early Modern Period', *Journal of Social History*, 41/4 (2008), 887–916.

Levy Peck, Linda, *Consuming Splendor: Society and Culture in Seventeenth-Century England* (Cambridge: Cambridge University Press, 2005).

Linkof, Ryan, '"The Photographic Attack on His Royal Highness": The Prince of Wales, Wallis Simpson and the Prehistory of the Paparazzi', *Photography & Culture*, 4/3 (2011), 277–92.

Lipovetsky, Gilles, *Il tempo del lusso* (Palermo: Sellerio, 2007).

Loos, Anita, *'Gentlemen Prefer Blondes': The Illuminating Diary of a Professional Lady* (1925; New York: Boni & Liveright, Inc., 1926).

Lu, Pierre Xiao, *Elite China: Luxury Consumer Behavior in China* (Singapore: John Wiley & Sons, 2008).

McNeil, Peter, 'The Duke of Windsor and the Creation of the "Soft Look"', in Patricia Mears (ed.), *Ivy Style: Radical Conformists* (New York, New Haven, and London: Yale University Press; Fashion Institute of Technology, 2012), 44–51.

Mandeville, Bernard, *The Fable of the Bees; or, Private Vices, Public Benefits ...* (London: C. Bathurst, 1795).

Mandler, Peter, *The Fall and Rise of the Stately Home* (New Haven: Yale University Press, 1997).

Marseille, Jacques (ed.), *Le Luxe en France du siècle des 'lumières' à nos jours* (Paris: ADHE, 1999).

Michaud, Yves, *Le Nouveau Luxe: Experiences, arrogance, authenticité* (Paris: Éditions Stock, 2013).

Miller, Maureen C., *Clothing the Clergy: Virtue and Power in Medieval Europe, c.800–1200* (Ithaca, NY: Cornell University Press, 2014).

Molà, Luca, *The Silk Industry of Renaissance Venice* (Baltimore: Johns Hopkins University Press, 2000).

Monnas, Lisa, *Merchants, Princes, and Painters: Silk Fabrics in Italian and Northern Paintings, 1300–1500* (New Haven and London: Yale University Press, 2008).

Morand, Paul, *The Allure of Chanel*, trans. Euan Cameron (London: Pushkin Collection, 2008). (French edn, 1976.)

Mosher Stuard, Susan, *Gilding the Market: Luxury and Fashion in Fourteenth-Century Italy* (Philadelphia: University of Pennsylvania Press, 2006).

Mowl, Timothy, *Horace Walpole: The Great Outsider* (London: John Murray Publishers, 1996).

Mowl, Timothy, *Elizabethan and Jacobean Style* (London: Phaidon, 2001).

Munhall, Edgar, *Whistler and Montesquiou: The Butterfly and the Bat* (New York and Paris: Frick Collection/Flammarion, 1995).

Parker, Grant, '*Ex Oriente Luxuria*: Indian Commodities and Roman Experience', *Journal of the Economic and Social History of the Orient*, 45/1 (2002), 40–95.

Pasols, Paul-Gérard, *Louis Vuitton: The Birth of Modern Luxury* (New York: Harry N. Abrams, 2012).

Perrot, Philippe, *Le Luxe: Une richesse entre faste et confort, XIIIe–XIXe siècle* (Paris: Seuil, 1995).

Philips, Tim, *Knock Off: The True Story of the World's Fastest Growing Crime* (London: Kogan Page, 2005).

Pinault, François-Henri, 'How I Did It', *Harvard Business Review* (March 2014), 42–5.

Pipponier, Françoise, and Perrine Manne, *Dress in the Middle Ages* (New Haven: Yale University Press, 2000).

Praz, Mario, *An Illustrated History of Interior Decoration: From Pompeii to Art Nouveau*, trans. William Weaver (London: Thames and Hudson, 1964).

Radziwill, Lee, *Happy Times* (New York: Assouline, 2000).

Ribeiro, Aileen, *Fashion and Fiction: Dress in Art and Literature in Stuart England* (New Haven and London: Yale University Press, 2005).

Ridley, Jane, *Bertie: A Life of Edward VII* (London: Chatto and Windus, 2012).

Robins, Rebecca, and Manfredi Ricca, *Meta-Luxury: Brands and the Culture of Excellence* (New York: Palgrave Macmillan, 2012).

Robinson, John Martin, *The Latest Country Houses, 1945–83* (London, Sydney, and Toronto: Bodley Head, 1984).

Saglia, Diego, 'Consuming Egypt: Appropriation and the Cultural Modalities of Romantic Luxury', *Nineteenth-Century Contexts*, 24/3 (2002), 317–32.

Sargentson, Carolyn, *Merchants and Luxury Markets. The* Marchands Merciers *of Eighteenth-Century Paris* (Malibu and London: Victoria and Albert Museum and the J. Paul Getty Museum, 1996).

Saumarez Smith, Charles, *Eighteenth-Century Decoration: Design and the Domestic Interior in England* (New York: H. N. Abrams, 1993).

Schama, Simon, *The Embarrassment of Riches: An Interpretation of Dutch Culture in the Golden Age* (London: HarperCollins, 1987).

Scheips, Charle, *Elsie de Wolfe's Paris: Frivolity before the Storm* (New York: Harry N. Abrams, 2014).

Schulze, Franz, *Philip Johnson. Life and Work* (Chicago: University of Chicago Press, 1994).

Scott, Jonathan, *The Pleasures of Antiquity: British Collectors of Greece and Rome* (New Haven: Yale University Press, 2003).

Scott, Katie, *The Rococo Interior: Decoration and Social Spaces in Early Eighteenth-Century Paris* (New Haven and London: Yale University Press, 1995).

Sekora, John, *Luxury: The Concept in Western Thought: Eden to Smollett* (Baltimore: Johns Hopkins University Press, 1977).

Silverman, Debora, *Selling Culture: Bloomingdale's, Diana Vreeland, & the New Aristocracy of Taste in Reagan's America* (New York: Pantheon, 1986).

Simmel, Georg, *Philosophie der Mode* (Berlin: Pan-Verlag, 1905).

Sombart, Werner, *Luxus und Kapitalismus* (Munich: Duncker & Humblot, 1913; English trans. *Luxury and Capitalism.* Ann Arbor: University of Michigan Press, 1967).

Stabel, Peter, '"Le Gout pour l'Orient": Demande cosmopolite et objets de luxe à Bruges à la fin du Moyen Âge', *Histoire urbaine*, 30/1 (2011), 21–39.

Staggs, Sam, *Inventing Elsa Maxwell: How an Irrepressible Nobody Conquered High Society, Hollywood, the Press and the World* (London: St Martin's Press, 2012).

Stuart, A. M., *Empress of Fashion: A Life of Diana Vreeland* (New York: HarperCollins, 2012).

Tapert, Annette, and Diana Edkins, *The Power of Style: The Women who Defined the Art of Living Well* (London: Aurum Press, 1994).

Teitelbaum, Mo Amelia, *The Stylemakers: Minimalism and Classic-Modernism, 1915–45* (London: Philip Wilson, 2010).

Thomas, Dana, *Deluxe: How Luxury Lost its Lustre* (London: Penguin, 2008).

Thomason, Allison Karmel, *Luxury and Legitimation: Royal Collecting in Ancient Mesopotamia* (Aldershot: Ashgate, 2005).

Thorold, Peter, *The London Rich: The Creation of a Great City from 1666 to the Present* (London: Viking, 1999).

Tungate, Mark, *Luxury World: The Past, Present and Future of Luxury Brands* (London and Philadelphia: Kogan Page, 2009).

Twitchell, James B., *Living it Up: Our Love Affair with Luxury* (New York: Columbia University Press, 2002).

Vanderbilt Balsan, Consuelo, *The Glitter and the Gold: The American Duchess—in her Own Words* (1953; London: Hodder & Stoughton, 2012).

Veblen, Thorstein, *The Theory of the Leisure Class: An Economic Study of Institutions* (New York: MacMillan, 1899).

Vogue's Book of Houses, Gardens, People: Photographed by Horst, Text by Valentine Lawford, Introduction by Diana Vreeland (London: Bodley Head, 1963, repr. every year until 1968 by Condé Nast publications).

Walker, Daniel, *Flowers Underfoot: Indian Carpets of the Mughal Era* (London: Thames and Hudson, 1998).

Wallace-Hadrill, Andrew, *Rome's Cultural Revolution* (Cambridge: Cambridge University Press, 2008).

Walter Lack, H., *Garden Eden: Masterpieces of Botanical Illustration* (Cologne: Taschen, 2001).

Welch, Evelyn, 'Public Magnificence and Private Display: Giovanni Pontano's "De Splendore" (1498) and the Domestic Arts', *Journal of Design History*, 15 (2002), 211–27.

Welch, Evelyn, *Shopping in the Renaissance: Consumer Cultures in Italy, 1400–1600* (New Haven and London: Yale University Press, 2005).

Wilson, Elizabeth, 'Luxury', *Luxury*, 1/1 (2014), 15–22.

Wilson, Richard, and Alan Mackley, *Creating Paradise: The Building of the English Country House 1660–1880* (London and New York: Hambledon and London, 2000).

Winks, Robin W., *Cloak and Gown: Scholars in the Secret War, 1939–1961* (London: Harvill Press, 1987).

Ziegler, Catherine, *Favored Flowers: Culture and Economy in a Global System* (Durham, NC, and London: Duke University Press, 2007).

Ziskin, Rochelle, *The Place Vendôme: Architecture and Social Mobility in Eighteenth-Century Paris* (Cambridge: Cambridge University Press, 1999).

PICTURE CREDITS

Figure 1.1. Abegg-Stiftung, CH-3132 Riggisberg, Inv no 9.45.81. © Abegg-Stiftung, CH-3132 Riggisberg, 2002; (photo: Christoph von Viràg)

Figure 1.2. Paris, Musée d'Orsay. © The Art Archive / DeA Picture Library

Figure 1.3. © The Trustees of the British Museum 1872, 0604.583

Figure 1.4. © The Trustees of the British Museum, Prints & Drawings Department 1936, 0717.2

Figure 1.5. © The Trustees of the British Museum. Prints & Drawings 1851, 0901.1045

Figure 1.6. © Victoria and Albert Museum, C.124:35-1979

Figure 1.7. © Trustees of the British Museum, Prints & Drawings, 1944, 1014.24

Figure 1.8. © Trustees of the British Museum, Prints & Drawings, 1917, 1208.2890

Figure 2.1. Abegg-Stiftung, CH-3132 Riggisberg, Inv no 232. © Abegg-Stiftung, CH-3132 Riggisberg, 2000; (photo: Christoph von Viràg)

Figure 2.2. Royal Collection Trust, Windsor Castle. © Her Majesty Queen Elizabeth II, 2015/Bridgeman Images

Figure 2.3. © Wallace Collection, London, UK/Bridgeman Images

Figure 2.4. Woburn Abbey, Bedfordshire, UK/Bridgeman Images

Figure 2.5. © Musée d'art et d'histoire, Ville de Genève, inv. no. 1825-23. Photo: Yves Siza

Figure 2.6. British Museum, Prints and Drawings 1881, 0611.309

Figure 2.7. Collection Hardwick Hall, Derbyshire. National Trust Inventory Number 1127744. © National Trust/Robert Thrift

Figure 2.8. British Museum, Prints and Drawings 1917, 1208.70.336

Figure 2.9. Victoria and Albert Museum, T.371-1977

Figure 2.10. Victoria and Albert Museum, Dr W.L. Hildburgh Bequest M.425-1956

Figure 3.1. Victoria and Albert Museum, IM.113-1921, bequeathed by Lady Wantage

Figure 3.2. Engraving © The Trustees of the British Museum, 1859, 0806.307

Figure 3.3. British Museum, WB.125

Figure 3.4. Victoria and Albert Museum, bequeathed by Claude D. Rotch, M.308:1,2-1962

Figure 3.5. Victoria and Albert Museum, 412:1, 2-1882

Figure 3.6. Victoria and Albert Museum, bequeathed by Lionel A. Crichton P.2-1939

Figure 3.7. © The Trustees of the British Museum, 1853, 1210.654

Figure 3.8. Author's Collection

Figure 4.1. Country Life Picture Library

Figure 4.2. Victoria and Albert Museum, 1736 to E-1869

Figure 4.3. © British Museum, 1889, 0724.69

Figure 4.4. Country Life Picture Library
Figure 4.5. Country Life Picture Library
Figure 4.6. Photograph courtesy Wikimedia commons
Figure 4.7. Museum of the City of New York/New York, NY/USA. The Museum of the City of New York Art Resource, NY Image Reference: ART497195
Figure 5.1. Miss Evans and friends, Montreal, QC, 1887 Wm. Notman & Son, Il-82850, McCord Museum, Montreal
Figure 5.2. Country Life Picture Library
Figure 5.3. Country Life Picture Library
Figure 5.4. Courtesy of the FIDM Museum at the Fashion Institute of Design & Merchandising, Los Angeles, CA; photo Brian Sanderson
Figure 5.5. Photograph Miss Fraser, Montreal, QC, 1897 Wm. Notman & Son, Il-119956, McCord Museum, Montreal.
Figure 5.6. FIDM Museum Library Inc., Museum Purchase 2011.5.20. Courtesy of the FIDM Museum at the Fashion Institute of Design & Merchandising, Los Angeles, CA; photo Brian Sanderson
Figure 5.7. FIDM Museum Library Inc., Museum Purchase 2013.5.80. Courtesy of
(a and b) the FIDM Museum at the Fashion Institute of Design & Merchandising, Los Angeles, CA; photo Brian Sanderson
Figure 5.8. FIDM Museum Library Inc., Gift of Mona Lee Nesseth 2013.975.2AB. Courtesy of the FIDM Museum at the Fashion Institute of Design & Merchandising, Los Angeles, CA; photo Brian Sanderson
Figure 5.9. Byron Company (New York), photographer, 1903, Museum of the City of New York/New York, NY/USA. The Museum of the City of New York/Art Resource, NY Image Reference: MNY1680
Figure 5.10. Image by © Bettmann/CORBIS
Figure 5.11. Courtesy Country Life Picture Library
Figure 5.12. Courtesy Country Life Picture Library
Figure 6.1. bpk / Kunstbibliothek, SMB / Dietmar Katz
Figure 6.2. Image and information courtesy Maureen Amelia Teitelbaum, London
Figure 6.3. Courtesy Sotheby's/ArtDigital Studio
Figure 6.4. Gift of Dr and Mrs Irwin R. Berman, 1976 (1976.414.3a-ggg). The Metropolitan Museum of Art, New York, NY, USA © The Metropolitan Museum of Art. Image source: Art Resource, NY. Image Reference: ART no. 425308
Figure 6.5. FIDM Museum Library Inc., Gift of Mona Lee Nesseth, FIDM Museum Library Inc. 2013.975.2AB; photo: Brian Sanderson
Figure 6.6. Author's collection
Figure 6.7. Author's collection
Figure 6.8. bpk / Kunstbibliothek, SMB / Dietmar Katz
Figure 6.9. Photograph by Gottscho-Schleisner, Inc. Acetate negative, 30 March 1955. Library of Congress Prints and Photographs Division Washington, DC. 20540 USA Gottscho-Schleisner Collection (Library of Congress) LC-G613-T-67025 (interpositive)
Figure 6.10. Author's Collection

Figure 6.11. International Centre for Photography
Figure 6.12. Virginia Museum of Fine Arts, Richmond. Collection of Mrs Paul Mellon. Photo: Katherine Wetzel © Virginia Museum of Fine Arts
Figure 7.1. Photo: Ed Uthman, MD. Euthman 23:54, 24 November 2006
Figure 8.1. Photographer: Alexander Su
Figure 8.2. Wikimedia Commons
Figure 8.3. Author's photograph

INDEX